DANIEL

A Book
for
Troubling Times

Alexander Di Lella

DANIEL

A Book
for
Troubling Times

Spiritual Commentaries

New City Press

Published in the United States by New City Press
202 Cardinal Rd., Hyde Park, NY 12538
©1997 Alexander Di Lella, O.F.M.

First published in Italian as
Il Libro di Daniele (1-6)
© 1995 Città Nuova, Rome, Italy

Cover design by Nick Cianfarani
Cover art: Daniel by Michelangelo; photo used with permission of Christus Rex et
Redemptor Mundi.

Library of Congress Cataloging-in-Publication Data:

Di Lella, Alexander A.
    Daniel : a book for troubling times / by Alexander Di Lella.
        p.   cm. — (Spiritual commentaries)
    Includes bibliographical references.
    ISBN 1-56548-087-2
    1. Bible.   O.T.   Daniel—Commentaries.   2. Bible.   O.T.   Daniel—
Devotional   I. Title.   II. Series.
BS1555.3.D55   1997
224'.5077—dc21   96-46248

Printed in the United States of America

Contents

Introduction

Why Read the Book of Daniel?

Why not read the Book of Daniel? After all, the book has something important to say; that's why it's in the Bible. Question is: Are we willing to listen? My intention in writing this spiritual commentary is to help you to read and reflect on Daniel and its enduring message and then to entice you to read the rest of the Bible. Jerome, patron of biblical students, once remarked, "Ignorance of the scriptures is ignorance of Christ."

You should read this commentary with a good modern translation of the Bible at your side. *The New American Bible* is the translation I have used for the text at the head of each chapter and for relevant citations in the commentary. But I have made references to hundreds of other biblical citations. Reading these texts will enrich your understanding of the book.

Title and Author

Daniel, the hero of the book, is not mentioned anywhere else in the Old Testament. The name, however, was not unusual. One of David's sons was called Daniel (1 Chr 3:1). One of the Jews returning from the Babylonian exile was also named Daniel (Ezr 8:2; Neh 10:7). But neither of these two men can be identified with the Daniel of our book. The name Daniel in Hebrew and Aramaic means "God has judged," or "God is my judge."

In Ezekiel 14:14, 20, there is mention of Noah, Daniel (or Danel), and Job. The context makes it clear, however, that these three are cited as outstanding examples of righteous individuals who lived in the far distant past and have become part of ancient Near Eastern folklore. They are not even Israelites but belong to foreign nations. In Ezekiel 28:3, the Lord orders the prophet to say to the prince of Tyre: "You are wiser than Daniel [or Danel]; there is no secret that is beyond you"—words that are clearly ironic. Some scholars think that this Daniel/Danel is the king with the same name in the Ugaritic "Tale of Aqhat," which dates to the fourteenth century B.C. In this story, King Daniel/Danel "judges the cause of the widow; he tries the case of the orphan." Such a statement could be behind the name of the hero in the Susanna story in chapter 13. It seems, therefore, that from ancient times in Syria-Palestine the name Daniel had been associated with persons of notable virtue and outstanding wisdom. We may conclude that the authors of the various parts of the book used the name Daniel precisely because of its association with this honored name in Near Eastern tradition.

The authorship of the book is a complex question. The principal reason is that, unlike any other book of the Bible, each of the several stories and apocalypses could have existed independently of the others. Accordingly, each could have been written by a different person. In fact, every one of the stories and apocalypses can be read independently of the others, with little or no loss in understanding. As we now have it, the book appears to be simply a series of relatively short works comprising a Daniel cycle that had been compiled and edited by some unknown person in about the middle of the second century B.C.

Scholars generally agree that the Book of Daniel represents the Hasidic mentality in outlook and perspective. The Hasidim, or Pious Ones, were those Jews who followed the Law of Moses strictly. The Pious Ones are mentioned by name in 1 Maccabees 2:42 and 7:13. They were distinguished from the more worldly Jews who compromised their faith by adjusting to the Greek allurements of the day. These lax Jews were not unlike many believers today whose values are determined more by a consumerist and pagan society than by biblical and Church teaching.

Place in the Canon

In the Jewish canon of scripture, which was fixed by the rabbis near the end of the first century A.D., there are four major divisions: the Torah (Genesis to Deuteronomy), the Earlier Prophets (Joshua to Kings), the Later Prophets (Isaiah to Malachi), and the Writings (Psalms to Chronicles). Daniel is found not among the prophets but among the Writings; it is located after Esther and before Ezra. The reason for this placement is not clear. Some think that the rabbis did not believe Daniel to be a prophetic book. Daniel is not a prophet like Amos, Hosea, Isaiah, or Jeremiah. Indeed Daniel, in both the stories and the apocalypses, seldom acts like a prophet nor is he ever called a prophet.

The book was probably too late to be included among the prophets, since it appeared about the middle of the second century B.C. Indeed, the rabbis taught that the prophetic corpus was closed after the prophet Malachi in the fifth century B.C. In the New Testament, however, Jesus makes reference to "the prophet Daniel" (Mt 24:15). The Jewish historian Josephus also speaks of Daniel as a prophet and refers to the contents of his book as prophecies (*Antiquities* x 11, 7). In the Greek translation called the Septuagint and in so-called Theodotion-Daniel (the second Greek form), Daniel in its long form is found among the Major Prophets either before Ezekiel and Isaiah (in that order) or after Isaiah as a fourth member of the group. In the Christian Old Testament, Daniel is found among the Major Prophets after Ezekiel—an arrangement already seen in the Latin Vulgate (fifth century).

The Jewish canon of Daniel does not include the deuterocanonical sections—the prayers in 3:24-90 and the stories of Susanna, Bel, and the Dragon in chapters 13 and 14. Protestants, who usually call the deuterocanonical books by the not entirely appropriate term Apocrypha (a Greek word that means "hidden or concealed"), follow the Jewish practice. In their editions of the Bible, Protestants either omit the deuterocanonical books altogether or, if they include them, they place them either between the Old Testament and New Testament or in an appendix. But Roman Catholics, following the ancient custom of the Church, believe that all the deuterocanonical portions of the Old Testament are sacred and inspired, and hence canonical.

Contents and Language

Daniel contains two types of literary materials: nine midrashic or homiletic stories (one each in chapters 1–6 and 13 and the stories of Bel and the Dragon in chapter 14) and five apocalypses (one in 2:29-45 inside the story of chapter 2, and one each in chapters 7, 8, 9, and 10–12). The stories are told in the third person about an ancient hero called Daniel and his three companions, who on account of their faith and their fidelity to the Law of Moses endured various trials among the Gentiles, but who triumphed in the end. The apocalypses or visions, narrated mostly in the first person, recount dreams and events that occurred to the same Daniel during the reigns of several Gentile kings. The purpose of these apocalypses was to strengthen and encourage those who were tempted to compromise their faith and abandon their religious practices in order to survive during the vicious persecution of Antiochus IV Epiphanes.

Daniel is extant in three different languages: Hebrew (1:1-2:4a and chaps. 8-12); Aramaic (2:4b-7:28, except for the long prayer in 3:24-90); and Greek (3:24-90 and chaps. 13-14). There are two Greek translations of the book: The Septuagint-form, surviving in only a few manuscripts, and so-called "Theodotion-Daniel," found in the rest of the Greek manuscripts. "Theodotion-Daniel" is not to be identified with the Theodotion who made a later revision of the Greek Old Testament. What is curious is that only two of the apocalypses now exist in Aramaic (2:29-45 and chap. 7); the other three are in Hebrew (chaps. 8, 9, and 10-12). The homiletic stories, on the other hand, are now found in Hebrew, Aramaic, and Greek. It seems certain, however, that the Greek portions (3:24-90 and chaps. 13-14) were originally composed in Hebrew though none of the Hebrew original has survived. Some scholars maintain that Aramaic was the original language of 1:1-2:4a and chapters 8–12. Those chapters were later translated into the Hebrew text that we now have.

10

Literary Genres

The homiletic stories in chapters 1–6 and 13–14 have as their literary genre a type of literature known as the tale of the successful courtier. This genre is found also in Genesis, Tobit, Judith, and Esther, as well as in the literature of the ancient Near East. The story of Joseph is a good example. Though he is sold by his jealous brothers into slavery, Joseph eventually does very well for himself. Several details from the Joseph story have echoes in the Daniel narratives. Like Joseph, who is "strikingly handsome" (Gn 39:6), Daniel and his companions are "handsome, intelligent and wise, quick to learn, and prudent in judgment" (Dn 1:4). Joseph refused to commit adultery with Potiphar's wife who had tried to seduce him (Gn 39:9). Daniel refused to "defile himself with the king's food or wine" (Dn 1:8). Because of God-given wisdom in interpreting the dreams of Pharaoh, Joseph was appointed vizier of all Egypt (Gn 41:1-57). Because Daniel was able to interpret Nebuchadnezzar's dream, the king "made him ruler of the whole province of Babylon" (Dn 2:48).

Apocalyptic is the literary genre of chapters 7–12 and also of 2:29-45, the core of the second story. Unlike the stories, which exhort and edify, the five apocalypses present a vision of divine intervention that will bring to an end the anguish of believers and usher in the kingdom of God. Apocalyptic is essentially resistance literature; it was written to address a crisis in the lives of believers. It became a popular literary form from the early second century B.C. until the second Jewish revolt (A.D. 132-35). Although parts of Ezekiel, Isaiah 24-27 and 40-66, Zechariah 9-14, and Joel may be considered proto-apocalyptic, the only portions of the Old Testament that are strictly speaking apocalyptic are Daniel 2:29-45 and chapters 7–12. Mark 13:1-37 (and parallels in Matthew 24:1-44; Luke 21:5-36) and Revelation are New Testament apocalypses. Many non-canonical writings, including several of the Dead Sea Scrolls, also employ apocalyptic.

The apocalypses of Daniel have these five literary characteristics: (1) pseudonymous or anonymous authorship; (2) dreams or visions; (3) "prophecies after the event"; (4) symbolic language; (5) esoteric content.

11

(1) Pseudonymity is the literary convention also found in other parts of the Old Testament—Proverbs, Qoheleth (Ecclesiastes), Tobit, Wisdom. It was used to add authority to a work. The pseudonymous author of chapters 7, 8, 9, and 10–12 identifies himself with Daniel, the hero of the book. The apocalypse in 2:29-45 is anonymous like the rest of the story in chapter 2.

(2) Dreams are the literary vehicle of God's revelation in chapters 2 and 7, which are similar to each other; visions are the vehicle in chapters 8, 9, 10–12. In both dreams and visions, however, the revelation deals with the future. The fictional time-frame of each apocalypse is the sixth century B.C.; each dream and vision tells what will take place in the following three or four centuries.

(3) "Prophecies after the event" are a literary convention employed in the visions and dreams. The author of each apocalypse actually wrote in the second century B.C. But from his fictional sixth-century B.C. time-frame he writes about past history as if he were predicting the future. This biblical convention was not used to deceive but rather to add authority to the work and to affirm the author's conviction that God is in control of human history.

(4) Symbolic language—highly imaginative and often extravagant—predominates. The four immense beasts of chapter 7, for example, aptly and graphically symbolize the four pagan empires—Babylonian, Median, Persian, and Greek.

(5) Esoteric content is the stuff of apocalyptic. God or his angel has revealed to Daniel that the four pagan empires will come to an end, at which time the faithful will inherit the kingdom of God. Daniel keeps the revelation secret (7:28; 8:26; 12:4) until the appointed time in the future, which happens to be the authors' own day—early second century B.C.

Historical Background

The historical outlook in the homiletic stories and in the apocalypses is generally the same. Daniel incorporates the popular but inaccurate Jewish tradition regarding the sequence of kingdoms and kings. Thus in the stories the sequence is: Nebuchadnezzar (chaps. 1-4) and Belshazzar (chap. 5), Babylonian kings, and

Darius the Mede and Cyrus the Persian (chap. 6). In the apocalypses, the sequence is: Belshazzar (chaps. 7-8), Darius the Mede (chap. 9), and Cyrus (chaps. 10-12, with clear references made also to the Hellenistic or Greek kingdoms and kings). The author's principal concern, however, was with the Greek-Seleucid kingdom of Antiochus IV Epiphanes.

Indeed Antiochus IV (175-64 B.C.) is the archvillain of the book, especially of the apocalypses of chapters 7–12, which were written during his reign. Totally unprincipled and unpredictable, he was given to extremes of generosity to his friends and of utter cruelty to his enemies. In his arrogance he assumed the title Epiphanes, which in Greek means "[god] Manifest." But because of his erratic and bizarre behavior, the people nicknamed him Epimanes, Greek for "Madman." Constantly in need of money, Antiochus plundered shrines and temples, including the Jewish temple in Jerusalem. To insure the unity of the disparate peoples in his kingdom, he insisted that Hellenism would be the way of life for all without exception. Hellenism was the civilization and international culture that had spread throughout the Mediterranean and Near Eastern world following the conquests of Alexander the Great (336-23 B.C.). Hellenism was attractive: it had one language, Greek; its center was the Greek *polis* (city); its politics was aristocratic with some democratic elements; its literature and philosophy were first-rate; it welcomed all peoples and their religions.

Some Jews went along with this policy, compromising their faith for economic gain and social advantage. The legitimate high priest Onias III was deposed by his brother Jason after he had offered Antiochus IV a huge bribe. Jason even erected a Greek gymnasium in Jerusalem, thus formally introducing Greek sports and culture. "The craze for Hellenism and foreign customs reached such a pitch, through the outrageous wickedness of the ungodly pseudo-high-priest Jason, that the priests no longer cared about the service of the altar. Disdaining the temple and neglecting the sacrifices, they hastened, at the signal for the discus-throwing, to take part in the unlawful exercises on the athletic field" (2 Mc 4:13-14). Since participants in sports were nude, many Jews underwent painful surgery to cover over "the mark of their circumcision" (1 Mc 1:15), which the Greeks considered a mutilation.

The final blow came in 167 B.C. when Antiochus IV abolished Jewish festivals and sacrifices, forbade circumcision and observance of the Sabbath and dietary laws, and ordered unclean animals to be sacrificed. Worst of all, he placed the statue of the bearded Olympian Zeus right over the great altar of holocausts in Jerusalem. This is "the desolating sin" and "the horrible abomination" of Daniel 8:13; 9:27; 11:31; and 12:11. "The Gentiles filled the temple with debauchery and revelry; they amused themselves with prostitutes and had intercourse with women even in the sacred court. They also brought into the temple things that were forbidden, so that the altar was covered with abominable offerings prohibited by the laws" (2 Mc 6:4-5). Later on Judas Maccabeus and his guerrilla forces won decisive victories over Antiochus' army. This enabled Judas to reconsecrate the Temple in December 164 B.C. (1 Mc 2:1-4:55; 2 Mc 8:1-36; 10:1-5).

A Spiritual Reading of Daniel

It is beyond question that the Book of Daniel had a profound and meaningful message for the Jews of the second century B.C. But what about us? What does the book mean for Christians striving to honor their spiritual and moral commitments and to live out their faith in the real world? It is questions like these that the present work attempts to address. This is not a verse-by-verse commentary. Rather, I shall present only those aspects of the historical-critical background that are necessary for an understanding of the book. My primary method will be literary criticism, which will help us appreciate the Christian significance of the book.

At the outset, I must emphasize that Daniel does not speak *of* our times, but rather *to* our times. The book does not provide a forecast of the future but a pattern or example of how God had entered into the history of the original readers on the one hand, and, on the other hand, how this same God wills to be involved in the lives of believers today. Thus, we must take into account what prompted the writing of the Book of Daniel in the second century B.C. Such a method will enable us to see how Daniel can speak to us today and to our spiritual lives. Reading *into* the text of Daniel and seeing there predictions of contemporary world affairs does

14

violence to the sacred text and gets us nowhere. What I hope to do is to guide the reader into reading *out* of the Book of Daniel what is significant for us today.

At the same time, however, we must take the fact that Daniel also has a future orientation seriously. After all, prophecy and apocalyptic were meant to be meaningful not only for one particular community in the past, but also for those who come afterwards. The plan and will of God were made manifest not just for the times when the biblical books were composed but for future generations as well. As Anthony de Mello, S.J., once observed, "The shortest distance between a human being and Truth is a story." More to the point, the poet Mona Van Duyn writes: "For what is story if not relief from the pain/ of the inconclusive, from dread of the meaningless?" ("Endings"). The stories of Daniel as well as the apocalypses address precisely the problem of meaning in a chaotic world.

Because of the turbulent times in which we live, many people are fascinated by the apocalyptic literature of the Bible. The peculiar imagery found in such books as Revelation and Daniel, especially the apocalyptic visions in chapters 2 and 7–12, seems to fuel the religious imagination. Those not acquainted with the methods of modern biblical studies may fancy that they can find in these books more or less clear allusions to political, military, and social upheavals happening in our time, or even see predictions of the future outcome of history. Such people even look to the apocalyptic literature of the Bible for solutions to complex problems facing our society today. Because the homiletic stories in Daniel 1-6 and 13-14 tell of divine interventions to rescue the faithful Jews, some people today believe that God will again intervene dramatically and perhaps spectacularly in human affairs. It will be only a matter of time. As we approach the turn of the millennium, we can expect even more speculations of this kind.

At the outset, we should lay to rest any interpretation that sees in the apocalypses of Daniel ancient predictions of the actual times in which we live, or even timetables of the end time, which some Christians imagine will occur in the not too distant future. Nor should we hope to find in the homiletic stories clear solutions to social, political, and moral problems of great complexity. If we accept Daniel on its terms and not on ours, then it has much more to offer than the often simple-minded solutions of misguided interpreters. The authors of the various parts of the book had a profound faith and hope in the God of revelation, who is Lord of history. They address the book to believers—ancient and modern—who share that faith and hope.

The perennial freshness of the Book of Daniel has intrigued and inspired artists and writers throughout the centuries. The story of Susanna and the wicked elders (chap. 13) was a favorite of artists from the Renaissance on because the bathing scene was made to order. The story of the three Jews in the fiery furnace (chap. 3) was also popular, for it symbolized resurrection from the dead. On the sarcophagus of Junius Bassus (d. 359) in St. Peter's grotto in Rome, Daniel is depicted at prayer between two lions (Dn 6:17-24), a scene painted by Rubens and many others. Bernini created a splendid sculpture of Daniel, which is now displayed in the Church of Santa Maria del Populo in Rome.

It is best to read this spiritual commentary one chapter at a time and then to reflect on the significance of the Daniel text for our personal life. In order to make each chapter more readable on its own without constant recourse to other chapters, I have repeated some biblical citations and key ideas as well as information about individuals and their times. I hope that this repetition will help rather than distract the reader. The reader, moreover, should not be put off by the repetitive accounts of kingdoms and kings in the apocalypses of the book.

I

"Daniel Was Resolved Not to Defile Himself"

(Daniel 1:1-21)

[1] In the third year of the reign of Jehoiakim, king of Judah, King Nebuchadnezzar of Babylon came and laid siege to Jerusalem. [2] The Lord handed over to him Jehoiakim, king of Judah, and some of the vessels of the temple of God, which he carried off to the land of Shinar, and placed in the temple treasury of his god.

[3] The king told Ashpenaz, his chief chamberlain, to bring in some of the Israelites of royal blood and of the nobility, [4] young men without any defect, handsome, intelligent and wise, quick to learn, and prudent in judgment, such as could take their place in the king's palace; they were to be taught the language and literature of the Chaldeans. [5] After three years' training they were to enter the king's service. The king allotted them a daily portion of food and wine from the royal table. [6] Among these were men of Judah: Daniel, Hananiah, Mishael, and Azariah. [7] The chief chamberlain changed their names: Daniel to Belteshazzar, Hananiah to Shadrach, Mishael to Meshach, and Azariah to Abednego.

[8] But Daniel was resolved not to defile himself with the king's food or wine; so he begged the chief chamberlain to spare him this defilement. [9] Though God had given Daniel the favor and sympathy of the chief chamberlain, [10] he nevertheless said to Daniel, "I am afraid of my lord the king; it is he who allotted your food and drink. If he sees that you look wretched by comparison with the other young men of your age, you will endanger my life with the king." [11] Then Daniel said to the steward whom the chief chamberlain had put in charge of Daniel, Hananiah, Mishael, and Azariah, [12] "Please test your servants for ten days. Give us vegetables to eat and water to drink. [13] Then see how we look in comparison with the other young men who

eat from the royal table, and treat your servants according to what you see." [14]He acceded to this request, and tested them for ten days; [15]after ten days they looked healthier and better fed than any of the young men who ate from the royal table. [16]So the steward continued to take away the food and wine they were to receive, and gave them vegetables.

[17]To these four young men God gave knowledge and proficiency in all literature and science, and to Daniel the understanding of all visions and dreams.

[18]At the end of the time the king had specified for their preparation, the chief chamberlain brought them before Nebuchadnezzar. [19]When the king had spoken with all of them, none was found equal to Daniel, Hananiah, Mishael, and Azariah; and so they entered the king's service. [20]In any question of wisdom or prudence which the king put to them, he found them ten times better than all the magicians and enchanters in his kingdom. [21]Daniel remained there until the first year of King Cyrus.

The first six chapters of Daniel as well as Susanna, Bel, and the Dragon in chapters 13 and 14 are independent stories that make a moral point, not only for the Jewish community of that day but for us too. Each story has the same basic elements: crisis for the Jewish heroes; resolve to remain faithful; trial or testing; successful resolution; praise of God. In this opening chapter, Daniel and his companions, chosen to be trained for the royal court, resolve to eat only vegetables and to drink water, refusing the rich food and wine from the royal table. Despite their diet the Jews turn out healthier and smarter than their fellow students and graduate at the head of their class.

Babylon and Jerusalem: A Study in Contrasts

Babylon and Jerusalem, the two cities mentioned in the opening verse, symbolize the principal concerns of this chapter and of the rest of the book. Babylon, a name which means "gate of the gods," was one of the most celebrated cities in the ancient world. The capital of the Neo-Babylonian (Chaldean) Empire, the city had an array of majestic buildings and broad avenues leading to the eight

18

gates in the city's double wall. The palace of Nebuchadnezzar II (605-562 B.C.), who is mentioned in 1:1, was adorned with the well-known hanging gardens, one of the seven wonders of the ancient world. In the time of Nebuchadnezzar, Babylon had fifty-three temples, the greatest of which was the temple of the god Marduk, chief of the Babylonian pantheon, with its impressive tower or ziggurat, which is probably the basis of the story of the City and Tower of Babel in Genesis 11:1-9. Each year on the anniversary of Marduk's coronation, a colossal statue of the god was hauled through the streets of the city and placed in his temple—a ceremony that may be reflected in the story of Daniel 3. That temple also contained the sacred vessels and gold and silver which Nebuchadnezzar had plundered from the Jerusalem temple (2 Kgs 25:13-15)—the background of Daniel 5. In striking contrast to mighty Babylon, Jerusalem at this time was a city under siege, soon to be destroyed by the Babylonian army.

Yet Babylon is no more. It is now nothing but an excavation site in an obscure village south of modern Baghdad, capital of Iraq. Babylon, however, continues to haunt us as an enduring symbol as well as a reminder of all that is corrupt, perverse, and immoral in human affairs and institutions (Is 47; Zec 5:5-11). In the Book of Revelation, Babylon—called "mother of prostitutes and of the abominations of the earth" (Rv 17:5)—stands for the Roman Empire and its wicked forces that try to do away with the infant Church. " 'Rejoice over her [Babylon], heaven, you holy ones, apostles, and prophets. For God has judged your case against her.' A mighty angel picked up a stone like a huge millstone and threw it into the sea and said: 'With such force will Babylon the great city be thrown down, and will never be found again. No melodies of harpists and musicians, flutists and trumpeters, will ever be heard in you again. No craftsmen in any trade will ever be found in you again. No sound of the millstone will ever be heard in you again. No light from a lamp will ever be seen in you again. No voices of bride and groom will ever be heard in you again. Because your merchants were the great ones of the world, all nations were led astray by your magic potion' " (Rv 18:20-23). But Babylon also stands for what is wrong with nations and societies that throughout history have suppressed the truth, crushed the innocent, and failed to protect the rights of the poor and helpless. Institutional sins like consumerism and militarism, nationalism and racism, and laws justifying the exploitation of third world nations, together with the evils they spawn, are just as pervasive and corrosive as personal sins.

Jerusalem, on the other hand, symbolizes the exact opposite of Babylon. Jerusalem, a name that is associated with the Hebrew word for peace, achieved its fame not because of its trappings of grandeur and might of which it had few, but because the city with its temple was the place where the living God, Lord of heaven and earth, had chosen to dwell here on earth (Ps 135:21; Sir 36:12; Is 27:13; Rv 21:9–22:5), and where God's people who remain faithful can live in safety and security, without fear (Tb 14:7).

The Babylon of history with its forces of evil besieged Jerusalem for the first time in 597 (2 Kgs 24:10-12) and again in 587 B.C. (2 Kgs 25:1-10). But the enduring Babylon has continued to lay siege to Jerusalem many times throughout history. In the second century B.C., Babylon was embodied in the wickedness of Antiochus IV Epiphanes who persecuted the Jews relentlessly. In our century, Babylon's evil dominion can be seen at work in the dungeons of the Hitlers, Stalins, Saddam Husseins, and other tyrants who confined, tortured, and murdered political dissidents and others they deemed unfit to live.

Babylon's evil hand is at work also in the systematic exploitation of the poor by rich and powerful transnational corporations as well as in the corruption of judges and other government officials. But the inhabitants of the spiritual Jerusalem by their fidelity and perseverance will win out in the end, as did Daniel and his three companions.

Daniel and His Companions in the Royal Court

The first chapter of Daniel serves as an introduction to the book and as an exhortation to be faithful to religious principles and to refrain from self-indulgence. The third year of King Jehoiakim (1:1) would be 606 B.C., a fictional date, which may be based on 2 Kings 24:1. The author of Daniel is not concerned with historical accuracy; he simply employs an historical framework in which to tell his story in order to make it more realistic. The account in 2 Chronicles 36:5-7 relates how Nebuchadnezzar captured Jehoiakim and brought some of the temple vessels to Babylon. In 1:2, the place is called Shinar, an ancient name for Babylonia (Gn 10:10; 11:2; 14:1; Jos 7:21; Is 11:11; Zec 5:11). Like "that which we call a rose/ By any other word would smell as sweet" (Shakespeare, *Romeo and Juliet*, II, ii, 43-44), so the name "Shinar" here has all the evil associations of Babylon.

The theology of history is an important feature of the Book of Daniel. So the author emphasizes that it was the Lord God of Israel who made all these disasters happen; it was not simply the military might of Babylon. In fact, Babylon was merely the instrument of God's justice in punishing his people for their infidelity (Dt 28:15-68). At the outset, the author reminds us that history is not just a series of seemingly unrelated events. Rather, history is the arena of God's domain and providence. God alone is in charge in Babylon as well as in Jerusalem and in every other place and time. It is good for us to realize this comforting truth. When we suffer disaster or depression, or when things go wrong in our personal life and family, we should not think that God has abandoned us or refuses to answer our prayers. God is indeed present to us with his loving care even when he chooses for his own mysterious reasons to remain silent.

Nebuchadnezzar wants only the best to be his courtiers. Only Israelite exiles of royal or noble stock are to be brought into the palace to serve at the Babylonian court (1:3). The author of Daniel may be alluding here to Isaiah's prophecy to King Hezekiah: "Some of your bodily descendants shall be taken and made servants in the palace of the king of Babylon" (Is 39:7). The Israelite exiles "were to be taught the language and literature of the Chaldeans" (1:4). This is a reference to the complicated cuneiform script and the sacred Babylonian rituals as well as the omen and dream literature. The term "Chaldean" is often the general term that refers to magicians, enchanters, and sorcerers as a group (cf. 2:2 and 2:4-5, 10).

The Jews were to be without any defect (1:4)—the same requirement for the Israelite priests (Lv 21:17-23) as well as the sacrificial animals (Lv 22:17-25). These men are to be handsome too.

Physical beauty is an attribute often associated with royalty. Saul, for example, "was a handsome young man. There was no other Israelite handsomer than Saul" (1 Sm 9:2; 10:23). David "was ruddy, a youth handsome to behold and making a splendid appearance" (1 Sm 16:12). In the Bible, physical beauty was also associated with wisdom, divine favor, and righteousness (Gn 39:6-23; 41:39; Jdt 8:7, 28-29; 11:20-21). These two features, priestly and royal, come together in Daniel and his companions. These narrative details anticipate how Daniel and his companions, because of their fidelity to the Law, turn out at the end of the story to be the best and brightest in the class. But there is an ironic twist in the story, which will become clearer in the rest of the book. Daniel receives his training in the pagan court. As a matter of fact, however, he serves not so much the interests of the various pagan monarchs as the interests of God. To insure that the trainees receive nothing but the best during their three years of schooling, they are to receive their food and wine from the king's own table (1:5).

The details about beauty seem to confirm an important value for many people today. In our society the young and beautiful seem invariably to receive preferential treatment and are often believed to be more intelligent than others. Consider the amount of time and money that people spend on their hair and their looks and clothes. The author of Daniel, however, employs these conventional details about beauty simply because they are needed for the plot. As Paul reminds Christians of all times, "Consider your own calling, brothers and sisters. Not many of you were wise by human standards, not many were powerful, not many were of noble birth. Rather, God chose the foolish of the world to shame the wise, and God chose the weak of the world to shame the strong, and God chose the lowly and despised of the world, those who count for nothing, to reduce to nothing those who are something, so that no human being might boast before God" (1 Cor 1:26-29). In a document dating to about A.D. 150, Paul is described as "a man small of stature, with a bald head and crooked legs, in a good state of body, with eyebrows meeting and nose somewhat hooked." If this description is accurate— and the uncomplimentary details seem to verify its authenticity—then there is hope for us all. Each of us—tall and short, fat and skinny, beautiful and plain, bright and average—are all precious in God's sight. Like Paul, we are called to use whatever talents we have in our service of God and neighbor.

The Four Jews Get Babylonian Names

After their introduction into the Babylonian court, Daniel and his three companions Hananiah, Mishael, and Azariah are given Babylonian names (1:7). It is significant that the Hebrew names of the Jewish heroes tell us something of the theology of the stories in the book. All the names are theophoric—they contain, as one of the elements of the name, the word for "God" or "Yahweh," which is the proper name of God in the Old Testament (Ex 3:13-15). These names foreshadow the gracious acts of God that will be told in the stories to follow. "Daniel" means "God has judged," or "My judge is God." This name anticipates the wise actions of Daniel as a judge in the story of Susanna (chap. 13). "Hananiah" means "Yahweh has taken pity." Yahweh has indeed been merciful to Israel even after he exiled the people in Babylon because of their infidelity to the Sinai covenant (Dn 3:95-96). "Mishael" means "Who is what God is?"—a name suggesting that there can be no god like the true God of Israel, who alone is God, who alone has power to save, who alone is present in all times and places (Dn 2:47; 3:14-18). "Azariah" means "Yahweh has helped." This name tells of the continuing presence of God by his providence and loving care for his people (1:9; 4:6; 6:27-28).

Daniel's name is changed to "Belteshazzar," which in Babylonian is a shortened form of "[Marduk or Bel,] protect the king's life" (cf. Is 46:1). The changing of the names means a change of destiny: *nomen est omen*. God changed the name of Abram, for example, to Abraham, because God was making him "the father of a host of nations" (Gn 17:5). By giving new names to the four Jews, the royal official was exercising his power over them, for naming a person or thing was a sign of power over that person or thing (Gn 1:5, 8, 10; 2:19-21; 2 Kgs 23:34; 24:17). But there is irony here, for despite the fact that the four Jewish heroes are given Babylonian names as functionaries in Nebuchadnezzar's court, the meanings of their Hebrew names are what prevail in the book. It is the God

23

of Israel who protects the king's life, and not the god Marduk or Bel (Dn 4:31-34). The changing of names was a hotly disputed question among the Jews in the second century B.C. Joshua, for example, bribed Antiochus IV to depose his brother Onias III, the legitimate high priest, so that he could become high priest. Joshua preferred to be called by his Greek name Jason (2 Mc 4:7-14). Here however, Daniel and his companions have no choice in the change of names.

The Jews Refuse to Eat from the Royal Table

Despite the fact that Daniel and his companions agree to be educated in a pagan court, they remain steadfast in the practice of their faith. They refuse to share in the royal food and drink lest they defile themselves (1:8). They put into practice the famous saying in Deuteronomy 8:3, "that not by bread alone does man live, but by every word that comes forth from the mouth of the LORD" (words quoted by Jesus when he was tempted after his long fast [Mt 4:4; Lk 4:4]). The reason for the defilement is not given. One of the possible reasons is that the food may have been unclean and hence forbidden by the dietary laws (Lv 11:4-47). If so, the author is encouraging his original readers to observe these laws (Tb 1:10-11; Jdt 10:5; 12:17-19; 1 Mc 1:63; Est 4:28).

The story in 2 Maccabees 6:18-28 of Eleazar, one of the foremost scribes, comes to mind. This old man of noble appearance preferred a glorious death to a life in which he would be defiled. During the persecution of Antiochus IV, he was forced to open his mouth to eat pork, but he immediately spat it out "and went forward of his own accord to the instrument of torture." The men in charge took Eleazar aside privately and urged him to bring his own lawful meat to the ritual meal prescribed by the king and to pretend to eat some of the forbidden meat in order to escape death. Eleazar absolutely refused to go along with this pretense lest he bring dishonor and shame on his old age.

A more likely reason for the defilement, however, may be that sharing in the royal table could signify a covenantal relationship with the king and his court, and accordingly a dependence of these Jews on the royal bounty. Sharing a meal was one of the ways of sealing a covenant in antiquity (Gn 26:28-30; 31:44-54; Ex 24:1-2, 9-11; 2 Sm 3:20-21). Today too, eating and drinking together are a sign of friendship and love and common concern. But such meals may also become the occasion for evildoing as, for example, when business associates with large expense accounts entertain clients in luxurious restaurants with the intention of increasing their profits, violating the moral law.

Daniel and his companions did not refuse to live in a pagan court and to study the Babylonian literature and science, for they believed that all wisdom, including that of the pagans, comes from God (Sir 1:1-10). Like Daniel, we too must live in an essentially secular, even pagan, society. We have no choice in the matter, unless of course we decide to retire to a cloister. Like Daniel, we too are called to live by our religious principles even when there is risk of failure. Like Daniel, we must study the secular sciences because of the demands of the world in which we live and work, but we should not let secularism and paganism influence our life or our decisions.

The Jews Prosper on Their Vegetarian Diet

The palace official, fearing for his own life because Daniel and his companions might lose weight and not look as healthy as those who shared in the royal table, at first refuses to provide the vegetarian diet. But the official gives in when Daniel proposes a ten-day test period to see if the four look any worse with their diet than the others with their food fit for a king. The result, of course, is that the four looked healthier and better fed than those who ate the royal cuisine (1:9-16). All of this sounds very convenient, and somewhat naive.

Some Points to Ponder

Daniel and his companions feel certain of the outcome of the test. But what about us who live in the real world of today where uncertainty and ambiguity are inevitable features of an adult faith? Faith is not always rewarded with good results. Sinners do prosper while the good suffer all sorts of adversities. The stories in Daniel are instructive for our faith in several ways. The author of Daniel, like the people who were exiled from the Holy Land, must have wondered where was the God who had made such great promises to Israel's ancestors. The Book of Daniel proves for all time that God is sovereign Lord even in Babylon with its grandiose temple to Marduk, and not just in Jerusalem, the only place assigned for the sacrificial cult (Dt 12:2-14). Many people in Israel considered Jerusalem to be sacred and inviolable because God had chosen the city and its temple to be the privileged place of his presence. But the prophet Jeremiah chastised the people for their superstitious attachment to the holy city and temple. He reminds the people that God will be present in their midst only if they reform their ways and their deeds by dealing justly with others and no longer oppressing the weak (Jer 7:1-15). As Christians, we also need to be reminded that any over-attachment to a place, even a sacred place like a church or a shrine, may become a form of idolatry leading to our condemnation. It is a wrong form of religion to believe that God can be present in one place more than in any other.

Daniel's example also demonstrates that believers can be true to their faith and at the same time live and flourish in a pagan society despite the trials and tribulations which they may have to undergo. God endows Daniel and his companions with superior understanding and knowledge. God also gave Daniel "the under-standing of all visions and dreams" (1:17). Daniel's ability to interpret dreams and visions will feature prominently in chapters 2 and 4. The four Jews graduate at the head of their class. King Nebuchadnezzar himself conducts the final oral examination and finds the four Jews ten times better than the magicians and astrologers in his whole kingdom (1:17-20). There is another ironic twist here: Daniel and his companions turn out to be superior to the pagan experts even with regard to the sciences in which the Babylonians prided themselves. Like a fairy tale, the story of course has a happy ending: The heroes live happily ever after.

Today's Christians, however, cannot always count on prosperity in their earthly life. Success is not invariably a sign of divine approval as the American Puritans naively thought. After all, as Jesus tells us, "Those who want to save their life will lose it, and those who lose their life for my sake will find it" (Mt 16:25; Mk 8:35; Lk9:24). Nor should Christians use secular criteria to evaluate whether or not their lives are successful. As Mother Teresa told a reporter after she received the Nobel Prize for Peace in 1979, "The Lord never calls us to be successful, only faithful."

Finally, this chapter teaches us today that we are to live out our faith commitment even in the pagan environment of today's world with all its blandishments and allurements, its temptations and compromises. There is no other place or time in which we can live. The Christian cannot live in the past nor in the future, but only in the present. Moreover, there are no ideal times or places in which to be Christian and to practice Christian virtues and live a Christian life-style. There are no golden ages in the Church; there is no Christian land of Camelot. The present time and place alone are where God meets us and we meet God. Fidelity in action is what this chapter dramatizes—fidelity to the Lord and to conscience in a pagan world.

II

"The Mystery Was Revealed to Daniel in a Vision"

(Daniel 2:1-23)

[1] In the second year of his reign, King Nebuchadnezzar had a dream which left his spirit no rest and robbed him of his sleep. [2] So he ordered that the magicians, enchanters, sorcerers, and Chaldeans be summoned to interpret the dream for him. When they came and presented themselves to the king, [3] he said to them, "I had a dream which will allow my spirit no rest until I know what it means." [4] The Chaldeans answered the king [Aramaic]: "O king, live forever! Tell your servants the dream and we will give its meaning." [5] The king answered the Chaldeans, "This is what I have decided: Unless you tell me the dream and its meaning, you shall be cut to pieces and your houses destroyed. [6] But if you tell me the dream and its meaning, you shall receive from me gifts and presents and great honors. Now tell me the dream and its meaning."

[7] Again they answered, "Let the king tell his servants the dream and we will give its meaning." [8] But the king replied: "I know for certain that you are bargaining for time, since you know what I have decided. [9] If you do not tell me the dream, there can be but one decree for you. You have framed a false and deceitful interpretation to present me with till the crisis is past. Tell me the dream, therefore, that I may be sure that you can also give its correct interpretation."

[10] The Chaldeans answered the king: "There is not a man on earth who can do what you ask, O king; never has any king, however great and mighty, asked such a thing of any magician, enchanter, or Chaldean. [11] What you demand, O king, is too difficult; there is no one who can tell it to the king except the gods who do not dwell among men." [12] At this the king became violently angry and ordered all the wise men of Babylon to be

put to death. ¹³When the decree was issued that the wise men should be slain, Daniel and his companions were also sought out.

¹⁴Then Daniel prudently took counsel with Arioch, the captain of the king's guard, who had set out to kill the wise men of Babylon: ¹⁵"O officer of the king," he asked, "what is the reason for this harsh order from the king?" When Arioch told him, ¹⁶Daniel went and asked for time from the king, that he might give him the interpretation.

¹⁷Daniel went home and informed his companions Hananiah, Mishael, and Azariah, ¹⁸that they might implore the mercy of the God of heaven in regard to this mystery, so that Daniel and his companions might not perish with the rest of the wise men of Babylon. ¹⁹During the night the mystery was revealed to Daniel in a vision, and he blessed the God of heaven:

²⁰"Blessed be the name of God forever and ever,
for wisdom and power are his.
²¹He causes the changes of the times and seasons,
makes kings and unmakes them.
He gives wisdom to the wise and knowledge to those
who understand.
²²He reveals deep and hidden things
and knows what is in the darkness,
for the light dwells with him.
²³To you, O God of my fathers,
I give thanks and praise, because you have given me
wisdom and power.
Now you have shown me what we asked of you,
you have made known to us the king's dream."

In this long chapter King Nebuchadnezzar has a disturbing dream. He calls in his "magicians, enchanters, sorcerers, and Chaldeans." He orders them to tell him, under penalty of death, both the content of the dream and its meaning. The Babylonian "experts," of course, cannot help the king. Only the Jewish outsider Daniel can honor the king's request. He tells the king that his apocalyptic dream concerns a colossal statue that symbolizes four successive kingdoms: Babylonian, Median, Persian, and Greek.

Dreams in the Bible

Dreams were considered important in the ancient Near Eastern world and in the Bible as well. In the Joseph cycle of stories in Genesis, dreams occur with regularity. Joseph had a dream in which he and his brothers were binding sheaves in the field, when suddenly his sheaf rose up above the others, and the sheaves of his brothers formed a ring around Joseph's and bowed down to it. His brothers asked him if he was going to be made king over them, and they hated him because he talked also about his other dreams (Gn 37:5-11). They then sell Joseph to caravan traders who in turn sell him in Egypt to Potiphar, a courtier of Pharaoh. Later, Joseph interprets the dreams of the royal cupbearer and baker who were in prison (Gn 40:1-19) and of Pharaoh (Gn 41:1-33). The result is that Joseph ends up a successful courtier in a Gentile land, becoming second in command at court (Gn 41:37-46). In the various narratives of our book, Daniel and his career are modeled to a great extent on the Joseph stories.

God often revealed himself in dreams. In a dream, Solomon is told by the Lord to ask for whatever he desires; he asks for wisdom (1 Kgs 3:5-15). In Genesis dreams are a normal means of divine communication in the stories of Abraham (15:12-20), Abimelech (20:3-7), Laban (31:24), and Jacob (46:2-4). In the New Testament the Magi are warned in a dream not to return to Herod (Mt 2:12). Later Joseph is told in a dream to take the child Jesus to Egypt to avoid Herod's attempt to kill him (Mt 2:13). Pilate's wife had a disturbing dream because of Jesus and tells her husband that Jesus is innocent (Mt 27:19) .

Yet the Bible also has stern warnings regarding those who rely on dreams. Thus, for example, Deuteronomy 13:2-6 imposes the death penalty on the prophet or dreamer who leads the people astray from the way of the Lord. The most extensive admonition regarding dreams is found in Sirach 34:1-6: "Empty and false are the hopes of the senseless, and fools are borne aloft by dreams. Like a man who catches at shadows or chases the wind, is the one who believes in dreams. What is seen in dreams is to reality what the reflection of a face is to the face itself. Can the unclean produce the clean? Can the liar ever speak the truth? Divination, omens and dreams all are unreal; what you already expect, the mind depicts. Unless it be a vision specially sent by the Most High, fix not your heart on it. For dreams have led many astray, and those who believed in them have perished." The profound insights of Sirach (Ben Sira) are valid in every time and place. This ancient sage rightly gives the lie to the practices of the so-called magical "arts" that attempt to forecast the future for gullible clients.

Interest in dreams, however, is perfectly legitimate as long as we do not exaggerate their significance. Sigmund Freud (1856-1939) proposed many theories about dreams, which he called "the royal road to the unconscious." Though psychologists today often disagree with Freud's theories, dreams can tell us something about ourselves, our hopes and fears as well as our talents and possibilities. When he accepted the Nobel Prize for physics in 1922, Niels Bohr (1885-1962) said that his dreams had shown him the makeup of the atom. Many others have reported similar experiences. The comments of Carl Jung (1875-1961), founder of analytic psychology, are worth pondering: "I have no theory about dreams. I do not know how dreams arise. On the other hand, I know that if we meditate on a dream sufficiently long and thoroughly—if we take it about with us and turn it over and over—something almost always comes of it."

The King's Dream

Nebuchadnezzar had a bad dream that disturbed him greatly (2:1). So he summoned "the magicians, enchanters, sorcerers, and Chaldeans"—the experts of his court to tell him what he had dreamt (2:2). The term "Chaldean" is used here almost as a synonym for astrologer. These were the men who had been trained in astrology, magic, and sorcery as well as dream interpretation. We are not told why the king asks these men for the content of the dream. It could be that Nebuchadnezzar did not remember his dream at all, as often happens also with us when we are awakened by a nightmare. It is also possible that the king is testing his wise men to see if their skills are for real, as 2:9 seems to indicate.

They ask the king to tell them the dream—a perfectly normal request. They will then interpret it for him (2:4). The king, however, refuses to tell them a thing. Instead, he insists that the experts tell him first the content of the dream and then its meaning. If they fail to do so, they will be cut to pieces and their houses destroyed (2:5). Such cruel and unusual punishment was not unheard of in antiquity. Assyrian-Babylonian forms of execution are graphically illustrated in the bas-reliefs that have been uncovered by archaeologists. The codes of Assyria and Babylonia likewise describe similar grisly modes of execution (cf. Dn 3:96; 6:25; and 2 Mc 1:16). Such barbarism was also practiced in the execution of Catholics in Elizabethan times in England and later during the Reign of Terror in the French Revolution. Unfortunately, government-sponsored torture and gruesome forms of execution occur also today in many parts of the world, even in so-called democratic countries.

The "Experts" Fail but Daniel Succeeds

The experts protest that no king had ever made such an unusual request before (2:10). When they add that the king is asking for something so difficult that only divine beings can reveal it to him (2:11), we can see the skillful hand of the author anticipating the outcome of the story. Indeed, of all Babylon's wise men only Daniel, under divine inspiration, is able to first describe Nebuchadnezzar's dream in detail and then to interpret it accurately. God alone knows all secrets as well as the hidden things of the human heart. God reveals such mysteries only to those whom he chooses.

Daniel proves to be superior in the very skills in which the Babylonian wise men had prided themselves. Despite all their efforts and education, the pagan experts could offer no help to their king. They fail again in the stories of chapters 4 and 5. God cannot be manipulated by the Babylonian magical devices into revealing what the king wanted to know. It may seem strange that these narratives place Daniel and his companions among Babylonian "magicians, enchanters, and sorcerers." Practitioners of these pagan "arts" are roundly condemned in many parts of the Old Testament. "Let there not be found among you anyone who immolates his son or daughter in the fire, nor a fortune-teller, soothsayer, charmer, diviner, or caster of spells, nor one who consults ghosts and spirits or seeks oracles from the dead. Anyone who does such things is an abomination to the LORD, and because of such abominations the LORD, your God, is driving these nations out of your way" (Dt 18:10-12; cf. Ex 22:17; Lv 19:26, 31; 20:6, 27; Is 47:9-15).

Superstitious Practices and Limits of Human Wisdom

Astrology, star gazing, palm reading, crystal ball consultation, reading of tea leaves and tarot cards, and other superstitious practices are all included in this biblical condemnation. It would be a serious mistake, therefore, to draw any theological conclusions for today regarding the presence of the four Jews among the Babylonian magicians. The author here is merely following the ironic plot lines of his own fiction. In other words, the author has Daniel and his companions beat the pagans at their own game. The story dramatizes the conflict between the Babylonian and the Israelite world-view. This conflict remains till this day. Christians must realize that it is impossible to reconcile the values of an essentially pagan society in which we live with the values of the revealed faith in which we entrust our lives.

The failure of the Babylonians emphasizes that there are clearly defined limits to human wisdom, intelligence, and training. In a scientific age like ours, we need to be reminded of this important truth. Science cannot solve all the problems we face or fill the empty spaces in the human spirit. Science cannot even answer all the critical questions posed by the sciences themselves. The ultimate nature of matter and energy still eludes the physicist. The human mind alone is unable to fathom the mysteries of the vast universe. In exquisite poetry, Job 39–41 dramatizes the limits of human understanding. Neither the philosopher nor the secular humanist can explain the reason for our existence as human beings and our ultimate destiny, which is loving communion with a personal God who cares and who has staked a claim in human affairs. This episode demonstrates what we were told earlier. God endowed Daniel with "the understanding of all visions and dreams" (1:18), and Nebuchadnezzar found Daniel and his companions "ten times better than all the magicians and enchanters in his kingdom" (1:20).

Daniel Seeks an Audience with the King

Because the Babylonian wise men were unable to honor the king's demands, he flies into a rage and orders that they all be put to death (2:12). Nebuchadnezzar, like tyrants throughout history, demands unquestioned obedience. It does not matter that the demand is difficult or impossible or against an enlightened conscience. Rulers like Hitler and Stalin and dictators in our own day will not be denied. Daniel and his companions are also included in the death warrant (2:13) because they were numbered among the wise men of the land (1:17-20). Daniel, however, is a man of action. He "prudently took counsel with Arioch, the captain of the king's guard" and asked why the king had issued such a harsh order. Arioch told him. Then Daniel asked for an audience with the king himself (2:14-16). At times, it is necessary to stand up to those in government, as Daniel did. But like Daniel, one must act *prudently* and respectfully, and not arrogantly or polemically. Otherwise, the intervention can turn into confrontation that may even make matters worse. By being humble and prudent, Daniel succeeded in getting an audience with Nebuchadnezzar. A drop of honey attracts more flies than a barrel of vinegar.

It was Christian gentleness and disarming humility that enabled Francis of Assisi and one of his brothers in 1219 to obtain an audience with Malik al-Kamil, the sultan of the Muslims in Egypt. The sultan was intrigued by the poor men, who stood in front of him with such charm and dignity. If they would become Muslims, he said, he would offer them the riches and pleasures of his court. Of course, they refused. Instead they told him that they were there to convert the sultan to the Christian faith. Instead of lopping off their heads, the sultan put the two friars through the ordeal of treading on the cross. A sumptuous carpet with crosses embroidered on it was spread out before Francis. Without hesitation the saint walked right on the crosses. Then he said to the sultan, "See, I have walked on the crosses of the bad thief. You can keep them if you wish. We keep our own which is the true cross." Totally disarmed by the saint's reply, the sultan agreed to hear about the Christian faith and then dismissed them in peace.

Daniel Prays for Enlightenment

When Arioch informs Daniel about what had happened, Daniel first tells his companions and then asks them to pray to "the God of heaven" about this "mystery," so that they may not be executed along with Babylon's wise men (2:17-18). Instead of consulting the Babylonian dream books in which he and his companions had been instructed (1:4, 17-20), Daniel, keenly aware of the limits even of his great knowledge (1:17), appeals to the Source of all wisdom. Daniel, the man of action, is also a man of prayer. Action, even of the most noble sort, should never extinguish the spirit of prayer. Worship of God together with daily prayer must go hand in hand with involvement in our culture—a culture that unfortunately looks upon belief in God as a naive curiosity.

Prayer is a prominent feature also in other parts of the book (3:24-45, 51-90; 6:11; 9:3-19; 13:42-43). Even Nebuchadnezzar and Darius the Mede pray to the God of Israel when Daniel resolves their problems (3:95, 100; 4:31-32; 6:27-28). Daniel, realizing the plight he and the Babylonian wise men faced together, called for divine help. So he enlists his companions in a group prayer. This may be the first instance in scripture of a house meeting for prayer. Group prayer establishes a common bond and solidarity among the participants and reinforces the faith of each. In the New Testament, we find Christians often praying in community in order to seek help from the Lord or to encourage each other in the faith (Acts 1:14; 4:23-31; 12:5, 12; Eph 6:10-18). The prayer of the four Jews is not self-centered. They also pray that the pagan wise men may be spared. Paul tells us, "Persevere in prayer, being watchful in it with thanksgiving" (Col 4:2). The New Testament also exhorts us to pray for our government leaders: "First of all, then, I ask that supplications, prayers, petitions, and thanksgivings be offered for everyone, for kings and for all in authority, that we may lead a quiet and tranquil life in all devotion and dignity" (1 Tm 2:1-2). Like Daniel, we should pray that those in authority refrain from violence and protect the innocent.

God Comes to the Rescue

The God of heaven answers the prayers of the four Jews. As Source of all knowledge and mystery, God reveals the king's dream and its meaning to Daniel, again at night in a vision (2:19). Daniel's reaction is instructive. He does not run off in great excitement to tell the king what God has revealed, but rather he immediately offers the Lord a hymn of praise and thanksgiving, in exquisite poetry, for having granted him what he had asked. Like the author of Psalm 113:2 and Job 1:21, Daniel first blesses the name (that is, the person or essence) of God "for wisdom and power are his" (2:20). There is no other source of human and angelic wisdom, and of earthly and heavenly power. Even the cycles of nature come under the dominion of the God of heaven who created them (cf. Dn 7:12; Acts 1:7). Kings come and go because their power derives from God who is in sovereign control of their destinies. Paul puts it this way, "Let every person be subordinate to the higher authorities, for there is no authority except from God, and those that exist have been established by God" (Rom 13:1; cf. Jn 19:10-11). Daniel is like Joseph who acknowledged that his ability to interpret dreams came from God (Gn 40:8; 41:16). Daniel also echoes (2:21) the words of the sage Ben Sira: "All wisdom is from the Lord, and with him it remains forever. . . . It is he who created her . . . ; he poured her out upon all his works, upon all the living according to his gift; he lavished her upon those who love him" (Sir 1:1, 9-10). Human wisdom is a gift of the Lord and not the result of study and effort alone, as Daniel 1 makes clear.

God alone can reveal "deep and hidden things," as Job 12:22 also confesses. God "knows what is in the darkness" since he is light itself (Mic 7:8), which is here used symbolically for God's knowledge of all "deep and hidden things" (2:22). The contrast between light and darkness forms a recurring theme in ancient Near Eastern literature. In the Old Testament, light is used as a symbol not only for knowledge as in Daniel 2:22 but also for such concepts as sight (Tb 10:5; 11:14), truth (Pss 37:6; 43:3; 119:105, 130), salvation (Ps 27:1), goodness (Jb 30:24), happiness (Pss 89:15; 97:11; Wis 18:1), and life itself (Is 53:11; Mic 7:9; Ps 49:19; Jb 3:20; 18:5-6; Tb 14:10; Sir 22:9). In the Dead Sea Scrolls and

36

the New Testament, light and darkness are used symbolically for truth and error (Lk 11:35), good and evil (Jn 1:4-9; 3:19), life and death (Jn 8:12; 12:46). The Qumran War Scroll speaks of the enmity between the children of light and the children of darkness. Jesus calls Christians "the light of the world" (Mt 5:14). Paul writes, "For you were once darkness, but now you are light in the Lord. Live as children of light" (Eph 5:8; cf. Jn 8:12; 12:36; 1 Thes 5:5; 1 Jn 1:7; 2:8-11).

At the conclusion of his prayer Daniel offers his thanks and praise to the "God of my fathers" for giving wisdom and power to him and for revealing to him the king's dream and its meaning (2:23). The expression, "God of my fathers," recalls the phrase, "God of your [i.e., Israel's] fathers," found elsewhere, especially in Deuteronomy (Dt 1:11, 21; 4:1; 6:3; 12:1; 27:3; Jos 18:3; 2 Chr 29:9; Ezr 8:28; 10:11; Acts 7:32). The expression emphasizes that this is the same God who was worshiped and honored by the Israel of old when God revealed to Moses his sacred name, Yahweh (Ex 3:13-15). It is the same God whom Jesus taught us to call "Our Father" (Mt 6:9-13) and whom Jesus addressed as "Holy Father" (Jn 17:11). We can come to this God with confidence and absolute trust when we approach him with a sincere heart (Heb 10:19-23). For God is a God of love (1 Jn 4:16) and compassion, utterly transcendent but also ever-present to those who put their faith in him.

III

"There Is a God in Heaven
Who Reveals Mysteries"

(Daniel 2:24-49)

[24]So Daniel went to Arioch, whom the king had appointed to destroy the wise men of Babylon, and said to him, "Do not put the wise men of Babylon to death. Bring me before the king, and I will tell him the interpretation of the dream." Arioch quickly brought Daniel to the king and said, [25]"I have found a man among the Judean captives who can give the interpretation to the king." [26]The king asked Daniel, whose name was Belteshazzar, "Can you tell me the dream that I had, and its meaning?" [27]In the king's presence Daniel made this reply:

"The mystery about which the king has inquired, the wise men, enchanters, magicians, and astrologers could not explain to the king. [28]But there is a God in heaven who reveals mysteries, and he has shown King Nebuchadnezzar what is to happen in days to come; this was the dream you saw as you lay in bed. [29]To you in your bed there came thoughts about what should happen in the future, and he who reveals mysteries showed you what is to be. [30]To me also this mystery has been revealed; not that I am wiser than any other living person, but in order that its meaning may be made known to the king, that you may understand the thoughts in your own mind.

[31]"In your vision, O king, you saw a statue, very large and exceedingly bright, terrifying in appearance as it stood before you. [32]The head of the statue was pure gold, its chest and arms were silver, its belly and thighs bronze, [33]the legs iron, its feet partly iron and partly tile. [34]While you looked at the statue, a stone which was hewn from a mountain without a hand being put to it, struck its iron and tile feet, breaking them in pieces. [35]The iron, tile, bronze, silver, and gold all crumbled at once, fine as the chaff on the threshing floor in summer, and the wind blew

them away without leaving a trace. But the stone that struck the statue became a great mountain and filled the whole earth.

³⁶"This was the dream; the interpretation we shall also give in the king's presence. ³⁷You, O king, are the king of kings; to you the God of heaven has given dominion and strength, power and glory; ³⁸men, wild beasts, and birds of the air, wherever they may dwell, he has handed over to you, making you ruler over them all; you are the head of gold. ³⁹Another kingdom shall take your place, inferior to yours, then a third kingdom, of bronze, which shall rule over the whole earth. ⁴⁰There shall be a fourth kingdom, strong as iron; it shall break in pieces and subdue all these others, just as iron breaks in pieces and crushes everything else. ⁴¹The feet and toes you saw, partly of potter's tile and partly of iron, mean that it shall be a divided kingdom, but yet have some of the hardness of iron. As you saw the iron mixed with clay tile, ⁴²and the toes partly iron and partly tile, the kingdom shall be partly strong and partly fragile. ⁴³The iron mixed with clay tile means that they shall seal their alliances by intermarriage, but they shall not stay united, any more than iron mixes with clay. ⁴⁴In the lifetime of those kings the God of heaven will set up a kingdom that shall never be destroyed or delivered up to another people; rather, it shall break in pieces all these kingdoms and put an end to them, and it shall stand forever. ⁴⁵That is the meaning of the stone you saw hewn from the mountain without a hand being put to it, which broke in pieces the tile, iron, bronze, silver, and gold. The great God has revealed to the king what shall be in the future; this is exactly what you dreamed, and its meaning is sure."

⁴⁶Then King Nebuchadnezzar fell down and worshiped Daniel and ordered sacrifice and incense offered to him. To Daniel the king said, "Truly your God is the God of gods and Lord of kings and a revealer of mysteries; that is why you were able to reveal this mystery." ⁴⁸He advanced Daniel to a high post, gave him many generous presents, made him ruler of the whole province of Babylon and chief prefect over all the wise men of Babylon. ⁴⁹At Daniel's request the king made Shadrach, Meshach, and Abednego administrators of the province of Babylon, while Daniel himself remained at the king's court.

After praising and thanking God, Daniel now comes to the rescue of the wise men of Babylon, including himself and his three companions. He goes to Arioch whom we first met in 2:14 and tells him not to go through with the king's execution order. Daniel tells the king the contents and interpretation of his dream. The king then promotes Daniel to a high post in government.

Daniel Lectures Nebuchadnezzar

Acceding to the request for an audience, Arioch brings Daniel into the presence of mighty Nebuchadnezzar (2:24). Arioch describes Daniel as one of "the Judean captives" (2:25), a description loaded with irony, for it is this Jewish "captive" who can free Nebuchadnezzar of the fear and apprehension he felt over his dream. We are told once again in 2:26 that Daniel's Babylonian name is Belteshazzar, which means "[Marduk or Bel,] guard his life." The irony should not be missed, for it is not Marduk or Bel or any other Babylonian deity that guarded Daniel's life but rather the true God of Israel.

When the king asks Daniel if he can tell him the dream and its meaning, Daniel could simply have answered yes, without explaining how he came to this knowledge. Instead of taking the credit for himself, Daniel sees an opening to give a polite but outspoken lecture about the failure of paganism and the truth about God. He first explains the inadequacy of Babylonian wisdom and magical practices, implying in effect that the pagan gods have no knowledge of anything, much less of something as mysterious as what the king dreamt. The prophets of Israel before Daniel ridiculed pagan idolatry, describing false gods as "the work of human hands, wood and stone" (Is 37:19). Idols are "gods that cannot save" (Is 45:20); they are utterly "useless" (Jer 2:8), "abominable" (Jer 7:30), and "deceptive" (Jer 8:5). Daniel then proclaims to the king that there is a true "God in heaven who reveals mysteries" and "what is to happen in days to come" (2:28). Daniel is quick to acknowledge that God alone has shown the king what he wants to know.

We can learn from Daniel how to seize the opportunity to talk about God and ultimate reality. Many today follow a life-style that is little more than the satisfaction of physical and social, psychological and sexual desires. Despite their prosperity and affluence, they are not content. They are restless. Something is missing. So in a futile attempt to find it, they pursue wealth, status, power, even sensual gratification. But in reality, what they are looking for is meaning—something that cannot be found in accumulating more and more or in indulging in an endless round of self-indulgence. Convinced Christians will seek and find opportunities to proclaim in a consumerist society that the Lord alone can provide the key to a meaningful human life. Mother Teresa of Calcutta is an outstanding example of Christian commitment, fearlessness, and outspokenness. She practices what the New Testament calls in Greek *parresia*, which means "frankness, plainness of speech, courage" that conceals nothing and overlooks nothing even in the presence of those in high places.

Especially after she was awarded the Nobel Prize for Peace in 1978, Mother Teresa was much in demand for interviews and speeches. Unafraid to speak out, she defended vigorously the Christian principles by which she lived—principles like reverence for the poor, the sanctity of marriage, and respect for all human life, especially the aged, the incurably ill, the unborn. Christians should follow the lead of Paul who prayed "that speech may be given me to open my mouth, to make known with boldness [*parresia*] the mystery of the gospel for which I am an ambassador in chains, so that I may have the courage to speak as I must" (Eph 6:19-20; cf. Acts 4:31).

The king's apocalyptic dream concerns the future about which no one can possibly know except "a God in heaven" who reveals mysteries (2:28-29). In 2:37 and 44, Daniel alters the phrase slightly, "the God of heaven." This threefold occurrence of the expression "God of/in heaven" adds emphasis. Repeating an expression three times is the Hebrew way of indicating the superlative degree, as in Isaiah 6:3, "Holy, holy, holy is Yahweh of hosts." This threefold repetition leads up to the expression "the great God" (2:45), which together with the phrase "God in/of heaven," suggests the utter transcendence of God. God is completely beyond and above our capabilities to understand. But that same God is also immanent. He has willed to involve himself in human history. The gods of Babylon, who were alleged to have power over the city and nation and whose images were made by human hands, could do nothing for Nebuchadnezzar. The reason is simple: They were not gods at all. Indeed, God in heaven alone has power and dominion over all nations, times, and peoples. It is only this God who is supreme. That is why this God can reveal secrets also in Babylon.

Daniel's Confession

Daniel humbly confesses that he knows the mystery only because God has revealed it to him, and that "he is not wiser than any other living person" (2:30). He is no more talented or better schooled than the other wise men. These men could not possibly know the king's mystery simply by means of their education. Daniel acknowledges the Source of his knowledge of such mysteries. The inability of the pagan wise men brings to mind what Paul observes in 1 Corinthians 1:19, "For it is written: 'I [God] will destroy the wisdom of the wise, and the learning of the learned I will set aside.' "

The second-century B.C. Jews who read the Book of Daniel must have been dazzled and attracted by Greek wisdom, science, and culture which seemed far superior to their own. They were tempted to question their own wisdom and religious heritage with its beliefs and practices that seemed out of touch with the new age. Christians today may feel the same about their own faith in our so-called post-Christian age. They may ask whether the old Christian beliefs have any validity in a world that has made such marvelous advances in technology, travel, communication, science, medicine, and standard of living. Paul's message to the first Christians, who were also awed by Greek literature and knowledge, is still valid today. "Where is the wise one? Where is the scribe? Where is the debater of this age? Has not God made the wisdom of the world foolish? For since in the wisdom of God the world did not come to know God through wisdom, it was the will of God through the foolishness of the proclamation to save those who have faith. For Jews demand signs and Greeks look for wisdom, but we proclaim Christ crucified, a stumbling block to Jews and foolishness to Gentiles, but to those who are called, Jews and Greeks alike, Christ the power of God and the wisdom of God. For the foolishness of God is wiser than human wisdom, and the weakness of God is stronger than human strength" (1 Cor 1:20-25).

Daniel Describes and Interprets the Apocalyptic Dream

Now comes Daniel's minute description of the king's dream. The king saw a colossal statue, "exceedingly bright" and "terrifying in appearance" (2:31). But this was no ordinary statue. It had a head of gold, chest and arms of silver, belly and thighs of bronze, legs of iron, and feet partly of iron and partly of tile (2:32-33). A stone or rock, which was "hewn from a mountain without a hand being put to it," then struck the iron and tile feet, causing the entire statue to come crumbling down into dust fine "as chaff on the threshing floor." The wind then blew away every trace. Nothing was left of the statue. But the stone that had struck it became "a great mountain and filled the earth" (2:31-35). This was a weird dream, to say the least—apocalyptic at its best.

Daniel now gives the interpretation, which is not at all consoling or flattering to the king's vanity. Daniel tells Nebuchadnezzar that he is "the king of kings," a title which means the most royal or powerful of kings. Ezekiel gives Nebuchadnezzar the same title (26:7). But in reality it is God alone who is "King of kings" (2 Mc 13:4). Nebuchadnezzar is the head of gold to whom the God of heaven had given "dominion and strength, power and glory." God gave the king control not only over human beings but also over "wild beasts and birds of the air" (2:37-38), an allusion to Genesis 1:26-28. As we learned from Daniel's prayer in 2:21, God alone "makes kings and unmakes them." The same idea is found in Jeremiah 27:5-6: "It was I [God] who made the earth, and man and beast on the face of the earth, by my great power, with my outstretched arm; and I can give them to whomever I think fit. Now I have given all these lands into the hand of Nebuchadnezzar, king of Babylon, my servant; even the beasts of the field I have given him for his use." Thus, without realizing it, mighty Nebuchadnezzar is God's servant just like the Persian King Cyrus who is called Yahweh's "anointed" in Isaiah 45:1. Despite Nebuchadnezzar's grandeur, however, another kingdom, though inferior to his, will take his place—the meaning of the chest and arms of silver. The third kingdom, of bronze, will be replaced by a fourth, "strong as iron," which will break and subdue all others. But this will be a divided kingdom, "partly strong" like iron and "partly fragile" like clay tile (2:39-42). The marriage alliances of this last kingdom will not last "any more than iron mixes with clay" (2:43).

It is generally agreed that the four kingdoms described here by the apocalyptic symbolism of metals are the Babylonian, Median, Persian, and Greek, including the Ptolemaic and Seleucid reigns that followed the death of Alexander the Great. This sequence is not historically accurate. The author simply took over a commonly held view regarding the succession of these kingdoms. The point of the author is not to teach a history lesson, but to show that the God of heaven is in control of history, and that this God can reduce to dust even the most powerful of kings and their empires (2:21). Though there was a steady decline in power and influence from the head of gold (the Babylonian kingdom) to the feet of clay and iron (the Ptolemaic and Seleucid kingdoms, which often fought against each other), each of these kingdoms, nevertheless, had frightful consequences for the Jews.

It was the Seleucid dynasty, however, which most concerned the Jews of that day. The earlier kingdoms had already disappeared and were nothing but a bad memory. But tyrants like the Seleucid Antiochus IV still had absolute power. He persecuted and martyred the Jews who were faithful to their spiritual heritage (2 Mc 6:1-7:41). For the Jews, therefore, it must have been a great consolation to believe that the Seleucid villainy would not endure, and that "in the lifetime of those kings the God of heaven will set up a kingdom that shall never be destroyed" (2:44). The mysterious stone, which demolished and pulverized the monstrous statue and became "a great mountain and filled the whole earth" (2:35), is that everlasting kingdom (2:45). Its members are those Jews who persevered to the end. The image of a great mountain comes from Isaiah 2:2 (cf. Mic 4:1). The idea of an eternal kingdom reserved for the loyal Jews will be taken up again in the apocalypse of Daniel 7. Kings and kingdoms, states and governments, even the most powerful and wealthy, come and go as we know from history. Only the great God and his kingdom will endure forever.

God's Kingdom

There is an important detail that must not be overlooked. The stone which strikes the statue was "hewn from a mountain without a [human] hand being put to it" (2:34, 45). Thus, the fifth kingdom, the everlasting kingdom, which will replace the kingdoms of the world, is completely the work of God and not the result of human efforts. This point may have been directed originally against the Maccabees, who used force against those Jews who capitulated to Antiochus IV (1 Mc 2:22-48). When people are oppressed, they long and pray for divine intervention. But deliverance does not come by taking up arms, but only in God's own time and manner. This lesson has often been forgotten. The result is the sad history of armed conflicts that continue to this day even among Christian groups like the Orthodox Serbs and Roman Catholic Croats, and Catholics and Protestants in Northern Ireland.

If one accepts Daniel's interpretation of the dream at face value, however, the fourth kingdom, including the dynasty of the Seleucids to which Antiochus IV belonged, would be the last earthly kingdom before the establishment of "a kingdom that shall never be destroyed or delivered up to another people" (2:44). Yet after the demise of the Seleucid dynasty, this everlasting kingdom, which would fill "the whole earth" (2:35), did not seem to leave any empirical signs of its presence. But the eschatological message of this story is clear. Those who remain faithful to God in any place and time may become members of the everlasting kingdom. It is this message that consoled the faithful Jews of that day.

The New Testament takes up the imagery of "stone" and applies it to Jesus Christ. Thus in 1 Peter 2:4-8, we read, "Come to him, a living stone, rejected by human beings but chosen and precious in the sight of God, and, like living stones, let yourselves be built into a spiritual house to be a holy priesthood to offer spiritual sacrifices acceptable to God through Jesus Christ. For it says in scripture: 'Behold, I am laying a stone in Zion, a cornerstone, chosen and precious, and whoever believes in it shall not be put to shame' [Is 28:16]. Therefore, its value is for you who have faith, but for those without faith: 'The stone which the builders rejected has become the cornerstone' [Ps 118:22], and 'A stone that will make people stumble, and a rock that will make them fall.' They stumble by disobeying the word, as is their destiny" (cf. Rom 9:31-33; Mk 12:10-11; Mt 21:42). The text of Luke 20:17-18 is even more explicit: "But he [Jesus] looked at them [the addressees of the parable of the tenant farmers] and asked, 'What then does this scripture passage mean: "The stone which the builders rejected has become the cornerstone"? Everyone who falls on that stone will be dashed to pieces; and it will crush anyone on whom it falls.' "

The mystery of God's kingdom is, of course, a central teaching of Jesus Christ. In the New Testament, the expression "kingdom of heaven (=God)" or "kingdom of God" occurs in ninety-seven verses. At the beginning of his ministry, "Jesus began to preach and say, 'Repent, for the kingdom of heaven is at hand' " (Mt 4:17). The kingdom is open to all who are sincere in their repentance, for as Jesus tells us, "Not everyone who says to me, 'Lord, Lord,' will enter the kingdom of heaven, but only the one who does the will of my Father in heaven" (Mt 7:21). As Christian disciples, our primary vocation is to follow Jesus and to "make this proclamation: 'The kingdom of heaven is at hand' " (Mt 10:7). Jesus has over-turned the values of his society as well as ours when he said, "Amen, I say to you, unless you turn and become like children, you will not enter the kingdom of heaven. Whoever humbles himself like this child is the greatest in the kingdom of heaven" (Mt 18:3-4).

These are difficult words for people today who strive at any cost to achieve success and advancement, power and prestige. After Jesus told the people the parable of the sower who sowed seed, the "disciples approached him and said, 'Why do you speak to them in parables?' He said to them in reply, 'Because knowledge of the mysteries of the kingdom of heaven has been granted to you, but to them it has not been granted' " (Mt 13:10-11). The meaning is clear: Only those who accept Jesus as Lord can understand what the mystery of the kingdom of God is all about. Paul writes, "The kingdom of God is not a matter of food and drink, but of righteousness, peace, and joy in the holy Spirit" (Rom 14:17). The apostle adds, "Do you not know that the unjust will not inherit the kingdom of God? Do not be deceived; neither fornicators nor idolaters nor adulterers nor boy prostitutes nor sodomites nor thieves nor the greedy nor drunkards nor slanderers nor robbers will inherit the kingdom of God" (1 Cor 6:9-10).

Because of our faith in Jesus, "He [God] delivered us from the power of darkness and transferred us to the kingdom of his beloved Son, in whom we have redemption, the forgiveness of sins" (Col

1:13-14). "Therefore, we who are receiving the unshakable kingdom should have gratitude, with which we should offer worship pleasing to God in reverence and awe" (Heb 12:28). The kingdom of God is "the mystery hidden from ages past in God who created all things, so that the manifold wisdom of God might now be made known through the Church to the principalities and authorities in the heavens" (Eph 3:9-10). This mystery is likewise the mystery of salvation through Jesus' suffering, and the mystery of eternal life through Jesus' death on the cross. The suffering, dying, and rising Christ is for those "who are called, Jews and Greeks alike, Christ the power of God and the wisdom of God" (1 Cor 1:24).

Daniel concludes his explanation of the apocalyptic dream by telling the king with complete confidence, "This is exactly what you dreamed, and its meaning is sure" (2:45). Nebuchadnezzar needs no proof of Daniel's words; he knows by intuition that the Jew has spoken the truth. According to 2:46, however, the king apparently has forgotten that Daniel was able to answer the king's questions only because of God's revelation, and not because of his training as a wise man (2:28-30). So the king gives Daniel what appear to be divine honors. When Paul healed the cripple at Lystra, the people thought he and Barnabas were Greek gods in human form (Acts 14:8-14). They called Barnabas "Zeus" and Paul "Hermes." When they wanted to offer sacrifice to the apostles, Paul exclaimed, "Why are you doing this? We are of the same nature as you, human beings. We proclaim to you good news that you should turn from these idols to the living God, 'who made heaven and earth and sea and all that is in them' " (Acts 14:15).

But here the divine honors given to Daniel may simply be the author's ironic way of turning the tables on pagan kings who often expected divine honors from their subjects. Antiochus IV took to himself the title Epiphanes, which means "[god] Manifest." That tyrant was, however, anything but godly; hence, his popular nickname Epimanes, "Madman." Jerome gives a different explanation. He writes that Nebuchadnezzar "worshiped not Daniel so much as in Daniel the God who reveals mysteries." In fact, Nebuchadnezzar proclaims in 2:47 that Daniel's God is "the God of gods and Lord of kings" as well as "revealer of mysteries." That is why, as the king confesses, Daniel was able to reveal the mystery.

However, there is also another irony involved here. Nebuchadnezzar, who in real life was head of a great empire and whom even Daniel calls "the king of kings" (2:37), now pays homage to Daniel, a captive from a fifth-rate people. This is a stunning reversal of human values and expectations.

As is usual in a narrative of the successful courtier (like Joseph in Genesis 42:37-44), the king lavishes gifts on Daniel and promotes him to a high position as "ruler of the whole province of Babylon and chief prefect over all the wise men of Babylon" (2:48). But unlike many today who forget their roots once they have climbed to the top of the social or political world, Daniel is mindful of his three companions. Daniel asks Nebuchadnezzar to give better jobs to his three companions (2:49).

But this happy ending should not be misunderstood. Dictators and other tyrants continue to act as if they were accountable to no one, not even God, and they persecute those who live by religious faith and principles. Moreover, as everyone is aware, the faithful are not always rewarded with honor and respect. Good people still suffer and are put to death unjustly. Being a mystery, the kingdom of God is not empirically verifiable in the world in which we live but is revealed only to the followers of Christ (Mt 13:11). The kingdom, nevertheless, is both a present reality and a future reality. The kingdom exists right now in the hearts of believers who live according to the law of Christ. The kingdom belongs to "the poor in spirit, for theirs is the kingdom of heaven" (Mt 5:3), and to those "who are persecuted for the sake of righteousness, for theirs is the kingdom of heaven" (Mt 5:10). The kingdom is also a future reality. As Jesus says in his trial before Pilate, "My kingdom does not belong to this world. If my kingdom did belong to this world, my attendants [would] be fighting to keep me from being handed over to the Jews. But as it is, my kingdom is not here" (Jn 18:36). The kingdom reaches its final destiny in the blessed immortality promised to the faithful (Mt 25:31-40).

IV

"King Nebuchadnezzar
Made a Golden Statue"
(Daniel 3:1-18)

[1] King Nebuchadnezzar had a golden statue made, sixty cubits high and six cubits wide, which he set up in the plain of Dura in the province of Babylon. [2] He then ordered the satraps, prefects, and governors, the counselors, treasurers, judges, magistrates and all the officials of the provinces to be summoned to the dedication of the statue which he had set up. [3] The satraps, prefects, and governors, the counselors, treasurers, judges, and magistrates and all the officials of the provinces, all these came together for the dedication and stood before the statue which King Nebuchadnezzar had set up. [4] A herald cried out: "Nations and peoples of every language, when you hear the sound of the trumpet, flute, lyre, harp, psaltery, bagpipe, and all the other musical instruments, [5] you are ordered to fall down and worship the golden statue which King Nebuchadnezzar has set up. [6] Whoever does not fall down and worship shall be instantly cast into a white-hot furnace." [7] Therefore, as soon as they heard the sound of the trumpet, flute, lyre, harp, psaltery, bagpipe, and all the other musical instruments, the nations and peoples of every language all fell down and worshiped the golden statue which King Nebuchadnezzar had set up.

[8] At that point, some of the Chaldeans came and accused the Jews [9] to King Nebuchadnezzar: "O king, live forever! [10] O king, you issued a decree that everyone who heard the sound of the trumpet, flute, lyre, harp, psaltery, bagpipe, and all the other musical instruments should fall down and worship the golden statue; [11] whoever did not was to be cast into a white-hot furnace. [12] There are certain Jews whom you have made administrators of the province of Babylon: Shadrach, Meshach, Abednego; these

men, O king, have paid no attention to you; they will not serve your god or worship the golden statue which you set up."

[13]Nebuchadnezzar flew into a rage and sent for Shadrach, Meshach, and Abednego, who were promptly brought before the king. [14]King Nebuchadnezzar questioned them: "Is it true, Shadrach, Meshach, and Abednego, that you will not serve my god, or worship the golden statue that I set up? [15]Be ready now to fall down and worship the statue I had made, whenever you hear the sound of the trumpet, flute, lyre, harp, psaltery, bagpipe, and all the other musical instruments; otherwise, you shall be instantly cast into the white-hot furnace; and who is the God that can deliver you out of my hands?" [16]Shadrach, Meshach, and Abednego answered King Nebuchadnezzar, "There is no need for us to defend ourselves before you in this matter. [17]If our God, whom we serve, can save us from the white-hot furnace and from your hands, O king, may he save us! [18]But even if he will not, know, O king, that we will not serve your god or worship the golden statue which you set up."

Though chapter 3 is the longest of the book because of the lengthy deuterocanonical additions, the story line is simple and straightforward. King Nebuchadnezzar makes a huge statue of gold and orders everyone, under penalty of death, to worship it at a given signal. Daniel's three companions remain loyal to their faith and defy the royal decree. The three Jews are then thrown alive into a raging furnace. But the heat and flames cause them no harm. When the king sees what has happened, he lets the three men out of the furnace and pays homage to their God. This chapter is also similar to chapter 6. Both stories deal with the rivalry, jealousy, and then betrayal of Jewish wise men by pagan courtiers.

Shadrach, Meshach, and Abednego Defy the King's Order

Curiously, Daniel, who is the hero of the first two chapters as well as of the other stories and apocalypses in the book, receives no mention here. Instead we find in center stage Daniel's three classmates and companions, who are called only by their Babylonian names—Shadrach, Meshach, and Abednego. The giving or changing of names was a sign of power. The use of the Babylonian names, therefore, should be taken as ironic. Though the pagan overlords gave the Jews these names, they could not, with all their power, force them to do what was against their enlightened conscience. Thus, the three Jews openly defy Nebuchadnezzar's order to worship the golden statue with the result that they are thrown into the blazing white-hot furnace. The angel of God comes to their rescue.

This story may be based on the words of Isaiah 43:1-2: "But now, thus says the LORD, who created you, O Jacob, and formed you, O Israel: Fear not, for I have redeemed you; I have called you by name: you are mine. When you pass through the water, I will be with you; in the rivers you shall not drown. When you walk through fire, you shall not be burned; the flames shall not consume you." Indeed, it is Yahweh who has called the three Jews by name—their Hebrew names which we know from chapter 1: Hananiah ("Yahweh has taken pity"), Mishael ("Who is what God is?"), and Azariah ("Yahweh has helped"). Precisely as the meanings of these names suggest, the God of mercy comes to the rescue of the three men. Our story may also be a midrash or edifying story based on Psalm 66:10-12: "For you have tested us, O God! You have tried us as silver is tried by fire. You have brought us into a snare; you laid a heavy burden on our backs. You let men ride over our heads; we went through fire and water, but you have led us out to refreshment." God's testing of human beings is a common motif in the Old Testament (Gn 22; Ex 16:4; 20:20; Dt 8:2, 16; 13:4; Jer 17:10; Tb 12:14). But human beings are never allowed to test God (Ex 17:2, 7; Dt 6:16; Jdt 8:12).

Nebuchadnezzar, like other absolute rulers throughout history, is not consistent. At the end of the story in chapter 2, he seemed to confess belief in the God of Israel as "the God of gods and Lord of kings and a revealer of mysteries," to quote his own words (2:47). In that story, moreover, he had a dream of a colossal statue made of gold, silver, bronze, iron, and clay tile; the statue terrified him. He seemed to have learned nothing from that disturbing experience. In the present story he gives orders to make a gigantic idol all of gold and tries to intimidate everybody to worship it. Of course, as we indicated in the introduction, such apparent inconsistencies may simply suggest that the author of this story is different from the author of the other story. Whatever the case, the final editor of the book did not see any literary or logical problem in allowing the two stories to follow each other.

The statue is to be "sixty cubits high and six cubits wide" (3:1), which in today's measurements would be ninety feet by nine. That immense piece of sculpture would have been even larger than the still famous Colossi of Memnon not far from Thebes in Egypt, each of which was carved out of a single block of stone almost sixty feet high. Nebuchadnezzar's idol would be taller than the massive granite statue of the most egotistical of Egypt's Pharaohs, Rameses II (1290-24 B.C.), in Thebes, which, if it had not been destroyed, would have been fifty feet high. When I visited Thebes in the spring of 1963 and viewed the ruins of that statue, I thought of what Percy Bysshe Shelly (1792-1822) wrote in his splendid poem, "Ozymandias of Egypt," Ozymandias being another name for Rameses II:

> I met a traveller from an antique land
> Who said: Two vast and trunkless legs of stone
> Stand in the desert. Near them on the sand,
> Half sunk, a shatter'd visage lies. . . .
> And on the pedestal these words appear:
> "My name is Ozymandias, king of kings:
> Look on my works, ye Mighty, and despair!"
> Nothing beside remains. Round the decay
> Of that colossal wreck, boundless and bare,
> The lone and level sands stretch far away.

These poignant words apply also to the mighty and arrogant Nebuchadnezzar and his monuments.

The dimensions of Nebuchadnezzar's idol—"sixty cubits high and six cubits wide"—should be understood symbolically and not realistically, as suggested by the disproportion (ten to one) of its height and breadth. In the human figure the proportion is usually five or six to one. Many numbers in the Bible have little or nothing to do with counting; rather, they have symbolic value. Thus, seven—the number of days in a week—symbolizes perfection or totality. In Revelation 5:6, Jesus is depicted as a lamb with seven eyes and seven horns. These images mean that Jesus has perfect (the number seven) knowledge (symbolized by eyes) and total (seven again) power (symbolized by horns). Another good number is four, which signifies the earth, for the ancients believed the earth had four corners. Twelve is also good; it is the number of the tribes of Israel and of the apostles. But the number six, being one less than seven, symbolizes imperfection. The number of the beast in Revelation 13:18 is "six hundred and sixty-six," where the number six is given three times, three being the number used to signify the superlative form. Thus, the beast is the worst creature imaginable. In like manner, the numbers in the dimensions of Nebuchadnezzar's idol suggest that it is indeed horrendous. This story was particularly relevant to the Jews of the second century B.C. because right in the temple of Jerusalem Antiochus IV erected the image of Olympian Zeus. This image was "the horrible abomination" referred to in 1 Maccabees 1:54; Daniel 9:27; 11:31, and the symbol of the Roman power that would profane the temple ("the abomination of desolation" in Matthew 24:15 and Mark 13:14).

The King Summons Everybody to Adore the Statue

As in Judith 2:2, Nebuchadnezzar summons the various dignitaries of the state when he decides to do something important. He orders them to come to the dedication of the statue, and they of course all show up (3:2-3). As absolute monarch, Nebuchadnezzar demands absolute obedience and tolerates no defiance. This kind of demand has been the hallmark of dictators throughout history. Hitler demanded that his troops take an oath of allegiance only to himself. His orders had to be followed to the letter, even when the orders contained actions forbidden by the moral law. That is why the dreaded SS troops of the Third Reich could commit such dreadful atrocities in the concentration camps like Auschwitz, Belsen, Buchenwald, Dachau, and Treblinka. At the Nuremberg trials after World War II, some of the Nazis, who were responsible for these camps with their crematory ovens, tried to justify their extermination of millions of Jews, Poles, Gypsies, homosexuals, and other "undesirable people" by alleging that they were not accountable for their actions because they were only following orders.

The king's herald then cries out to the "nations and peoples of every language," presumably an indication of the large extent of the Babylonian empire. At "the sound of the trumpet, flute, lyre, harp, psaltery, bagpipe, and all the other musical instruments," everyone is ordered to bow down in worship of the golden statue. Those who refuse to do so will "be instantly cast into a white-hot furnace" (3:4-6). According to Jeremiah 29:22, two false prophets, whose names were Zedekiah and Ahab, were roasted in the flames by King Nebuchadnezzar. Burning a person to death is a penalty found also in Law 110 of the Code of Hammurabi (1776-1686 B.C.). When the orchestra played its song, everybody fell down and worshiped the idol. But not the three Jews.

Not much has changed since Nebuchadnezzar's day. There are still many people who hear that orchestra and immediately bow down to the idols of today's society—popular singers, actors, or the heroes of the political, social, and financial worlds. Others live their lives according to the insatiable demands of hedonism, consumerism, and utilitarianism that are incompatible with the law of God and the informed Christian conscience.

Heroism of Shadrach, Meshach, and Abednego

Rabbi Elchanan Wasserman, the greatest rabbinic authority of Europe before World War II, taught that heroism meant something totally different from armed resistance. Heroism meant the willingness to remain true to the faith even when confronted with barbarism, cruelty, and chaos. In 1941, Rabbi Wasserman assembled the Jewish community of Kovno and asked them to proclaim their loyalty to their faith in spite of the dreadful deportation and death that awaited them at the hands of the Nazis. For such believers, martyrdom was heroism. The same is true of Shadrach, Meshach, and Abednego. Though they were "administrators in the province of Babylon," they unequivocally refused to go along with the crowd. They were good and law-abiding citizens of the state. There were limits, however, to what the state could demand. Unlike the Maccabees who engaged in armed opposition to the forces of Antiochus IV, the three Jews engaged in civil disobedience and non-violent resistance and were willing to suffer martyrdom.

This is the kind of resistance which Mahatma Gandhi (1869-1948) and Martin Luther King, Jr. (1929-68) employed in their efforts to bring about civil, social, and political change. Nebuchadnezzar's law was immoral and against the conscience of the three Jews, because it was based on legal positivism—the pernicious philosophy that an action is permissible simply because the political powers pass a law permitting or even demanding it.

Despite the threat of an excruciating death, Shadrach, Meshach, and Abednego would not compromise their religious principles simply to be "politically correct" or even to save their lives. They took a firm stand against the political establishment and its legal but immoral demands, as did the young German Lutheran theologian Dietrich Bonhoeffer, who was martyred by the Nazis in 1945. The Christians of the early Church were accused of the civil crime of atheism because they, like the three Jews before them, refused to worship the gods and goddesses of the Roman state religion. These Christians were also martyred for their faith.

As servants of the living God in heaven, the three Jews would not serve a pagan god or worship a lifeless idol made of solid gold (3:7-12). Here we see the Jewish confessors following the glorious tradition of the martyrs. In fact, the story may be an exhortation to follow the example of the heroic martyrs, who preferred death to a life of defilement, compromise, and infidelity (1 Mc 1:57, 60-63; 2 Mc 6:8-11, 18-31). In 2 Maccabees 7, there is the story of an unnamed Jewish mother and her seven sons, "who were arrested and tortured with whips and scourges by the king, to force them to eat pork in violation of God's law. One of the brothers, speaking for the others, said: 'What do you expect to achieve by questioning us? We are ready to die rather than transgress the laws of our ancestors.' At that the king [Antiochus IV], in a fury, gave orders to have pans and caldrons heated. While they were being quickly heated, he commanded his executioners to cut out the tongue of the one who had spoken for the others, to scalp him and cut off his hands and feet, while the rest of his brothers and his mother looked on. When he was completely maimed but still breathing, the king ordered them to carry him to the fire and fry him. As a cloud of smoke spread from the pan, the brothers and their mother encouraged one another to die bravely." Five of the remaining brothers were cruelly maimed and executed in the same way. Only the youngest son was still alive. Antiochus promised "on oath, to make him rich and happy if he would abandon his ancestral customs: He would make him his friend and entrust him with high office. When the youth paid no attention to him at all, the king appealed to the mother, urging her to advise her boy to save his life. . . . She leaned over close to her son and said in their native language: 'Son, have pity on me, who carried you in my womb for nine months, nursed you for three years, brought you up, educated and supported you to your present age. I beg you, child, to look at the heavens and the earth and see all that is in them. . . . Do not be afraid of this executioner, but be worthy of your brothers and accept death, so that in the time of mercy I may receive you again with them.' " The young son refused to obey the king's demands. Enraged, the king treated him even worse than his brothers. Finally, the mother was executed.

The Chaldeans Report the Jews to the King

In our story it is interesting that "some of the Chaldeans" are the ones who report to the king that Shadrach, Meshach, and Abednego have defied the king's orders. The expression "the Chaldeans" is, as we noted before, a collective name for the Babylonian wise men who are also mentioned in 2:2, 4, 5, 10. The implication seems to be that some of these experts were jealous of Shadrach, Meshach, and Abednego, because the three Jews as well as Daniel graduated at the head of the class in chapter 1. So here was their chance to get rid of the three Jews once and for all. But these Chaldeans are also ungrateful, for in the story of chapter 2 they owed their life to Daniel and his companions. Because these Jews prayed, God revealed to Daniel the mystery of Nebuchadnezzar's dream. So the king's order to slay all the wise men was not put into effect. As the French poet J. de La Fontaine (1621-95) once wrote: "The symbol of ingratitude/ is not the serpent, but man."

King Nebuchadnezzar flies into a rage when he learns about the defiance of Shadrach, Meshach, and Abednego. The king apparently realized, however, that it was out of jealousy that the Chaldeans had betrayed their Jewish friends. So when the three are brought before him, he gives them a chance to defend themselves by asking if the report is true that they would not serve his god or worship the gold statue which he had set up. He then urges them to fall down and worship the idol whenever the orchestra plays its song. If they do not obey, they will suffer a horrible death by burning. Then he asks them the arrogant and blasphemous question, "Who is the God that can deliver you out of my hands?" (3:15).

This sneering question is reminiscent of the words of the Assyrian commander, who speaks in the name of the King Sennacherib: "Thus says the king: 'Do not let Hezekiah deceive you, since he cannot deliver you. Let not Hezekiah induce you to rely on the LORD, saying, The LORD will surely save us; this city will not be handed over to the king of Assyria. Do not listen to Hezekiah. . . . Do not let Hezekiah seduce you by saying, The LORD will save us. Has any of the gods of the nations ever rescued his land from the hand of the king of Assyria? . . . Which of all the gods of these lands ever rescued his land from my hand? Will the LORD then save Jerusalem from my hand?' " (Is 36:14-16, 18, 20). The Lord did indeed save Jerusalem from Sennacherib's hand. "The angel of the LORD went forth and struck down one hundred and eighty-five thousand in the Assyrian camp. Early the next morning, there they were, all the corpses of the dead. So Sennacherib, the king of Assyria, broke camp and went back home to Nineveh" (Is 37:36-37). Such is the downfall of blasphemous arrogance, for as Proverbs 16:18 rightly observes, "Pride goes before disaster, and a haughty spirit before a fall."

In their overweening pride Nebuchadnezzar and Sennacherib believe that there are no limits to their power and authority. Similarly, Hitler thought his Third Reich would last a thousand years. Assyria, Babylon, and the Third Reich are no more. But Jerusalem lives on in the Israel of faith, the spiritual descendants of Abraham. "Realize then that it is those who have faith who are children of Abraham. Scripture, which saw in advance that God would justify the Gentiles by faith, foretold the good news to Abraham, saying, 'Through you shall all the nations be blessed.' Consequently, those who have faith are blessed along with Abraham who had faith" (Gal 3:7-9).

The Three Jews Confess Their Faith in God

Shadrach, Meshach, and Abednego now speak up fearlessly. Their conduct calls to mind the words of Jesus: "They will hand you over to the courts. . . . You will be arraigned before governors and kings because of me. . . . When they lead you away and hand you over, do not worry beforehand about what you are to say. But say whatever will be given to you at that hour. For it will not be you who are speaking but the holy Spirit" (Mk 13:9-11). The three Jews tell the king that they feel no need to defend themselves or to explain why they refuse to honor his requests (3:16). Then they give the king a short lesson in Israelite theology. God, if he so wills, can save them from the white-hot furnace; and they pray for deliverance. But if God does not will to save them, they will not serve a pagan god or worship the gold statue the king had made (3:17-18). Here we see in dramatic action the unwavering faith and the unflinching courage of the three confessors. They let God be God. They make no attempt to control God. God alone is the one who decides if and when he will intervene miraculously in human affairs. To expect anything else is to make God a labor-saving device or a celestial convenience at our beck and call.

V

"In the Fire Azariah Stood Up
and Prayed Aloud"
(Daniel 3:19-45)

[19]Nebuchadnezzar's face became livid with utter rage against Shadrach, Meshach, and Abednego. He ordered the furnace to be heated seven times more than usual [20]and had some of the strongest men in his army bind Shadrach, Meshach, and Abednego and cast them into the white-hot furnace. [21]They were bound and cast into the white-hot furnace with their coats, hats, shoes and other garments, [22]for the king's order was urgent. So huge a fire was kindled in the furnace that the flames devoured the men who threw Shadrach, Meshach, and Abednego into it. [23]But these three fell, bound, into the midst of the white-hot furnace.

[24]They walked about in the flames, singing to God and blessing the Lord. [25]In the fire Azariah stood up and prayed aloud:

[26]"Blessed are you, and praiseworthy,
O Lord, the God of our fathers,
and glorious forever is your name.
[27]For you are just in all you have done;
all your deeds are faultless,
all your ways right, and all your judgments proper.
[28]You have executed proper judgments
in all that you have brought upon us
and upon Jerusalem, the holy city of our fathers.
By a proper judgment you have done all this
because of our sins;
[29]For we have sinned and transgressed
by departing from you,
and we have done every kind of evil.
[30]Your commandments we have not heeded or observed,
nor have we done as you ordered us for our good.
[31]Therefore all you have brought upon us,
all you have done to us,
you have done by a proper judgment.

[32] You have handed us over to our enemies,
    lawless and hateful rebels;
    to an unjust king, the worst in all the world.
[33] Now we cannot open our mouths;
    we, your servants, who revere you,
    have become a shame and a reproach.
[34] For your name's sake, do not deliver us up forever,
    or make void your covenant.
[35] Do not take away your mercy from us,
    for the sake of Abraham, your beloved,
    Isaac your servant, and Israel your holy one,
[36] To whom you promised to multiply their offspring
    like the stars of heaven,
    or the sand on the shore of the sea.
[37] For we are reduced, O Lord, beyond any other nation,
    brought low everywhere in the world this day
    because of our sins.
[38] We have in our day no prince, prophet, or leader,
    no holocaust, sacrifice, oblation, or incense,
    no place to offer first fruits, to find favor with you.
[39] But with contrite heart and humble spirit
    let us be received;
[40] As though it were holocausts of rams and bullocks,
    or thousands of fat lambs,
So let our sacrifice be in your presence today
    as we follow you unreservedly;
    for those who trust in you cannot be put to shame.
[41] And now we follow you with our whole heart,
    we fear you and we pray to you.
[42] Do not let us be put to shame,
    but deal with us in your kindness and great mercy.
[43] Deliver us by your wonders,
    and bring glory to your name, O Lord:
[44] Let all those be routed
    who inflict evils on your servants;
Let them be shamed and powerless,
    and their strength broken;
    [45] Let them know that you alone are the Lord God,
    glorious over the whole world."

Nebuchadnezzar's rage against Shadrach, Meshach, and Abednego knows no bounds. You just don't cross tyrants like him. So he

60

orders "the furnace to be heated seven times more than usual" (3:19). Here again the number is symbolic; "seven" signifies totality or perfection. Thus, the furnace is made as hot as possible. Then the king calls in not just his ordinary servants but "the strongest men in his army" to bind up the three dissident Jews and to cast them into the white-hot furnace. Irony is at work here. The strongest soldiers are needed to bind up not powerful adversaries but defenseless Jews, who rely only on the power of God for their protection. The three confessors are cast into the furnace "with their coats, hats, shoes, and other garments" (3:21)—important details that will feature in the climax of the story in 3:94.

Shadrach, Meshach, and Abednego Thrown into the Furnace

The fire in the furnace was so huge "that the flames devoured the men who threw Shadrach, Meshach, and Abednego into it" (3:22). Our author uses irony again. The king's strongest soldiers are consumed by the very fire they made to roast the three apparently helpless Jews. But "these three fell, bound, into the midst of the white-hot furnace" and "walked about in the flames, singing to God and blessing the Lord" (3:23-24). Note the striking contrasts: Mighty Nebuchadnezzar in a flaming rage, who is surrounded by his strongest soldiers; and Shadrach, Meshach, and Abednego in the white-hot furnace, who sing their joyful praises to God. Many other martyrs have gone to their death singing hymns to the Lord.

Azariah's Prayer

Azariah now prays aloud. His prayer (3:26-45) is a penitential lament like Psalms 51 and 106 and the prayers in Ezra 9:6-15; Daniel 9:4-19; and Baruch 1:13–3:8. It is a poignant review of Israel's past sins—all violations of the Sinai Covenant. These acts of disloyalty caused the nation to suffer defeat and exile precisely as God had promised in Leviticus 26:14-43 and Deuteronomy 28:15-68. Azariah begins, nevertheless, with words of praise: "Blessed are you, and praiseworthy, O Lord, the God of our fathers" (3:26). Some hymns in the Qumran Dead Sea Scrolls begin with

61

similar words. The reason is that God has been righteous and just in what he had done to Israel (3:27-33). Indeed God is absolutely true to his promises even when it means the destruction of the nation and the exile of the Chosen People. God's righteousness—praised also in Psalms 119:137; Tobit 3:2; and 13:6— is a theme likewise taken up in the New Testament (Rv 16:7 and 19:2). Even Nebuchadnezzar exalts and glorifies "the King of heaven, because all his works are right and his ways just" (Dn 4:34).

Of particular significance in 3:27-33 is what the author affirms concerning the reasons why these disasters came upon the Jews. He states: "You [God] have handed us over to our enemies, lawless and hateful rebels; to an unjust king, the worst in all the world" (3:32). That king is of course Nebuchadnezzar. Because of his savagery, which is described earlier in this chapter, a pious Jew could readily describe the tyrant as the worst in the world. But the author makes it clear that Nebuchadnezzar was able to destroy Jerusalem and exile the people not simply because of his military might but because God had made the Babylonian army the instrument of his judgment (3:31). The same idea is expressed in Daniel 1:2. The phrase, "we cannot open our mouths," means that the people because of their disloyalty have no right to lament that God has made them "a shame and a reproach" (3:33).

Nevertheless, Azariah, speaks up in the name of the faithful remnant of the people (3:34-37). His words are instructive as to how we should approach God in prayer. "For your name's sake, do not deliver us up forever, or make void your covenant" (3:35). Azariah reminds God that his own honor should prompt him to come to the rescue of his people. The faithful should have no fear to approach God and tell him frankly of their distress. The key to this intimate approach to God is repentance and humility. In his attempt to save Sodom, Abraham boldly haggles with God over the number of innocent people needed to spare the wicked city. Abraham even reminds God that the innocent should not die with the guilty and that "the judge of all the world should act with justice" (Gn 18:23-32). Prayer is being open with a God who loves us and having no fear to speak what is in our heart.

The great Jeremiah serves as an example. He had a difficult time in his prophetic ministry; so he complained bitterly to God: "You duped me, O LORD, and I let myself be duped; you were too strong for me, and you triumphed. All the day I am an object of laughter; everyone mocks me. Whenever I speak, I must cry out, violence and outrage is my message; the word of the LORD has brought me derision and reproach all the day. I say to myself, I will not mention him, I will speak in his name no more. But then it becomes like fire burning in my heart, imprisoned in my bones; I grow weary holding it in, I cannot endure it. . . . Cursed be the day on which I was born! May the day my mother gave me birth never be blessed! Cursed be the man who brought the news to my father, saying, 'A child, a son, has been born to you!' filling him with great joy. Let that man be like the cities which the LORD relentlessly overthrew; let him hear war cries in the morning, battle alarms at noonday, because he did not dispatch me in the womb! Then my mother would have been my grave, her womb confining me forever. Why did I come forth from the womb, to see sorrow and pain, to end my days in shame?" (Jer 20:8-9, 14-18). These deeply moving words may seem to us out of line and close to disrespect, even blasphemy. But this is real prayer, a profoundly emotional and heartfelt prayer, of a prophet who takes his mission seriously and has the emotional integrity to tell God exactly how he feels about it (cf. the prophet's other "confessions" in Jer 12:1-4; 15:10-11, 15-21; 17:14-18; 18:18-23).

Azariah Appeals for Mercy

Azariah now pulls out all the stops. He pleads with God not to take away his mercy "for the sake of Abraham, your beloved" (3:35). Biblical tradition considers Abraham "the friend of God" (Is 41:8; 2 Chr 20:7; Jam 2:23). It was to Abraham that God first revealed himself. Abraham was called out of paganism to a land that God would show him. God would make of him a great nation, and all the nations of the earth would be blessed in him. Abraham obeyed God's call (Gn 12:1-4), and thus became our father in faith (Rom 4:16). The multiplying of offspring "like the stars of heaven, or the sand on the shore of the sea" (3:36) was promised to Abraham in Genesis 15:5 and 22:17. Israel, whom Azariah calls "your holy one" (3:35), is more often called "the servant of God" (Is 41:8; 44:1-2, 21; 45:4; 48:20; 49:3).

Azariah alludes to Deuteronomy 28:62 in describing how few there are left of the Chosen People, and then he confesses once again that it was because of their sins that they have been "brought low everywhere in the world this day" (3:37). Jerome applies this verse to the Church when it undergoes trial because of the sins of Christians. Azariah's confession is a wholesome reminder that sin cannot be dismissed as if it were of no consequence to a person or nation or religious community. Nations and empires as mighty as the Egyptian, Babylonian, and Persian have been built by force of arms and flourished for a time, only to decline and disappear completely, chiefly because of the decay of the moral fabric of the people and their leaders. The vast Roman Empire in the West rotted from within long before the outside forces of the Germanic chieftain Odoacer destroyed it in the year 476. In our own day the Soviet empire has been dissolved primarily because of the bank- ruptcy of the Marxist-atheist philosophy of government and eco- nomics as well as its denial of basic civil and political rights. Corruption in government, business, and private life, the exploita- tion of the poor, the violation of the right to life, and other types of sin will affect a society and lead to its ultimate decay. A nation and people ignore the law of God at their own peril. This is the point Azariah makes so eloquently and passionately when he laments that in his day they have "no prince, prophet, or leader" (3:38). A similar lament, composed after the destruction of Jeru- salem by the Babylonians in 587 B.C., is heard in Lamentations 2:9.

Since the people can no longer offer the prescribed liturgical sacrifices, Azariah asks the Lord to accept instead a "contrite and humble spirit . . . as though it were holocausts of rams and bullocks . . . as we follow you unreservedly; for those who trust in you cannot be put to shame" (3:38-40). Here we see the essence and spirit of true religion: prayer, repentance, humility, following the way of the Lord without reservation. Without these, liturgy and sacrifice are worthless. Recall the words of Isaiah: "What care I for the number of your sacrifices? says the LORD. I have had enough of whole- burnt rams and fat of fatlings. In the blood of calves, lambs and goats I find no pleasure. When you come in to visit me, who asks these things of you? Trample my courts no more! Bring no more worthless offerings; your incense is loathsome to me. New moon and sabbath, calling of assemblies, octaves with wickedness: These I cannot bear. Your new moons and festivals I detest; they weigh me down, I tire of the load. When you spread out your hands, I close my eyes to you. Though you pray the more, I will not listen. Your hands are full of blood! Wash yourselves clean! Put away your misdeeds from before my eyes; cease doing evil; learn to do good. Make justice your aim: Redress the wronged, hear the orphan's plea, defend the widow (Is 1:11-17; cf. Am 5:21-24).

Liturgy—no matter how beautiful, artistic, and emotionally satisfying—is worse than a waste of time if a person makes it a substitute for upright living. Isaiah calls it detestable to the Lord. Liturgy, if it is to be acceptable to the Lord, must be a celebration of the believer's life with God, a life of justice and compassion, of moral behavior and concern for the poor and oppressed (Sir 34:21-27; 35:1-5). The people's failure to follow such a life is what Azariah laments.

Azariah's Resolve

Now Azariah's prayer turns to a firm resolve to follow the Lord unreservedly, "with our whole heart" (3:41), a phrase taken from the well-known words of Deuteronomy 6:5: "Therefore, you shall love the LORD, your God, with all your heart, and with all your soul, and with all your strength." Azariah concludes with a fervent appeal to the Lord's kindness and great mercy. He begs for deliverance so as to "bring glory to your name, O Lord" (3:43). He even prays for the defeat of his enemies so that they may "know that you alone are the Lord God, glorious over the whole world" (3:45). A similar appeal is voiced also in Daniel 4:14; 1 Kings 20:28; 2 Kings 19:19; Psalm 59:13; Isaiah 37:20; Ezekiel 25:11; 30:19; Baruch 2:14-15.

Jesus, however, commands us to have a different attitude toward our enemies. "You have heard that it was said, 'You shall love your neighbor and hate your enemy.' But I say to you, love your enemies, and pray for those who persecute you, that you may be children of your heavenly Father, for he makes his sun rise on the bad and the good, and causes rain to fall on the just and the unjust" (Mt 5:43-45).

VI

"In the Furnace the Three Men Sang with One Voice"

(Daniel 3:46-90a)

[46]Now the king's men who had thrown them in continued to stoke the furnace with brimstone, pitch, tow, and faggots. [47]The flames rose forty-nine cubits above the furnace, [48]and spread out, burning the Chaldeans nearby. [49]But the angel of the Lord went down into the furnace with Azariah and his companions, drove the fiery flames out of the furnace, [50]and made the inside of the furnace as though a dew-laden breeze were blowing through it. The fire in no way touched them or caused them pain or harm. [51]Then these three in the furnace with one voice sang, glorifying and blessing God:

[52]"Blessed are you, O Lord, the God of our fathers,
  praiseworthy and exalted above all forever;
And blessed is your holy and glorious name,
  praiseworthy and exalted above all for all ages.
[53]Blessed are you in the temple of your holy glory,
  praiseworthy and glorious above all forever.
[54]Blessed are you on the throne of your kingdom,
  praiseworthy and exalted above all forever.
[55]Blessed are you who look into the depths
  from your throne upon the cherubim,
  praiseworthy and exalted above all forever.
[56]Blessed are you in the firmament of heaven,
  praiseworthy and glorious forever.
[57]Bless the Lord, all you works of the Lord,
  praise and exalt him above all forever.
[58]Angels of the Lord, bless the Lord,
  praise and exalt him above all forever.
[59]You heavens, bless the Lord,
  praise and exalt him above all forever.

⁶⁰All you waters above the heavens,
   bless the Lord, praise and exalt him above all forever.
⁶¹All you hosts of the Lord, bless the Lord;
   praise and exalt him above all forever.
⁶²Sun and moon, bless the Lord;
   praise and exalt him above all forever.
⁶³Stars of heaven, bless the Lord;
   praise and exalt him above all forever.
⁶⁴Every shower and dew, bless the Lord;
   praise and exalt him above all forever.
⁶⁵All you winds, bless the Lord;
   praise and exalt him above all forever.
⁶⁶Fire and heat, bless the Lord;
   praise and exalt him above all forever.
⁶⁷[Cold and chill, bless the Lord;
   praise and exalt him above all forever.
⁶⁸Dew and rain, bless the Lord;
   praise and exalt him above all forever.]
⁶⁹Frost and chill, bless the Lord;
   praise and exalt him above all forever.
⁷⁰Ice and snow, bless the Lord;
   praise and exalt him above all forever.
⁷¹Nights and days, bless the Lord;
   praise and exalt him above all forever.
⁷²Light and darkness, bless the Lord;
   praise and exalt him above all forever.
⁷³Lightnings and clouds, bless the Lord;
   praise and exalt him above all forever.
⁷⁴Let the earth bless the Lord,
   praise and exalt him above all forever.
⁷⁵Mountains and hills, bless the Lord;
   praise and exalt him above all forever.
⁷⁶Everything growing from the earth,
   bless the Lord; praise and exalt him above all forever.
⁷⁷You springs, bless the Lord;
   praise and exalt him above all forever.
⁷⁸Seas and rivers, bless the Lord;
   praise and exalt him above all forever.
⁷⁹You dolphins and all water creatures, bless the Lord,
   praise and exalt him above all forever.
⁸⁰All you birds of the air, bless the Lord;
   praise and exalt him above all forever.

[81] All you beasts, wild and tame,
    bless the Lord;
        praise and exalt him above all forever.
[82] You sons of men, bless the Lord;
        praise and exalt him above all forever.
[83] O Israel, bless the Lord;
        praise and exalt him above all forever.
[84] Priests of the Lord, bless the Lord;
        praise and exalt him above all forever.
[85] Servants of the Lord, bless the Lord;
        praise and exalt him above all forever.
[86] Spirits and souls of the just, bless the Lord;
        praise and exalt him above all forever.
[87] Holy men of humble heart, bless the Lord;
        praise and exalt him above all forever.
[88] Hananiah, Azariah, Mishael, bless the Lord;
        praise and exalt him above all forever.
For he has delivered us from the nether world,
    and saved us from the power of death;
He has freed us from the raging flame
    and delivered us from the fire.
[89] Give thanks to the Lord, for he is good,
    for his mercy endures forever.
[90a] Bless the God of gods, all you who fear the Lord;
        praise him and give him thanks,
        because his mercy endures forever."

Curiously in the Theodotion-form of this account, the statement in 3:46, "the king's men . . . continued to stoke the furnace," contradicts what was said in 3:22, "the flames devoured the men who threw Shadrach, Meshach, and Abednego into it." But this contradiction may indicate that this section may have a different translator from the one who translated the earlier account. The Septuagint-form avoids this difficulty by distinguishing between the men who threw the three Jews into the furnace and the men who kept stoking the flames. Now it's the turn of the three Jews to sing a hymn of praise in the blazing furnace.

The Raging Furnace

We are told a new detail: "The flames rose forty-nine cubits above the furnace" (3:47). Here again the number should be understood not literally but symbolically. The number forty-nine equals the number seven (symbolizing totality or perfection) multiplied by itself. Thus, the flames rose to a perfect height so as to dramatize the power of God to save even in such a raging inferno. In contrast, Nebuchadnezzar's gold idol is sixty cubits high and six cubits wide—two numbers symbolizing imperfection, as we saw above in 3:1. These flames are perfect for God's purposes: They burn the Chaldean henchmen nearby (3:48).

The Angel Comes to the Rescue

Now comes an even more spectacular intervention to neutralize the flames that rose so high. "The angel of the Lord" comes down and drives "the fiery flames out of the furnace" (3:49). In other parts of the Old Testament, "the angel of the Lord" is a personification of God's power or represents God himself (Gn 16:7-11; 22:11, 15; Ex 3:2; Nm 22:22-35; Jgs 6:11-12). But here we have a person with an angelic nature who appears as a fourth individual in the furnace (3:92). We should observe that the angel comes down only at the conclusion of Azariah's prayer (3:26-45). Not only does the angel drive out the flames but he also transforms the inside of the furnace, making it "as though a dew-laden breeze were blowing through it" (3:50). This is hyperbole at its colorful best in service of theology as story. Human wickedness embodied in the towering flames is no match for the mercy and fidelity of God embodied in the angel and the fresh breeze he brings.

The Song of the Three Jews

The three Jews now sing their song to glorify and bless the Lord. Nebuchadnezzar had his orchestra with its "trumpet, flute, lyre, harp, psaltery, bagpipe, and all the other musical instruments" (3:4, 7, 10, 15) to dazzle the crowds to obey the king's command to worship the idol. But the music in the words of Shadrach, Meshach, and Abednego is far more beautiful to hear and more satisfying to the human spirit. The song is divided into three parts: (1) direct praises of God, "Blessed are you. . ." (3:52-56); (2) indirect praises in which various creatures are invited to participate (3:57-88b); and (3) praises for the special reasons of the three Jews (3:88c-90). All three parts have the same literary genre (lyric poetry) in the form of a hymn. There are a pair of set formulas in each of the first two parts: (1) "Blessed are you" and "praiseworthy and exalted above all forever" (3:52-56); (2) "Bless the Lord" and "Praise and exalt him above all forever" (3:57-88b). Such formulas are found also in other psalms. For example, Psalm 136 has at the end of every verse the refrain, "for his mercy endures forever" (cf. Pss 103:1-2, 20-23; 150:1-5). These formulas are in the style of acclamations or refrains in litanies.

Francis of Assisi followed the technique of set formulas in his famous "Canticle of Brother Sun" in which he uses the phrase, "All praise be yours, my Lord," eight times. Bonaventure writes: "In all things fair, he [Francis] beheld him who is most fair, and by his footprints in created things he found his Beloved everywhere, making a ladder of all things by which to ascend to him who is all lovely." Francis of Assisi never lost his childlike sense of wonder at the beauty and splendor of God's creatures. The same is true of the inspired author of the hymn of the three confessors.

The introduction to the hymn (3:52-56) is an expanded form of the praises voiced by Azariah in his prayer (3:26). The Lord is indeed "the God of our fathers," the same God who revealed himself to Moses (Ex 3:14-15). It is this God who is Father of our Lord Jesus Christ. "In times past, God spoke in partial and various ways to our ancestors through the prophets; in these last days, he spoke to us through a son, whom he made heir of all things and through whom he created the universe" (Heb 1:1-2). The temple of God's "holy glory" (3:53) is not the Jerusalem temple, which had been destroyed by Nebuchadnezzar in 587 B.C. (as alluded to in 3:38). It is, rather, the palace of the heavens in which God has "the throne of [his] kingdom" (3:54). The palace is located "in the firmament of the heaven" (3:56), where God has a "throne above the cherubim" from which he looks "into the depths," the abyss

(3:55), because he knows all things (Ps 11:4). The phrase, "above the cherubim," is a poetic expression that originated in the cultic language associated with the Ark of the Covenant that was placed in the sanctuary (Ex 25:17-22). The cherubim on the Ark were images of creatures with wings outstretched as if to support the deity. "The LORD is king; the peoples tremble; he is throned upon the cherubim; the earth quakes" (Ps 99:1; cf. Ps 80:2; Is 37:16).

Call to All Creatures to Bless the Lord

Now comes the famous *Benedicite* in which the three confessors invite all creatures to bless the Lord (3:57-88b). Part of this lovely poem is used on Sundays and other festivals in the morning Liturgy of the Hours recited by those in holy orders and by many laypeople. The invitation to all creatures collectively (3:57) is now extended to particular creatures, beginning with the celestial. First come the angels (3:58), who are invited to praise the Lord also in Psalm 148:2. The angels are attendants at God's throne above (Ps 103: 20; Tb 12:15; Lk 1:19; Rv 8:2). In 3:59-60, by way of the literary device of personification, the author addresses the heavens (as in Is 44:23; Pss 19:1; 97:6) and then the waters above the heavens (Gn 1:6-7 and Ps 148:4). In Hebrew cosmography these waters are the source of rainfall (Gn 7:11). Taking the idea from Psalms 103:21 and 148:2b, he invites as a group "all you hosts of the Lord" (3:61), which are God's heavenly armies (Gn 2:1). Among these, in 3:62-63, are the sun and moon and stars, which are created in that order in Genesis 1:14-16; also in Psalm 148:3 these are called to praise the Lord.

The meteorological phenomena, however, receive the lion's share of personifications, ten verses (3:64-73), the number ten signifying a round number (for example, the Ten Commandments referred to as such in Ex 34:28; Dt 4:13; 10:4) or a minimum number (Gn 18:32; Nm 11:32; at least ten are required for the Jewish Passover meal). The importance of showers and rain, as well as dew and frost, ice and snow (3:64, 68, 70)—all sources of moisture—is obvious to anyone who has lived in the Holy Land for a period of time. Sufficient water, which we often take for granted but which is crucial to survival, often is lacking in that part

71

of the world. When I was a fellow at the American School of Oriental Research in Jerusalem in 1962-63, rain was so scarce that water had to be rationed.

"The winds," in Greek *pneumata* which can also mean "spirits," are invited to bless the Lord (3:65), for these bring in the moisture-laden clouds from the Mediterranean Sea. Interestingly, the Vulgate understands the Greek word as referring to "the spirits" and then adds "of God." Apparently, the inspired poet, who composed this song, enjoyed cold weather and what it brings, for he devotes three verses to "cold and chill," "frost and chill," and "ice and snow" (3:67, 69, 70). A snowfall can transform an ordinary countryside with its trees into a thing of dazzling beauty—a frequent motif in paintings. In 3:71, the author places "nights" before "days" because in Jewish thought the day was said to begin at sunset. So, for example, after God created the light and separated it from darkness and called the light "day" and the darkness "night," "evening came, and morning followed—the first day" (Gn 1:3-5). Following the text of Genesis, however, the poet places "light" before "darkness" (3:72). Then the three confessors call on "lightnings and clouds" to praise the Lord. A powerful thunder and lightning storm can put on an awesome spectacle of light and sound, which the poet seemed to enjoy, as indeed I do myself.

After an introductory call to the earth (3:74), the three confessors invite the various creatures of the earth to praise the Lord— seven in number (3:75-81), seven symbolizing totality or perfection. First are the "mountains and hills" (Ps 148:9; Is 44:23; 49:13), probably because God revealed himself to Moses on the mountain at Sinai/Horeb, "the mountain of God" (Ex 3:1; 4:27; 18:5; Nm 10:33). Mount Zion was also called "the Mountain of Yahweh" (Ps 24:3) or Yahweh's "holy mountain" (Pss 2:6; 48:3; Is 11:9; 65:25). Next comes "everything growing from the earth," a collective way of referring to trees, plants, and flowers as well as the various cereal grains that are food for humans and animals alike. All-important water receives two verses: "springs" with their "living [= fresh, flowing] water" (Jer 2:13; 17:13; Zec 14:8) as opposed to the flat (often unpleasant) water stored in cisterns; and "seas and rivers" (Ps 69:35). Next come the living creatures which are capable of motion, beginning with the majestic "dolphins" (Ps

74:14) and the rest of the "water creatures." In Semitic mythology, the sea contained fearful chaotic monsters that terrified people. Not so, says the Old Testament. All water creatures, great and small, are good since they come from the hand of God. "God created the great sea monsters and all kinds of swimming creatures with which the water teems, and all kinds of winged birds. God saw how good it was" (Gn 1:21). Finally, the poet, in imitation of Psalm 148:10, invites the "beasts, wild and tame, to praise the Lord." All living creatures in their countless species and endless varieties should be respected and not abused, for they proclaim the glory of their Creator. The loss of an animal species due to the senseless destruction of the environment is a loss to us all as well as to future generations.

What must be noted about 3:59-81 is that for our inspired poet all these creatures are natural phenomena, all parts of God's good creation. Many of these creatures were the objects of worship by the pagans. But here the poet proclaims loudly and clearly that all creatures even in heaven are nothing more than the "works of the Lord" (3:57). The author of the Wisdom of Solomon makes a similar point: "For all were by nature foolish who were in ignorance of God, and who from the good things seen did not succeed in knowing him who is, and from studying the works did not discern the artisan. But either fire, or wind, or the swift air, or the circuit of the stars, or the mighty water, or the luminaries of heaven, the governors of the world, they considered gods. Now if out of joy in their beauty they thought them gods, let them know how far more excellent is the Lord than these; for the original source of beauty fashioned them. Or if they were struck by their might and energy, let them from these things realize how much more powerful is he who made them" (Wis 13:1-4).

Futility of Idolatry and Superstition

Any form of animism, in which the forces of nature are thought to be divine, is out of the question for the believer. The Akkadians and Babylonians worshiped the moon god, called "Sin," and in both ancient Mesopotamia and Egypt the people venerated a large number of sky deities. The Egyptians also worshiped various animals—a practice called theriolatry, which the author of the Wisdom of Solomon ridicules: "They worship the most loathsome beasts—for compared as to folly, these are worse than the rest, nor for their looks are they good or desirable beasts, but they have escaped both the approval of God and his blessing. Therefore they were fittingly punished by similar creatures, and were tormented by a swarm of insects" (Wis 15:18–16:1). For the Chosen People the sun was merely the bearer of light (Gn 1:14-18), and nothing more. To avoid even the hint of pagan polytheism, the priestly author of Genesis 1 does not even use the Hebrew words for "sun," and "moon," but instead uses the unusual expressions, "the two great lights, the greater one to govern the day, and the lesser one to govern the night" (Gn 1:16). The stars likewise are mere creatures whose purpose is for light and for reckoning time (Gn 1:16; Pss 8:4; 136:9; Jer 31:35). On the day when God created the universe, "the morning stars sang in chorus and all the sons of God [the angels] shouted for joy" (Jb 38:7). Despite their spectacular beauty, the stars are dim before God (Jb 25:5). In Daniel 12:3, the righteous "shall be like the stars forever." The Old Testament roundly condemned the heavenly cults of Mesopotamia (Dt 4:19; Am 5:26). In view of what the scriptures say, it is nothing but superstition to "read" the stars, as the astrologers have pretended to do for gullible clients throughout history.

Animism and other superstitions have not disappeared despite the technologically sophisticated age in which we live. According to the recent International Social Survey Program study, fifty percent of the British people believed in faith healers, forty percent in fortune tellers, thirty-three percent in good luck charms and astrology. In Great Britain it seems that those who believe in God are also likely to believe in such animistic practices. Sociologist Andrew Greeley concludes from this study: "The Reformations, the Enlightenment, the Industrial and Scientific Revolutions have not banished magic from the 'civilized' world."

The poet reserves the conclusion of the song (hence, the most emphatic position) to human beings who without exception are all invited to praise the Lord (3:82-88b). It is noteworthy that here again in a unified section we have seven poetic lines. After the invitation to all the children of Adam, which includes the Gentiles

74

too, the poet calls on Israel (as in Psalm 135:19), for God had chosen Israel from all the peoples of the earth to be his own (Dt 7:6; 14:2; 1 Sm 12:22; 1 Kgs 3:8; Ps 33:12). Next come the "priests of the Lord" who serve at the altar and intercede for the people (Ex 40:13-15). All human beings are called to be "servants of the Lord" (3:85) by doing his will. God, however, bestows the title "my servant" on certain Old Testament characters: Abraham (Gn 26:24), Moses (Nm 12:7-8; Jos 1:2), Caleb (Nm 14:24), David (2 Sm 3:18; 7:5, 8), Job (2:3; 42:7-8), and Isaiah (Is 20:3). But God calls even a scoundrel like Nebuchadnezzar "my servant" (Jer 25:9; 27:6; 43:10), because this king would do God's will in destroying the kingdom of Judah because of its disloyalty.

The mention of "spirits and souls of the just [or righteous]" (3:86) is an allusion to the interiority of the human person, who also possesses a body, the exteriority. Thus, upright human beings, who do God's will, are called to praise God with their whole being, with their spirit and soul as well as their body. The "holy men of humble heart" (3:87) are of course people like Shadrach, Meshach, and Abednego whom Nebuchadnezzar had thrown into the fiery furnace for their refusal to worship the king's gold idol. Finally, the poet has the three Jews inviting themselves to bless the Lord (3:88ab). Here they are addressed by their Hebrew names, Hananiah, Azariah, and Mishael, which we first saw in 1:6 but in a different order. The reason for the Hebrew names is that the three confessors are no longer under Nebuchadnezzar's power but unmistakably under God's sovereign control. In 3:88cdef, there is a switch from the third person to the first person, for these lines give the reason why the three confessors are to bless the Lord. God "has delivered us" (stated twice, by way of the literary device called inclusion) and "has saved us" and "has freed us." The expressions, "the nether world," "the power of death," and "the raging flames" are in synonymous parallelism. The song concludes with a quotation in 3:89 from Psalms 106:1 and 136:1, and with an allusion in 3:90 from Psalm 136:2.

Among the heroes of Israel, 1 Maccabees 2:59 lists Hananiah, Azariah, and Mishael, who "for their faith were saved from the fire." The scene of the three Jews praising and blessing the Lord inside the flaming furnace became a theme in Christian art because it symbolized the resurrection.

VII

"Blessed Be the God of Shadrach, Meshach, and Abednego"

(Daniel 3:90b-97)

[90b]Hearing them sing, and astonished at seeing them alive, [91]King Nebuchadnezzar rose in haste and asked his nobles, "Did we not cast three men bound into the fire?" "Assuredly, O king," they answered. [92]"But," he replied, "I see four men unfettered and unhurt, walking in the fire, and the fourth looks like a son of God." [93]Then Nebuchadnezzar came to the opening of the white-hot furnace and called to Shadrach, Meshach, and Abednego: "Servants of the most high God, come out." Thereupon Shadrach, Meshach, and Abednego came out of the fire. [94]When the satraps, prefects, governors, and nobles of the king came together, they saw that the fire had had no power over the bodies of these men; not a hair of their heads had been singed, nor were their garments altered; there was not even a smell of fire about them. [95]Nebuchadnezzar exclaimed, "Blessed be the God of Shadrach, Meshach, and Abednego, who sent his angel to deliver the servants that trusted in him; they disobeyed the royal command and yielded their bodies rather than serve or worship any god except their own God. [96]Therefore I decree for nations and peoples of every language that whoever blasphemes the God of Shadrach, Meshach, and Abednego shall be cut to pieces and his house destroyed. For there is no other God who can rescue like this." [97]Then the king promoted Shadrach, Meshach, and Abednego in the province of Babylon.

Shadrach, Meshach, and Abednego must have had strong voices inside the furnace; according to the Septuagint-form of the book, Nebuchadnezzar could hear them singing from his palace. Amazed that the three were still alive, the king gets up quickly and comes to the furnace. Not only are the three confessors alive; not even their hair or clothing had the smell of fire! The king then praises God and gives the three men a big promotion.

The King Finds the Three Jews Alive and Well

Nebuchadnezzar calls in his nobles because he is baffled by what he sees in the furnace. He asks them, "Did we not cast three men bound into the fire?" The nobles answer in the affirmative (3:91). But now the king sees "four men unfettered and unhurt walking in the fire, and the fourth looks like a son of God" [as the Theodotion-form has it, or, "a son of the gods," according to the Aramaic] (3:92). Nebuchadnezzar's towering rage at being defied and the flaming fire forty-nine cubits high (3:47) could do no harm to the three confessors who put their faith and trust in God. Spared by a miraculous intervention of God, they walk about freely inside the furnace. No king on earth, no matter how strong and influential, can bind up the power of God.

The mysterious "man like a son of the gods" is an angel, or "an angel of God," as the Septuagint-form translates the Aramaic, for angels are often called "sons of God" (Dt 32:8; Jb 1:6; 2:1; 38:7; Ps 89:7). In fact, Nebuchadnezzar himself in 3:95 calls this strange person God's angel. It is presumably the same angel of the Lord who had come "down into the furnace with Azariah and his companions and drove the flames out of the furnace, and made the inside of the furnace as though a dew-laden breeze were blowing through it" (3:49-50). But earlier Christian interpreters, going one better than the Theodotion-form of the text, understood the mysterious person as "the Son of God." Jerome comments on this phrase: "I do not know how an impious king deserved to see the Son of God."

The King Releases the Jews

Nebuchadnezzar had witnessed the spectacular deliverance of the three Jews. So he "came to the opening of the white-hot furnace and called to Shadrach, Meshach, and Abednego: 'Servants of the most high God, come out' " (3:93). No further mention is made of the angel, for once he has performed his function as God's emissary he disappears. Only God, who sent the angel, is acknowledged. Mighty Nebuchadnezzar finally confesses that Shadrach, Meshach, and Abednego are "servants of the most high God." The title, "the most high God," which occurs often in the older biblical books (Gn 14:18-20, 22; Pss 57:2; 78:35, 56) is found also in 3:99 (the introduction to the next story) and 5:18, 21; and "the Most High" in 4:14, 21-22, 29; 7:18, 22, 25 (twice), 27. In the Wisdom of Ben Sira (Sirach) the title "the Most High" occurs forty-one times. It is found also in the New Testament, mostly in Luke and Acts of the Apostles (Lk 1:32, 35, 76; 6:35; 8:28; Acts 7:48; 16:17). It appears with some frequency likewise in the Genesis Apocryphon and other Qumran Dead Sea scrolls.

It is a title of great dignity and profound respect. It conveys the idea that God as ruler of all the universe is absolutely supreme over everyone and everything. "All you peoples, clap your hands, shout to God with cries of gladness, for the LORD, the Most High, the awesome, is the great king over all the earth" (Ps 47:2-3). God's sovereignty extends likewise to the so-called gods of the Gentiles. "For the LORD is a great God, and a great king above all gods; in his hands are the depths of the earth, and the tops of the mountains are his. His is the sea, for he has made it, and the dry land, which his hands have formed. Come, let us bow down in worship; let us kneel before the LORD who made us" (Ps 95:3-6). But here the pagan king uses the august title, "the most high God." Thus, Nebuchadnezzar finally acknowledges that the God of Israel has dominion even in Babylon.

The Jews Come Out of the Furnace

Shadrach, Meshach, and Abednego now emerge from the white-hot furnace, unscathed, untouched, and none the worse for the experience. In their curiosity "the satraps, prefects, governors, and nobles of the king came together" to see for themselves. Ironically, it is these same individuals who earlier in the story came to the dedication of the gold idol when the king had summoned them. When the orchestra played its song, they all bowed down and worshiped the statue (3:2-7). Some of them also were informers who told the king about the civil disobedience of Shadrach, Meshach, and Abednego (3:8-12). Now, however, the king's officials stand in awe next to the three Jews. With their own eyes they "saw that the fire had had no power over the bodies of these men; not a hair of their heads had been singed, nor were their garments altered; there was not even a smell of fire about them" (3:94). Not only were the three confessors unharmed; but they did not lose a single hair in the fire. The words of Jesus come to mind: "You will be hated by all because of my name, but not a hair on your head will be destroyed. By your perseverance you will secure your lives" (Lk 21:17-19). Even the clothing of the three Jews remained untouched. Nor did they have to air out their garments to get rid of the smell of fire and smoke. In the amazement of the officials we again see hyperbole at work in service of theology. Notice that the pagans themselves verify and authenticate the stupendous miracle.

The King Praises the God of the Jews

The story comes full swing when "Nebuchadnezzar exclaimed, 'Blessed be the God of Shadrach, Meshach, and Abednego, who sent his angel to deliver the servants that trusted in him; they disobeyed the royal command and yielded their bodies rather than serve or worship any god except their own God' " (3:95). There is subtle irony in this scene. Earlier in the story (3:4-5) when the orchestra played its song, nations and peoples were ordered to bow down and worship the king's idol. But here as if in response to the song of the three Jews to all human beings to bless the Lord (3:82), the king now blesses the God of Israel. The simple song of the three Jews has more effect on the king than his elaborate orchestra had on them.

Nebuchadnezzar even praises the three confessors for defying the royal command and yielding their bodies to the flames. Finally, he decrees "for nations and peoples of every language that whoever blasphemes the God of Shadrach, Meshach, and Abednego shall be cut to pieces and his house destroyed. For there is no other God who can rescue like this" (3:96). There is delicious irony in this decree. In 3:4-7, the king had commanded that when the orchestra played its song "nations and peoples of every language" should "fall down and worship the golden statue," and they all did exactly that. Now these same "nations and peoples" are ordered not to blaspheme the God of Israel. Moreover, the three confessors are apparently exempted from worshiping the king's gold idol.

Nebuchadnezzar's calling the three confessors "servants of the Most High" (3:93), however, does not mean that the God of Israel is now the God of the king. He simply acknowledges that the Most High is the God of the three Jews, and their religion is now legitimate in the pagan kingdom. His decree (3:96) reinforces the legitimacy and respect that all his subject nations and people must give to the Jewish religion. It was precisely this kind of religious toleration which was desired by the Jews of the second century B.C., but which was denied them during the brutal regime of Antiochus IV Epiphanes. In the conclusion of this long story, Nebuchadnezzar gives Shadrach, Meshach, and Abednego a promotion (3:97). By their fidelity to the law of God and their perseverance even in the face of excruciating death, the three Jews not only survive the ordeal but also achieve a more prominent position in their civil service career.

Some Reflections

It is important to keep in mind that the three Jews did not escape the flames; they were saved in the flames. Only after they deliberately chose to be thrown into the white-hot furnace in order to be true to the demands of their faith did they experience God's dramatic rescue. The fact that the Jews are faithful to the point of death puts no constraints on God. God is absolutely free to do as he wills. God may choose to do nothing, as Shadrach, Meshach, and Abednego declare to the king before he throws them into the blazing furnace. This is faith at its best, with no strings attached. Thus, the speech of the three confessors to the king (3:16-18) clearly implies that faith in God's power to save does not mean that God will suspend the laws of nature or step in to prevent wicked people from doing wicked things simply in order to make life more pleasant for good people. God is not a *deus ex machina*, a

80

convenient God to call on to get us out of a fix. Nor is God a labor-saving device or a celestial pain reliever, as is evident from what Jesus experienced in his agony and death on the cross. But the God and Father, who did not spare his own Son, will enable believers to transcend, to go beyond, their natural instincts by choosing to die instead of giving in to the immoral demands of the state. In other words, authentic faith in the God of revelation empowers those who believe to remain faithful and constant even when God decides for his own reasons to remain silent. The story of the three confessors dramatizes that loyalty to God is more important and ultimately more meaningful than the prolongation of life and social and economic prosperity acquired at the expense of religious principles.

Ambrose (340-97) in his Commentary on Psalm 118 writes: "As there are many kinds of persecution, so there are many kinds of martyrdom. Every day you are a witness to Christ. You were tempted by the spirit of fornication . . . and did not want your purity of mind and body to be defiled: You are a martyr for Christ. You were tempted by the spirit of avarice to seize the property of a child and violate the rights of a defenseless widow, but remembered God's law and saw your duty to give help, and not act unjustly: You are a witness to Christ. . . . You were tempted by the spirit of pride but saw the poor and the needy and looked with loving compassion on them, and loved humility rather than arrogance: You are a witness to Christ. . . . The true witness is one who bears witness to the commandments of the Lord Jesus and supports that witness by deeds."

Thus, what the three confessors say to Nebuchadnezzar in 3:16-18 is that the problem of God and of faith in God who loves us and cares for us is difficult to resolve even when one believes in the true God who revealed himself to Israel. But that problem, which every man and woman must face if they are to lead an examined life, becomes impossible to resolve when one puts faith in the pagan gods, which are as lifeless and powerless as Nebuchadnezzar's gold statue. As we know from such ancient myths as the Mesopotamian *Enuma Elish*, these gods were believed to be not much different from human beings. They have parents, and thus they came into existence through birth. They are graphically described as sexual beings often with unrestrained erotic urges. They had spouses and children who would fight against one another. They had faults and passions. They had to contend with rival gods and were often replaced by supposedly superior gods.

The Old Testament often ridicules the pagan "gods fashioned by the hands of man out of wood and stone, gods which can neither see nor hear, neither eat nor smell" (Dt 4:28; cf. Dn 14:5, 27). The God of Israel, however, is neither male nor female; he is pure spirit. Consequently, God has no consort and no offspring. God always existed. God is supreme; there is no other. But this God is also a God who cares, a God who saves, a God who wills to be involved in human affairs, a God who holds us accountable for our decisions and actions.

In the story of 2 Maccabees 7 the mother and her seven sons are not spared despite their outstanding faith and constancy. Instead, like other persecuted believers throughout history, they suffer a grisly death. The author of that story tells us of course that the martyrs will be vindicated in the afterlife where they will receive the reward for their loyalty. In our story, however, Shadrach, Meshach, and Abednego are spared at the last minute by God's stupendous intervention. But the author certainly knew that real fire really burns and that God does not ordinarily interfere with the laws of nature. The miraculous climax described so graphically in 3:24-45, 49-94 may simply be another way for the author to allude to the doctrine of the resurrection or life after death that is described explicitly in 12:1-3.

Burning to death was a penalty practiced not just by barbarous rulers of antiquity. In the history of the Church many stalwart Christians also met their death by being burned alive. Saint Lawrence, the Roman deacon, was martyred during the persecution of Valerian in the year 258. According to a legend, well known to Ambrose and Augustine, Saint Lawrence was burned to death. But he never lost his sense of humor. While being roasted on the grill, he said to the judge, "It is well done; turn it over and eat it." In the sixteenth and seventeenth centuries, hundreds of Japanese martyrs met their death by crucifixion, beheading, or being burned alive in the hot springs of Unzen, a place of pilgrimage I visited in the spring of 1972. During the persecutions, the Japanese authorities placed on the ground *Fumi-e*, "Tread Pictures," which were images of Jesus on the cross or of Mary and her child surrounded by the saints. Those who were suspected of being Christians were ordered to trample on the images. Anyone who refused to do so was tortured and put to death.

Nebuchadnezzar's grisly form of execution and disposal of assumed enemies lives on, even in our own century. After gassing with hydrogen cyanide millions of Jews, Gypsies, Poles, and others considered undesirable, the Nazis used furnaces or incinerators to burn the corpses. According to reliable reports, these atrocities in the death camps were committed to the sound of music playing in the background. Nebuchadnezzar's brutality, unfortunately, lives on also in our own day in the torture and imprisonment, exile and death, of many innocent victims. In dozens of places around the world, even in some so-called democracies, prisoners of conscience are subjected to the most degrading forms of punishment and execution. Their only crime is refusal to fall down and worship the gold statue of the state when the music plays.

Fear of the furnace is still being used by unscrupulous governments to keep political and religious dissidents in line. The 1993 Annual Report of Amnesty International gives an account of the ways in which human rights are trampled upon in 161 countries. Authorities in these countries use such practices as the jailing of prisoners of conscience, political murders by "security forces," unfair trials, judicial torture, detentions, and abductions. Shadrach, Meshach, and Abednego show the way to overcome the fear of the furnace—their faith in a God of justice and mercy who loves us and who can save us. They prove that lively faith can quench fires and can move mountains. Indeed, Jesus tells us, "Amen, I say to you, if you have faith the size of a mustard seed, you will say to this mountain, 'Move from here to there,' and it will move. Nothing will be impossible for you" (Mt 17:20). And again, "Amen, I say to you, if you have faith and do not waver . . . even if you say to this mountain, 'Be lifted up and thrown into the sea,' it will be done" (Mt 21:21).

How first Azariah (3:25-45) and then Shadrach, Meshach, and Abednego (Azariah's Babylonian name) react after being thrown into the raging furnace (3:51-90ab) is instructive for believers today. Azariah confesses the sins of the people and praises God for his "proper judgments" in punishing the nation by handing it over to Nebuchadnezzar (3:27-32). Then Azariah pleads for mercy and deliverance from oppressors, so that they may know that the Lord alone is God "glorious over the whole world" (3:33-45). When the angel of the Lord came to the rescue and "made the inside of the furnace as though a dew-laden breeze were blowing through it" (3:49-50), Shadrach, Meshach, and Abednego, break out into exuberant song. Thus, the confession of sin and the prayer for mercy are followed by praise of the Lord.

The prayer of Azariah is a wholesome reminder that the Lord will extend his mercy and forgiveness to those who turn to him in repentance. No one is hopeless or helpless. No one is too far gone. No one is beyond the pale of God's love and concern.

The prayer of Azariah is somber. The song of Shadrach, Meshach, and Abednego is exuberant, prompting us to raise our own voices in praise to the Lord for the beauties of creation, above all for mother earth that we often take for granted. As the great German exegete Gerhard von Rad once wrote, "Praise is our most characteristic mode of existence: Praising and not praising stand over against one another like life and death."

Praise is also the highest form of prayer. We proclaim the goodness of the Lord as well as his mercy and majesty, and at the same time we acknowledge our total dependence on God and on the bounty with which he sustains us. Praise also helps us preserve our sense of wonder and reverence in this vast and awesome universe.

VIII

"I, Nebuchadnezzar, Had a Terrifying Dream"

(Daniel 3:98–4:15)

3:98King Nebuchadnezzar to the nations and peoples of every language, wherever they dwell on earth: abundant peace! 99It has seemed good to me to publish the signs and wonders which the most high God has accomplished in my regard.

100How great are his signs, how mighty his wonders;
> his kingdom is an everlasting kingdom,
> and his dominion endures through all generations.

4:1I, Nebuchadnezzar, was at home in my palace, content and prosperous. 2I had a terrifying dream as I lay in bed, and the images and the visions of my mind frightened me. 3So I issued a decree that all the wise men of Babylon should be brought before me to give the interpretation of the dream. 4When the magicians, enchanters, Chaldeans, and astrologers had come in, I related the dream before them; but none of them could tell me its meaning. 5Finally there came before me Daniel, whose name is Belteshazzar after the name of my god, and in whom is the spirit of the holy God. I repeated the dream to him: 6"Belteshazzar, chief of the magicians, I know that the spirit of the holy God is in you and no mystery is too difficult for you; tell me the meaning of the visions that I saw in my dream.

7"These were the visions I saw while in bed: I saw a tree of great height at the center of the world. 8It was large and strong, with its top touching the heavens, and it could be seen to the ends of the earth. 9Its leaves were beautiful and its fruit abundant, providing food for all. Under it the wild beasts found shade, in its branches the birds of the air nested; all men ate of it. 10In the vision I saw while in bed, a holy sentinel came down from heaven, 11and cried out:

> " 'Cut down the tree and lop off its branches,
> strip off its leaves and scatter its fruit;

let the beasts flee its shade, and the birds its branches.
¹²But leave in the earth its stump and roots,
    fettered with iron and bronze, in the grass of the field.
Let him be bathed with the dew of heaven;
    his lot be to eat, among beasts, the grass of the earth.
¹³Let his mind be changed from the human;
    let him be given the sense of a beast,
    till seven years pass over him.
¹⁴By decree of the sentinels is this decided,
    by order of the holy ones, this sentence;
That all who live may know
    that the Most High rules over the kingdom of men:
He can give it to whom he will,
    or set over it the lowliest of men.'
¹⁵"This is the dream that I, King Nebuchadnezzar, had. Now, Belteshazzar, tell me its meaning. Although none of the wise men in my kingdom can tell me the meaning, you can, because the spirit of the holy God is in you."

The chapter division of this section, as well as the division of all the other chapters of the Bible, comes from the Latin Vulgate. Stephen Langton, an English theologian and archbishop of Canterbury, introduced this division around the year 1225. Langton made an error in attaching the first three verses of the story, 3:98-100, to the end of the story in chapter 3. These verses clearly belong to the story in chapter 4.

King Nebuchadnezzar again figures prominently in this story. But unlike the other narratives in the book, this story has the form of a letter or epistle written by the king himself. In it, he gives a description of a terrifying dream, which his Babylonian wise men could not interpret for him. Daniel again comes before the king and tells him the meaning of the dream. As is normal in a letter, Nebuchadnezzar writes in the first person; but a small portion, 4:25-30, is written in third person. A similar shift occurs also in the Book of Tobit. In 1:3–3:6, Tobit tells the story in the first person; then the rest of the book (3:7–14:15) is written in the third person.

Nebuchadnezzar's Letter

The letter-form here follows the style used in the Akkadian letters of the Neo-Babylonian era, the Aramaic letters of the Persian period, and the Greek letters of the Hellenistic era (1 Mc 10:18-20; 15:2, 16; 2 Mc 1:1). The sender of the letter is "King Nebuchadnezzar," the addressees, "the nations and peoples of every language, wherever they dwell on earth," and the greeting, "abundant peace" (3:98). The expression, "The nations and peoples of every language," is found also in the previous story (3:4, 7, 96) as well as in 5:19; 6:26; and 7:14. The greeting, "abundant peace," occurs also in 6:26 (cf. 1 Pt 1:2 and 2 Pt 1:2). "Peace," Hebrew *shalom*, is the usual greeting Jews have given each other right to the present day. "Into whatever house you enter, first say, 'Peace to this household' " (Lk 10:5). This formal introduction is followed by a statement of the purpose of the letter: "It has seemed good to me to publish the signs and wonders which the most high God has accomplished in my regard" (3:99). Then the king offers a brief hymn of praise to God (3:100), a feature found also in such letters as 2 Corinthians 1:3-4; Ephesians 1:3-6; 1 Peter 1:3-5. The body of the letter (4:1-34) tells the story of Nebuchadnezzar's dream and what happened to him afterwards.

Nebuchadnezzar's Dream

As in the narrative of Daniel 2, Nebuchadnezzar has a dream that frightened the wits out of him. The dream seemed especially out of place, for the king was at home in his palace, "content and prosperous" (4:1). He is utterly pleased with himself and with his position in life. When he had been troubled by the earlier dream and sought Daniel, who told the king the contents of the dream and its meaning, he acknowledged that Daniel's God "is the God of gods and Lord of kings and a revealer of mysteries" (2:47). But now that things have returned to normal, and he once again enjoys his riches and power, he forgot about God or, what is worse, he thought he no longer needed God. This recalls the parable of the rich fool. "There was a rich man whose land produced a bountiful harvest. He asked himself, 'What shall I do, for I do not have space to store my harvest?' And he said, 'This is what I shall do: I shall tear down my barns and build larger ones. There I shall store all my grain and other goods and I shall say to myself, "Now as for you, you have so many good things stored up for many years, rest, eat, drink, be merry!" ' But God said to him, 'You fool, this night your life will be demanded of you; and the things you have prepared, to whom will they belong?' " (Lk 12:16-20).

It is when people are prosperous and affluent that they tend to forget about God. "Then Jesus said to his disciples, 'Amen, I say to you, it will be hard for one who is rich to enter the kingdom of heaven. Again I say to you, it is easier for a camel to pass through the eye of a needle than for one who is rich to enter the kingdom of God' " (Mt 19:23-24). "Blessed are the poor in spirit, for theirs is the kingdom of heaven" (Mt 5:3).

It was Nebuchadnezzar's good fortune that should have given him cause for concern. His kingdom was secure and the economy was thriving. What could possibly go wrong? The king would soon find out. He would learn his lesson the hard way. The king's serenity and security are completely shattered by the "images and visions" he saw in his dream (4:2). The king's nightmare, however, did not vanish when he awoke. Unlike the dream in chapter 2, the contents of the present dream are all too clear. Nevertheless, the king does not know what to make of it. So, as in the previous case, Nebuchadnezzar calls in his experts, "all the wise men of Babylon," "the magicians, enchanters, Chaldeans, and astrologers" (4:3-4). But unlike in the earlier story, the king takes it easy on his soothsayers, telling them the content of the dream and then simply asking them to give him its meaning. But once again these wise men had no idea what the dream meant.

Daniel Appears in Court

Finally on the scene comes Daniel, whose name, the king says, "is Belteshazzar after the name of my god." This name in Babylonian is a shortened form of "[Marduk or Bel,] protect the king's life." The king then adds that in Daniel "is the spirit of the holy God" (4:5). This expression is a literal reminiscence of the Joseph story. After Joseph had given his wise advice to store up grain from the seven good years as a reserve for the coming seven lean years, we are told, "This advice pleased Pharaoh and all his officials. 'Could we find another like him,' Pharaoh asked his officials, 'a man so endowed with the spirit of God?' " (Gn 41:37-38). The comment about Daniel's Babylonian name is ironic, for the pagan gods Marduk and Bel could not possibly help the king's wise men to interpret the dream. Only Daniel with the help of the God of Israel can honor the king's request. Addressing Daniel/Belteshazzar as "chief of the magicians," because of what he had done for the king in chapter 2, Nebuchadnezzar confesses, "I know that the spirit of the holy God is in you and no mystery is too difficult for you; tell me the meaning of the visions that I saw in my dream" (4:6). In 4:15 the king repeats the phrase, "the spirit of the holy God is in you," after he finishes telling Daniel about the dream. This literary device, called inclusion, emphasizes the significance of the phrase. Thus, Nebuchadnezzar acknowledges that Daniel has the ability to interpret dreams not because of the training he received in the Babylonian court schools (1:3-5), but because he has received this gift from God. The implication of the king's statement in 4:6 is clear. Only God knows what the future holds in store. The Babylonian "magical arts" are useless, being mere fantasies to delude the gullible and the superstitious.

Addressing Babylon in mocking tones, the prophet Isaiah says, "Keep up, now, your spells and your many sorceries. Perhaps you can make them avail, perhaps you can strike terror! You wearied yourself with many consultations, at which you toiled from your youth. Let the astrologers stand forth to save you, the stargazers who forecast at each new moon what would happen to you. Lo, they are like stubble, fire consumes them; they cannot save themselves from the spreading flames. This is no warming ember, no fire to sit before. Thus do your wizards serve you with whom you have toiled from your youth; each wanders his own way, with none to save you" (Is 47:12-15). Yet despite strong biblical condemnation, astrology and fortune telling continue to influence millions today. Some consult the astrological charts and horoscopes as an "innocent pastime." Others take astrology seriously and allow it to be a major influence in their decisions and actions. But every form of fortune telling and astrology is superstition and ultimately idolatry, which is of course contrary to faith in the true God.

The King's Dream

In chapter 2, Daniel first had to tell the king the content of the dream and then its interpretation. Here Nebuchadnezzar himself tells Daniel what he had dreamt. The king's dream is of a gigantic tree "at the center of the earth . . . with its top touching the heavens, and it could be seen to the ends of the earth" (4:7-8). The imagery of a tree is found also in Ezekiel 31:3-9, where the prophet compares Pharaoh to a magnificent cedar towering up in the sky of Lebanon. "Behold, a cypress [cedar] in Lebanon, beautiful of branch, lofty of stature, amid the very clouds lifted its crest. Waters made it grow, the abyss made it flourish, sending its rivers round where it was planted, turning its streams to all the trees of the field. Thus it grew taller than every other tree of the field, and longer of branch because of the abundant water. In its boughs nested all the birds of the air, under its branches all beasts of the field gave birth, in its shade dwelt numerous peoples of every race. It became beautiful and stately in its spread of foliage, for its roots were turned toward abundant water. The cedars in the garden of God were not its equal, nor could the fir trees match its boughs, neither were the plane trees like it for branches; no tree in the garden of God matched its beauty. I made it beautiful, with much foliage, the envy of all Eden's trees in the garden of God" (Ez 31:3-9). Because of its pride and wickedness, the cedar was cut down ignominiously by foreigners and its branches broken (Ez 31:10-13). Herodotus (vii, 19) records that Xerxes had a dream in which he saw himself crowned with the shoot of an olive tree; its boughs covered the whole earth until suddenly the crown about his head disappeared. As in the case with Pharaoh in Ezekiel 31 and Xerxes, Nebuchadnezzar's appalling dream of the tree was occasioned by his arrogant self-sufficiency. He even thought he could take the place of God, who alone sustains the lives of all human beings and animals and birds.

Our author, while utilizing the tree imagery of earlier writers, was also creative and independent. The tree, which symbolizes the empire of Nebuchadnezzar, will be cut down but not destroyed, so that all may come to know that God alone is supreme over all human governments (4:14). Our author here alludes to the universalism we find also in Second Isaiah (Is 40-55). "All you who are thirsty, come to the water! You who have no money, come, receive grain and eat; come, without paying and without cost, drink wine and milk! Why spend your money for what is not bread; your wages for what fails to satisfy? Heed me, and you shall eat well, you shall delight in rich fare. Come to me heedfully, listen, that you may have life" (Is 55:1-3).

The dream in chapter 2 merely kept the king from falling back to sleep, but the dream here scared him to no end. The most likely reason is that the king had an inkling that the dreadful sentence pronounced in the dream (4:11-14) somehow applied to himself. Nebuchadnezzar saw "a tree of great height at the center of the world" (4:7). This gigantic tree is of course a symbol of Nebuchadnezzar and his enormous empire which seemed to the ancients as if it were at the center of the earth, at least in terms of its political and social significance. The tree is "large and strong," and its top is "touching the heavens." In his haughtiness Nebuchadnezzar considered himself more than a mere mortal; he was not like the rest of human beings. The tree "could be seen to the ends of the earth" (4:8), a colorful expression to indicate the scope of the empire. The tree had lush and beautiful leaves and its fruit was plentiful, "providing food for all." It provided protective shade for wild beasts, and "in its branches the birds of the air nested." All human beings ate of it (4:9). The thoughts expressed by the symbolism of the huge tree reflect the actual historical facts regarding the commanding position of Nebuchadnezzar's kingdom as well as its extensive power, earthly glory, and great prosperity. Included in the symbolism is the protection and support that this kingdom in fact provided for the people who belonged to it and to those who were desirous of enjoying its privileges and advantages. Nebuchadnezzar had thought of himself as a benevolent despot. The images in 4:7-9 convey what he had always wanted to be: a world renowned monarch as well as the beloved benefactor of his people and even of all humankind. But as often happens with other totalitarian rulers, Nebuchadnezzar's noble sentiments and goals were intermingled with self-importance and pride which would eventually undo him.

History knows of other benevolent and not so benevolent despots who have followed Nebuchadnezzar's example. In our own century rulers like Lenin, Hitler, Mussolini, Stalin, Mao Tse-tung and Saddam Hussein have all thought of themselves as saviors and benefactors of their people. If these tyrants had to deprive their people of their freedom and their dignity in order to achieve the utopian new world order, so be it. The new kingdom they will usher in is what counts even at the price of bloodshed and the trampling of truth and human dignity. The leaves of the Nebuchadnezzar tree, though beautiful, are not for healing the nations as is the tree of life in the New Testament. "Then the angel showed me the river of life-giving water, sparkling like crystal, flowing from the throne of God and of the Lamb down the middle of its street. On either side of the river grew the tree of life that produces fruit twelve times a year, once each month; the leaves of the trees serve as medicine for the nations" (Rv 22:1-2; cf. Ez 47:1-12).

The Nebuchadnezzar tree can give abundant fruit to his subjects and lots of shade. But little else could grow in that shade. Freedom and truth cannot thrive in such an environment. But there is another tree under which every aspiration of the human heart can flourish and hundreds of other fruits can grow as well. "He [Jesus] proposed another parable to them. 'The kingdom of heaven is like a mustard seed that a person took and sowed in a field. It is the smallest of all the seeds, yet when full-grown it is the largest of plants. It becomes a large bush, and the "birds of the sky come and dwell in its branches' " (Mt 13:31-32). Here Jesus quotes Daniel 4:9 and Ezekiel 17:23, where the birds also represent people. But in contrast to Nebuchadnezzar's people who were deprived of their liberty, the birds in the parable of Jesus represent all peoples and nations who are called to come freely and dwell in the branches of the large bush that is the kingdom of God. "For freedom Christ set us free; so stand firm and do not submit again to the yoke of slavery" (Gal 5:1). "For you were called for freedom, brothers and sisters. But do not use this freedom as an opportunity for the flesh; rather, serve one another through love" (Gal 5:13).

Nebuchadnezzar's pleasant dream of prosperity and affluence for the people of his empire (4:7-9) now turns frightful. Down from heaven came "a holy sentinel," an angel, who cried out his message of doom. The immense tree is to be cut down, its branches lopped off, its leaves stripped, its fruit scattered. Beasts and birds will flee in terror. In spite of his good intentions and philanthropy, Nebuchadnezzar is cut down to size because of pride. The king now gets back some of what he had dished out to others. In the siege of Tyre, the city is told that Nebuchadnezzar "shall pound your walls with battering-rams and break down your towers with his weapons" (Ez 26:9). Now the axes are in the hand of God who has passed judgment on Nebuchadnezzar, and for the same reason that judgment was passed on the king of Tyre. "Son of man, say to the prince of Tyre: Thus says the Lord GOD: Because you are haughty of heart, you say, 'A god am I! I occupy a godly throne in the heart of the sea!'— And yet you are a man, and not a god, however you may think yourself like a god. . . . Because you have thought yourself to have the mind of a god, therefore I will bring against you foreigners, the most barbarous of nations. They shall draw their swords against your beauteous wisdom, they shall run them through your splendid apparel. They shall thrust you down to the pit, there to die a bloodied corpse, in the heart of the sea. Will you then say, 'I am a god!' when you face your murderers? No, you are a man, not a god, handed over to those who will slay you" (Ez 28:2, 6-9).

Hope for the King

There is a glimmer of hope for Nebuchadnezzar. The stump and roots of the tree will be left in the earth but will be "fettered with iron and bronze." The king will "be bathed with the dew of heaven," and he will "eat, among beasts, the grass of the earth" (4:11-12). For seven years he will lose his mind, having "the sense of a beast." The number seven here has symbolic value, denoting completeness or perfection, as in 3:19. All this was decreed by the sentinels or watchers, also called "the holy ones," another expression denoting the angels (Jb 5:1; 15:15; Ps 89:6; Zec 14:5), who attend the throne of the Almighty and are members of the divine council (1 Kgs 22:19-22; Jb 1:6; 2:1; 15:8; Ps 89:8; Jer 23:18). Thus, "all who live may know that the Most High rules over the kingdom of men: He can give it to whom he will, or set over it the lowliest of men." These words are reminiscent of Ezekiel 17:24: "And all the trees of the field shall know that I, the LORD, bring low the high tree, lift high the lowly tree, wither up the green tree, and make the withered tree bloom."

Having concluded the account of his dream, Nebuchadnezzar now asks Daniel/Belteshazzar to tell him its meaning because none of the wise men can do so. Daniel of course obliges.

IX

"His Dominion Is an Everlasting Dominion"

(Daniel 4:16-34)

[16]Then Daniel, whose name was Belteshazzar, was appalled for a while, terrified by his thoughts. "Belteshazzar," the king said to him, "let not the dream or its meaning terrify you." [17]"My lord," Belteshazzar replied, "this dream should be for your enemies, and its meaning for your foes. The large, strong tree that you saw, with its top touching the heavens, that could be seen by the whole earth, [18]which had beautiful foliage and abundant fruit, providing food for all, under which the wild beasts lived, and in whose branches the birds of the air dwelt— [19]you are that tree, O king, large and strong! Your majesty has become so great as to touch the heavens, and your rule extends over the whole earth. [20]As for the king's vision of a holy sentinel that came down from heaven and proclaimed: 'Cut down the tree and destroy it, but leave in the earth its stump and roots, fettered with iron and bronze in the grass of the field; let him be bathed with the dew of heaven, and let his lot be among wild beasts till seven years pass over him'—[21]this is its meaning, O king; this is the sentence which the Most High has passed upon my lord king: [22]You shall be cast out from among men and dwell with wild beasts; you shall be given grass to eat like an ox and be bathed with the dew of heaven; seven years shall pass over you, until you know that the Most High rules over the kingdom of men and gives it to whom he will. [23]The command that the stump and roots of the tree are to be left means that your kingdom shall be preserved for you, once you have learned it is heaven that rules. [24]Therefore, O king, take my advice; atone for your sins by good deeds, and for your misdeeds by kindness to the poor; then your prosperity will be long."

[25]All this happened to King Nebuchadnezzar. [26]Twelve months later, as he was walking on the roof of the royal palace

in Babylon, [27]the king said, "Babylon the great! Was it not I, with my great strength, who built it as a royal residence for my splendor and majesty?" [28]While these words were still on the king's lips, a voice spoke from heaven, "It has been decreed for you, King Nebuchadnezzar, that your kingdom is taken from you! [29]You shall be cast out from among men, and shall dwell with wild beasts; you shall be given grass to eat like an ox, and seven years shall pass over you, until you learn that the Most High rules over the kingdom of men and gives it to whom he will." [30]At once this was fulfilled. Nebuchadnezzar was cast out from among men, he ate grass like an ox, and his body was bathed with the dew of heaven, until his hair grew like the feathers of an eagle, and his nails like the claws of a bird. [31]When this period was over, I, Nebuchadnezzar, raised my eyes to heaven; my reason was restored to me, and I blessed the Most High, I praised and glorified him who lives forever:

His dominion is an everlasting dominion,
    and his kingdom endures through all generations.
[32]All who live on the earth are counted as nothing;
    he does as he pleases with the powers of heaven
    as well as with those who live on the earth.
There is no one who can stay his hand
    or say to him, "What have you done?"

[33]At the same time my reason returned to me, and for the glory of my kingdom, my majesty and my splendor returned to me. My nobles and lords sought me out; I was restored to my kingdom, and became much greater than before. [34]Therefore, I, Nebuchadnezzar, now praise and exalt and glorify the King of heaven, because all his works are right and his ways just; and those who walk in pride he is able to humble.

When Daniel/Belteshazzar hears the account of Nebuchadnezzar's dream, he is terrified and his face blanches. The king himself notices Daniel's consternation. "Belteshazzar," the king said to him, "let not the dream or its meaning terrify you" (4:16). After deferentially wishing that what is depicted in the vision should befall the king's enemies, Daniel proceeds to interpret the details of the dream. The king's towering pride is flattened. He is to live like an animal for seven years before being restored to his throne.

The Meaning of the King's Dream

Daniel does not waffle, but acts like Nathan the prophet who confronted King David fearlessly about his adultery with Bathsheba, his attempted cover-up, and his murder of Uriah, her husband (2 Sm 12:1-12). Daniel begins by saying, "The large, strong tree that you saw . . . you are that tree, O king, large and strong! Your majesty has become so great as to touch the heavens, and your rule extends over the whole earth" (4:17-18). Now comes the hard part—the king will be cut down and live "among wild beasts till seven years pass over him" (4:20). "This is the sentence which the Most High has passed upon my lord king." Nebuchadnezzar's overweening pride has caused his downfall. "Pride goes before disaster, and a haughty spirit before a fall" (Prv 16:18).

The King's Illness

The king will suffer from a disease known as zoanthropy in which he believes himself to be changed into an animal and behaves like one—a fitting punishment for Nebuchadnezzar's totalitarian behavior and exploitation of his people. Daniel tells him, "You shall be cast out from among men and dwell with wild beasts; you shall be given grass to eat like an ox and be bathed with the dew of heaven." Nebuchadnezzar will suffer from this disease for seven years, the number seven symbolizing, as noted before, totality or perfection. Thus, the king will have the perfect amount of time in which to suffer so as to be led to repentance. Daniel tells the king he will be afflicted that long, "until you know that the Most High rules over the kingdom of men and gives it to whom he will" (4:22). The command that the stump and roots be left in the ground means that Nebuchadnezzar's kingdom will be preserved for him, once he has learned that it is heaven (that is, God) that rules (4:23). Daniel urges the king to repent and to atone for his sins by good works and for his misdeeds "by kindness to the poor; then your prosperity will be long" (4:24). The king is given a chance to make up for his past injustices. He is to show mercy to those he had wronged. Repentance is not simply a change of heart; it is also a change of direction. It is not only confession of sin to God; it is

97

also willingness to make reparation and restitution to those we have sinned against.

The Value of Almsgiving

Especially in later Judaism, kindness to the poor by means of almsgiving was considered a serious obligation as well as a means of expiation for sin. "Give alms from your possessions. Do not turn your face away from any of the poor, and God's face will not be turned away from you. Son, give alms in proportion to what you own. If you have great wealth, give alms out of your abundance; if you have but little, distribute even some of that. But do not hesitate to give alms" (Tb 4:7-8). "Almsgiving frees one from death, and keeps one from going into the dark abode. Alms are a worthy offering in the sight of the Most High for all who give them" (Tb 4:10-11). "Give to the hungry some of your bread, and to the naked some of your clothing. Whatever you have left over, give away as alms; and do not begrudge the alms you give" (Tb 4:16). "Prayer and fasting are good, but better than either is almsgiving accompanied by righteousness. A little with righteousness is better than abundance with wickedness. It is better to give alms than to store up gold; for almsgiving saves one from death and expiates every sin. Those who regularly give alms shall enjoy a full life" (Tb 12:8-9). "Because Ahiqar had given alms to me, he escaped from the deadly trap Nadab had set for him. But Nadab himself fell into the deadly trap, and it destroyed him. So, my children, note well what almsgiving does, and also what wickedness does—it kills!" (Tb 14:10-11). "Water quenches a flaming fire, and alms atone for sins" (Sir 3:29). "Be not impatient in prayers, and neglect not the giving of alms" (Sir 7:10). "Store up almsgiving in your treasure house, and it will save you from every evil" (Sir 29:12). "In works of charity one offers fine flour, and when he gives alms he presents his sacrifice of praise" (Sir 35:2). " 'Cornelius, your prayer has been heard and your almsgiving remembered before God' " (Acts 10:31).

The King Does Not Repent

Nebuchadnezzar listened attentively to Daniel but apparently saw no need for immediate conversion and repentance. The great Augustine (354-430) also postponed his conversion—something he later lamented bitterly. In his *Confessions* he wrote: "Late have I loved you, O Beauty ever ancient, ever new, late have I loved you! You were within me, but I was outside, and it was there that I searched for you. In my unloveliness I plunged into the lovely things which you created. You were with me, but I was not with you. Created things kept me from you; yet if they had not been in you they would not have been at all."

For Nebuchadnezzar a year had passed and nothing had happened. So he persisted in his peacock-strutting and self-complacency. "Twelve months later, as he was walking on the roof of the royal palace in Babylon, the king said, 'Babylon the great! Was it not I, with my great strength, who built it as a royal residence for my splendor and majesty?' " (4:26-27). While these words of insufferable hubris were still on the king's lips, the voice from heaven passed judgment on him. "It has been decreed for you, King Nebuchadnezzar, that your kingdom is taken from you!"

The sound of the ax is heard in both Old and New Testaments. "When he [John the Baptist] saw many of the Pharisees and Sadducees coming to his baptism, he said to them, 'You brood of vipers! Who warned you to flee from the coming wrath? Produce good fruit as evidence of your repentance. And do not presume to say to yourselves, "We have Abraham as our father." For I tell you, God can raise up children to Abraham from these stones. Even now the ax lies at the root of the trees. Therefore every tree that does not bear good fruit will be cut down and thrown into the fire' " (Mt 3:7-10).

Though the judgment of God on human sin and evil may be delayed, it is nonetheless inevitable. Nebuchadnezzar had been warned explicitly about the punishment to follow if he did not repent (4:22); yet he persisted twelve more months in his smug complacency (4:26-27). If we are tempted to delay our own repentance, we should recall Paul's words: "By your stubbornness and impenitent heart, you are storing up wrath for yourself for the day of wrath and revelation of the just judgment of God, who will repay everyone according to his works: eternal life to those who seek glory, honor, and immortality through perseverance in good works, but wrath and fury to those who selfishly disobey the truth and obey wickedness" (Rom 2:5-8). So now God's judgment "was fulfilled. Nebuchadnezzar was cast out from among men, he ate grass like an ox, and his body was bathed with the dew of heaven, until his hair grew like the feathers of an eagle, and his nails like the claws of a bird" (4:30). No more hair styling and fancy manicures for the king. Mighty Nebuchadnezzar now lives like a beast, deprived of his human will and intelligence. His mental illness will last for the seven-year period that had been decreed. Then the king finally comes to his spiritual senses. He raises his eyes to heaven, and his reason is restored. Then he blesses, praises, and glorifies the Most High "who lives forever" (4:31).

We too have to be knocked off our high horse and brought low before we come to acknowledge that God in heaven will indeed pass judgment on our pride, lust, sensuality, anger, greed, insensitivity to the needs of the poor, the downtrodden, and the weak. God may allow us a time to repent and to "know that the Most High rules over the kingdom of men" and to learn "that it is heaven that rules" (4:22-23). Indeed as another inspired author says about God: "You have mercy on all, because you can do all things; and you overlook the sins of men that they may repent. For you love all things that are and loathe nothing that you have made; for what you hated, you would not have fashioned. And how could a thing remain, unless you willed it; or be preserved, had it not been called forth by you? But you spare all things, because they are yours, O LORD and lover of souls, for your imperishable spirit is in all things! Therefore you rebuke offenders little by little, warn them, and remind them of the sins they are committing, that they may abandon their wickedness and believe in you, O LORD!" (Wis 11:23-12:2).

But we should not presume on God's mercy. God will not be mocked. The moment of salvation is now. Jesus tells us: "This is the time of fulfillment. The kingdom of God is at hand. Repent, and believe in the gospel" (Mk 1:15). Paul writes, "Working together, then, we appeal to you not to receive the grace of God in vain. For he says: 'In an acceptable time I heard you, and on the day of salvation I helped you.' Behold, now is a very acceptable time; behold, now is the day of salvation" (2 Cor 6:1-2).

As a matter of historical record, there is no evidence that Nebuchadnezzar suffered from mental illness or was deprived of his throne for seven years. From reliable sources we know enough of the forty-three-year reign of this king to make it impossible to fit in what Daniel 4 tells us about him. After T. G. Pinches published the "Nabonidus Chronicle" in 1882, scholars began to suspect that in an earlier form of the folktale the insane king was not Nebuchadnezzar II (605-562 B.C.), who appears here and in the other chapters of the book, but rather his fourth successor, Nabunaid or Nabonidus (556-39). This view was confirmed by the fragmentary "Prayer of Nabonidus" from Qumran Cave 4.

The author of our story, however, was not interested in conveying historical information about either Babylonian ruler. The original audience would see in Nebuchadnezzar's insanity the antics of the Seleucid king of their own time, Antiochus IV (175-64 B.C.). In 169 this despot took on himself the title "Epiphanes," which means "[God] Manifest." But because of his behavior that ranged from the outrageous to the barbaric, the people nicknamed him "Epimanes," "Madman." The ancient historian Polybius describes in detail the conduct of Antiochus: his carousing with strangers of the lowest rank, his walking the streets in disguise, his visiting the shops of the silversmiths and goldsmiths and seeking to impress them with his knowledge and love of art, his lavish generosity to utter strangers, his perverse practical jokes in the public baths. On one occasion a man said to him in the public baths, "You kings are fortunate to have such ointments of exquisite fragrance." The next day Antiochus went to the baths and had a large container of precious ointment poured all over that man. Others rushed forward to get their share of the perfume. But because the floor became slippery from the ointment, many slipped and fell, to the insane laughter of the king.

The King's Health Restored

At the end of seven years, Nebuchadnezzar's reason was restored, and he finally acknowledges God as supreme. "His dominion is an everlasting dominion, and his kingdom endures through all generations" (4:31). Because of his sinful hubris and failure to recognize that all power comes from God, Nebuchadnezzar has experienced God's judgment, a judgment not only on himself but also on the people he rules. The king and people are called upon to repent. Only with genuine repentance will Nebuchadnezzar and his empire experience God's open-armed mercy.

Daniel's prophetic voice to repent echoes down to our own day. But where are the prophetic voices today? Mother Teresa of Calcutta is received with affection by most people, even unbelievers, but her voice lamenting the crimes of our society goes unheeded. Nebuchadnezzar received a punishment that befitted his sins. The same will be true with us. Sin will be requited; it is only a matter of time. The warnings are here in scripture. If there is no systemic conversion and repentance, the ax will be laid to the root.

Nebuchadnezzar's first act after his reason was restored is to make an act of faith that God's kingdom alone "endures through all generations" and that God holds sway both in heaven and on earth (4:31-32). Only then were the glory of his kingdom, his majesty, and his splendor returned to him, and he "became much greater than before" (4:33). He then praises and glorifies "the King of heaven, because all his works are right and his ways just," and then confesses what he knows from personal experience, that "those who walk in pride he is able to humble" (4:34). Nebuchadnezzar had been reduced to an animal-like state. Only when he was restored to full humanity was he able to praise and bless the Most High.

The Sin of Oppression

Like the repentant Nebuchadnezzar, we are all destined by God to be in full possession of our humanity. Accordingly, to deprive the weak in third world countries of their basic dignity and freedom that make a decent life possible is to obstruct God's plan for humanity. God made all human beings without exception in his own image and likeness and gave them dominion "over the fish of the sea, the birds of the air, and the cattle, and over all the wild animals and all the creatures that crawl on the ground" (Gn 1:26).

It is, therefore, morally perverse for transnational corporations with the collusion of their respective governments to dehumanize and make virtual slaves of men, women, and children, so that they can produce consumer goods at low prices for the affluent nations of the West.

Citizens of the third world are not chattel to be exploited. Christian moral sense compels us to help them by taking political and economic steps to remedy the causes of social injustice. Daniel said to Nebuchadnezzar, "O king, take my advice; atone for your sins by good deeds, and for your misdeeds by kindness to the poor" (4:24). Daniel gives that same advice to us today. It is significant that Nebuchadnezzar's repentance, his restoration to full humanity, and his recognition of the supreme dominion of God happened at the same time. When we repent and honor God as we should, we value the lives of the downtrodden as being as precious as our own. But when we disdain the lives of the poor, we dishonor the God who hears them when they cry out to him. "For the LORD hears the poor, and his own who are in bonds he spurns not" (Ps 69:34). "He who shuts his ear to the cry of the poor will himself also call and not be heard" (Prv 21:13).

X

"King Belshazzar Gave a Great Banquet"

(Daniel 5:1-16)

[1] King Belshazzar gave a great banquet for a thousand of his lords, with whom he drank. [2] Under the influence of the wine, he ordered the gold and silver vessels which Nebuchadnezzar, his father, had taken from the temple in Jerusalem, to be brought in so that the king, his lords, his wives and his entertainers might drink from them. [3] When the gold vessels taken from the temple which is the house of God in Jerusalem had been brought in, and while the king, his lords, his wives and his entertainers were drinking [4] wine from them, they praised their gods of gold and silver, bronze and iron, wood and stone.

[5] Suddenly, opposite the lampstand, the fingers of a human hand appeared, writing on the plaster of the wall in the king's palace. When the king saw the wrist and hand that wrote, [6] his face blanched; his thoughts terrified him, his hip joints shook, and his knees knocked. [7] The king shouted for the enchanters, Chaldeans, and astrologers to be brought in. "Whoever reads this writing and tells me what it means," he said to the wise men of Babylon, "shall be clothed in purple, wear a golden collar about his neck, and be third in the government of the kingdom." [8] But though all the king's wise men came in, none of them could either read the writing or tell the king what it meant. [9] Then King Belshazzar was greatly terrified; his face went ashen, and his lords were thrown into confusion.

[10] When the queen heard of the discussion between the king and his lords, she entered the banquet hall and said, "O king, live forever! Be not troubled in mind, nor look so pale! [11] There is a man in your kingdom in whom is the spirit of the holy God; during the lifetime of your father he was seen to have brilliant knowledge and god-like wisdom. In fact, King Nebuchadnezzar, your father, made him chief of the magicians, enchanters, Chal-

deans, and astrologers, [12]because of the extraordinary mind possessed by this Daniel, whom the king named Belteshazzar. He knew and understood how to interpret dreams, explain enigmas, and solve difficulties. Now therefore, summon Daniel to tell you what this means."

[13]Then Daniel was brought into the presence of the king. The king asked him, "Are you the Daniel, the Jewish exile, whom my father, the king, brought from Judah? [14]I have heard that the spirit of God is in you, that you possess brilliant knowledge and extraordinary wisdom. [15]Now, the wise men and enchanters were brought in to me to read this writing and tell me its meaning, but they could not say what the words meant. [16]But I have heard that you can interpret dreams and solve difficulties; if you are able to read the writing and tell me what it means, you shall be clothed in purple, wear a gold collar about your neck, and be third in the government of the kingdom."

This well-known story of the handwriting on the wall is a mixture of legend, folktale, and history, all of which have made a profound theological point for the original audience as well as for those who read the book today. Although Belshazzar was a genuine historical individual, he was not strictly speaking king of Babylon. He could not, for example, preside over the Babylonian New Year's Day festival that required the king's presence. Nebuchadnezzar, moreover, was not the father of Belshazzar, as 5:2 states. Rather Nabonidus, who was not even a descendant of Nebuchadnezzar but a usurper, was Belshazzar's father. Belshazzar was, however, crown prince, and in the third year of his father's seventeen-year rule, he was made coregent with his father and served in that capacity from 549-39 B.C. Moreover, during Nabonidus' many long absences from the capital, Belshazzar was practically speaking king of the neo-Babylonian empire. It is also historically correct that he was in charge when Babylon was captured in 539 B.C. But the author of our story is not interested in these historical details. His interest is purely theological and spiritual.

This story, though independent in itself, is closely related to the preceding one regarding Nebuchadnezzar's insanity (3:98–4:34). In fact, part of the earlier story is retold here in practically the same words (5:18-21). As in other parts of the book, the present story

105

has as its principal theme Daniel's God-given wisdom, which is far superior to the combined expertise of all the Babylonian wise men. Only because of this wisdom is Daniel able to interpret the mysterious handwriting. The theological and spiritual lesson of the story is clear. God will severely punish the king for his drunken orgy and the sacrilege he committed in allowing his guests to drink wine from the gold and silver vessels Nebuchadnezzar had taken from the temple in Jerusalem.

Belshazzar's Sacrilegious Feast

This story was written during the persecution of the Jews under Antiochus IV Epiphanes. The Jews, therefore, must have taken comfort in the thought that, just as God punished Belshazzar's desecration, God would surely chasten Antiochus for violating the Jerusalem temple in 167 B.C., when he placed there a statue of Olympian Zeus. The story is told in 2 Maccabees 6:1-5: "The king [Antiochus IV] sent an Athenian senator to force the Jews to abandon the customs of their ancestors and live no longer by the laws of God; also to profane the temple in Jerusalem and dedicate it to Olympian Zeus, and that on Mount Gerizim to Zeus the Hospitable, as the inhabitants of the place requested. This intensified the evil in an intolerable and utterly disgusting way. The Gentiles filled the temple with debauchery and revelry; they amused themselves with prostitutes and had intercourse with women even in the sacred court. They also brought into the temple things that were forbidden, so that the altar was covered with abominable offerings prohibited by the laws."

The setting of the present story is, as in the Book of Esther, a great banquet in the royal palace. From archeological excavations we know that in ancient Near Eastern palaces, particularly in the royal palace in Babylon, there were huge halls that could easily accommodate hundreds of people for a dinner and drinking party as described in 5:1. Everybody who was anybody was present at Belshazzar's "great banquet." In addition to "a thousand of his lords," the king was surrounded by his wives and entertainers. This was no ordinary party. There was food galore, delicacies of every sort, and plenty of wine.

The Babylonians, as a matter of historical record, were known to have a weakness for alcohol. In our story Belshazzar got drunk rather early in the banquet. His misuse of wine occasioned his sacrilegious order to bring in the gold and silver vessels from the Jerusalem temple, so that he, "his lords, his wives and his entertainers might drink from them" (5:2). Drunkenness has been the occasion of many other sinful decisions. Alcohol loosens inhibitions with the result that under its influence people tend to perform immoral acts that they would not otherwise do. The words of Ben Sira serve as a wholesome warning. "Let not wine-drinking be the proof of your strength, for wine has been the ruin of many. As the furnace probes the work of the smith, so does wine the hearts of the insolent. Wine is very life to man if taken in moderation. Does he really live who lacks the wine which was created for his joy? Joy of heart, good cheer and merriment are wine drunk freely at the proper time. Headache, bitterness and disgrace is wine drunk amid anger and strife. More and more wine is a snare for the fool; it lessens his strength and multiplies his wounds" (Sir 31:25-30).

Many years after Belshazzar, there was a similar party. "Herod, on his birthday, gave a banquet for his courtiers, his military officers, and the leading men of Galilee." For entertainment the daughter of Herodias "came in and performed a dance that delighted Herod and his guests. The king said to the girl, 'Ask of me whatever you wish and I will grant it to you.'" In his drunken stupor Herod swore an oath, "I will grant you whatever you ask of me, even to half of my kingdom." When the girl, at the prompting of Herodias who had bided her time to get revenge, asked for the head of John the Baptist, Herod quickly sobered up and realized how foolish he had been. But his guests were looking on to see what he would do. So in order for Herod to save face John the Baptist had to lose his head (Mk 6:21-28).

Belshazzar outdid himself in villainy by ordering that *the gold and silver vessels which Nebuchadnezzar, his father, had taken from the temple in Jerusalem, to be brought in"* (5:2). The author in the original Aramaic of 5:3 employs the common biblical device of "phrasal repetition" with slight changes, indicated by my italics, to make a significant point: "When *the gold vessels* taken from the temple *which is the house of God* in Jerusalem had been brought in . . ." The author omits details in 5:3 that might make the repetition wearisome but adds a significant description—the phrase after the temple, "which is the house of God" to emphasize the horror of Belshazzar's profanation of the temple vessels. Belshazzar and his guests then committed the further abomination of raising these sacred cups in praise of "their gods of gold and silver, bronze and iron, wood and stone" (5:3-4).

The misuse and abuse of sacred things has continued into our own time. On the infamous Kristallnacht, "Crystal Night," the night of 9-10 November 1938, the Nazis organized throughout Germany a pogrom against the Jews. In addition to breaking the windows of Jewish shops, these thugs desecrated and burned synagogues, stealing their sacred biblical scrolls and other precious items. This shocking event would eventually lead to Hitler's "ultimate solution," the annihilation of six million European Jews. In other places, churches have also been violated and turned into museums or stables. Sacred works of art became collector's items for the conqueror. Church and synagogue appointments of gold and silver were melted down and sold. Worse still, sacred vessels designed for sacramental purposes were desecrated and used as ordinary drinking goblets, as in our story. Treasured Bibles and other church books became curios for the dilettante.

God is indeed patient, as the psalmist writes: "You, O Lord, are a God merciful and gracious, slow to anger, abounding in kindness and fidelity" (Ps 86:15; also Ex 34:6; Nm 14:18; Neh 9:17; Wis 15:1; Jl 2:13; Jon 4:2). There is, however, a limit to God's forbearance. Presumption is a serious sin, as King Saul learned too late in his career: "For a sin like divination is rebellion, and presumption is the crime of idolatry. Because you have rejected the command of the LORD, he, too, has rejected you as ruler" (1 Sm 15:23). Paul also reminds us, "Make no mistake: God is not mocked, for a person will reap only what he sows, because the one who sows for his flesh will reap corruption from the flesh, but the one who sows for the spirit will reap eternal life from the spirit" (Gal 6:7-8). Belshazzar would soon experience the truth of these words.

The Handwriting on the Wall

There seemed to be no limit to the drunken carousing of Belshazzar and his guests, their debauchery, and their sacrilegious use of sacred vessels in idolatrous worship. Inhibitions were out. Excess was in. Belshazzar wanted this to be a party to remember. Little did he or his guests suspect why it would indeed become memorable. The party would be their last. The enemy was at the gates. Soon Babylon would be no more. Amid the raucous merry-making, out of nowhere, "suddenly, opposite the lampstand, the fingers of a human hand appeared, writing on the plaster of the wall in the king's palace" (5:5). Here the author uses a clever literary device to make his point: the Aramaic verb *npq* of 5:2-3, translated "to be brought in," is repeated in 5:5, in a different form, meaning "to appear." The purpose of this wordplay is to focus on the arrogant blasphemy of Nebuchadnezzar who brought *(npq)* the temple vessels to Babylon (5:2) and of Belshazzar who brought *(npq)* these vessels into the banquet hall (5:3). The third (hence most emphatic) use of *npq* to describe the appearing of the mysterious hand (5:5) dramatizes God's response to these insolent acts.

Belshazzar Fails to Repent

The moment of divine judgment has arrived. Belshazzar sobers up quick. He turns white. He is literally shaking in his boots, "and his knees knocked" (5:6). He has no idea at all what the hand has written, but he has an intuition that it spells out disaster. But he did not repent. Belshazzar followed the example of his predecessors in similar circumstances and summoned "the enchanters, Chaldeans, and astrologers" to interpret the handwriting on the wall. To motivate these wise men to do their best, the king offers rich rewards to the one who can tell the king the meaning of the writing—purple clothing, the clothing of royalty (Mk 15:17); a golden collar about the neck, a sign of authority (Gn 41:42); and a big promotion in the government of the kingdom (5:7). But money cannot buy the meaning of this mystery that only God can reveal. As in the earlier stories, the Babylonian wise men cannot help at all. Their wisdom is utterly useless. They cannot even make out the words, much less interpret the writing. So Belshazzar's terror intensifies, "his face went ashen." Even his lords "were thrown into confusion" (5:9). The party was over, for good.

Throughout history God has provided a hand which writes, not mysteriously, but clearly on the wall. Today the handwriting has global implications. God chooses the events and persons whom he wills to do the writing. What scientists tell us about ecological devastation, especially in the rain forests, and about environmental pollution from industrial wastes, vehicle emissions, and agricultural pesticides—all this is handwriting which we as a race ignore at our peril. The nuclear disaster at Chernobyl is handwriting that we can all see and interpret. The time to address these issues is now. The clock is ticking. We cannot presume that later we will have time to act.

Daniel Summoned to the Hall

Belshazzar's queen was not present at the banquet. It may be that the party would be too wild for the queen, or principal consort, to be invited. But more likely the reference is rather to the queen-mother, Nitocris, the widow of Nebuchadnezzar. According to Herodotus (I, 185-87), she had a reputation of being wise. When she hears "the discussion between the king and his lords," she enters the banquet hall. She came not to scold her drunken son but to offer help. She addresses the king with the customary greeting, "O king, live forever!" (5:10). Only the reader can see the irony of her words. Before the night is over, Belshazzar will be dead (5:30). She tells the king about Daniel, a man "in whom is the spirit of the holy God" (5:11), the description found also in 4:4, 15. She gives a brief summary of Daniel's career. He has "brilliant knowledge and god-like wisdom." He became "chief of the magicians, enchanters, Chaldeans, and astrologers" because of his extraordinary mind. He knows "how to interpret dreams, explain enigmas, and solve difficulties" (5:11-12). She then tells the king to summon Daniel into the hall.

Belshazzar does just that. He first asks Daniel, "Are you the Daniel, the Jewish exile, whom my father, the king, brought from Judah?" The irony of this question is striking. The high and mighty

Babylonian king has to call on the helpless and powerless "Jewish exile" to read the writing and interpret its meaning. The king then tries to flatter Daniel by telling him that he had heard about his "brilliant knowledge and extraordinary wisdom" (5:14). The king is forced to admit that his own wise men and enchanters could not help him. If Daniel can read and interpret the writing, the king promises him the same lavish gifts he had offered his own wise men.

Flattery and riches—these are offered to men and women of faith also today to entice them to blunt the divine message of judgment on human waywardness and vice. The Roman satiric poet Juvenal (ca. A.D. 60-127) once wrote, *Omnia Romae/ Cum pretio*, "At Rome, all things can be had at a price." Bribes and status, however, are too high a price to pay when our soul is involved. Daniel sees through Belshazzar's manipulative tactics. No gift or honor will prevent him from pronouncing God's judgment on the king.

This story has been immortalized by Rembrandt (1606-69) in his famous painting, "Belshazzar's Feast."

XI

"The Writing I Will Read for You, O King"

(Daniel 5:17–6:1)

[17]Daniel answered the king: "You may keep your gifts, or give your presents to someone else; but the writing I will read for you, O king, and tell you what it means. [18]The Most High God gave your father Nebuchadnezzar a great kingdom and glorious majesty. [19]Because he made him so great, the nations and peoples of every language dreaded and feared him. Whomever he wished, he killed or let live; whomever he wished, he exalted or humbled. [20]But when his heart became proud and his spirit hardened by insolence, he was put down from his royal throne and deprived of his glory; [21]he was cast out from among men and was made insensate as a beast; he lived with wild asses, and ate grass like an ox; his body was bathed with the dew of heaven, until he learned that the Most High God rules over the kingdom of men and appoints over it whom he will. [22]You, his son, Belshazzar, have not humbled your heart, though you knew all this; [23]you have rebelled against the Lord of heaven. You had the vessels of his temple brought before you, so that you and your nobles, your wives and your entertainers, might drink wine from them; and you praised the gods of silver and gold, bronze and iron, wood and stone, that neither see nor hear nor have intelligence. But the God in whose hand is your life breath and the whole course of your life, you did not glorify. [24]By him were the wrist and hand sent, and the writing set down.

[25]"This is the writing that was inscribed: MENE, TEKEL, and PERES. These words mean: [26] MENE, God has numbered your kingdom and put an end to it; [27] TEKEL, you have been weighed on the scales and found wanting; [28] PERES, your kingdom has been divided and given to the Medes and Persians."

[29]Then by order of Belshazzar they clothed Daniel in purple, with a gold collar about his neck, and proclaimed him third in

the government of the kingdom. ³⁰The same night Belshazzar, the Chaldean king, was slain: ^{6:1}And Darius the Mede succeeded to the kingdom at the age of sixty-two.

Belshazzar's offer of rich rewards and advancement in his kingdom is a futile attempt to bribe Daniel to change God's judgment now at hand. This attempt calls to mind the story of King Balak of Moab, who tried in vain to bribe Balaam to curse Israel (Nm 22-24). Instead of cursing Israel, Balaam under divine inspiration blessed Israel. "Balak beat his palms together in a blaze of anger at Balaam and said to him, 'It was to curse my foes that I summoned you here; yet three times now you have even blessed them instead! Be off at once, then, to your home. I promised to reward you richly! . . .' Balaam replied to Balak, 'Did I not warn the very messengers whom you sent to me, "Even if Balak gave me his house full of silver and gold, I could not of my own accord do anything, good or evil, contrary to the command of the LORD"? Whatever the LORD says I must repeat' " (Nm 24:10-13). Money acquired by devious means or, worse, from the exploitation of the poor will not become untainted by being given away even to noble causes. Such "philanthropy" will not cleanse a guilty conscience. Repentance and restitution alone will restore right order and lead the way to divine forgiveness.

Daniel Lectures the King

Daniel does not fall for Belshazzar's flattery or his lavish presents. He refuses to accept a thing, telling the king bluntly but courteously to keep the gifts or to give them away. Before reading and interpreting the mysterious handwriting, Daniel gives the king a short but powerful homily (5:17-24). The homily has two balanced parts, one beginning with "You, O King" (5:17), and the other with "You, his son, Belshazzar" (5:22). As James A. Montgomery wrote in his famous commentary, "There is no finer example of the preacher's diction in the Bible than this stern and inexorable condemnation." Daniel reviews the history of Belshazzar's father as described in detail in chapter 4. God had given Nebuchadnezzar "a great kingdom and glorious majesty." But

113

because this king became proud and insolent, "he was put down from his royal throne and deprived of his glory." He was cast out to live "with wild asses" and to eat grass "like an ox" until "he learned that the Most High God rules over the kingdom of men and appoints over it whom he will" (5:18-21).

Despite this clear warning, however, Belshazzar persisted in following his father's arrogant example. Instead of humbling himself, he "rebelled against the Lord of heaven" by bringing into his banquet hall the vessels from the Jerusalem temple and violating them when he and his nobles, his wives, and his entertainers drank from them. To add to the sacrilege, Belshazzar and his guests while drinking from the sacred vessels "praised the gods of silver and gold, bronze and iron, wood and stone, that neither see nor hear nor have intelligence" (5:23). Here we have another example of the literary device called "phrasal repetition," which I mentioned in chapter X above. In 5:4, the gods are described simply in terms of the materials of which they are made, "gold and silver, bronze and iron, wood and stone." But in 5:23, the author adds to this repetition the significant words: "that neither see nor hear nor have intelligence." This clause derives from Deuteronomy 4:28: "There [in exile] you [the unfaithful Israelites] shall serve gods fashioned by the hands of man out of wood and stone, gods which can neither see nor hear, neither eat nor smell." The pagan gods of even gold and silver are utterly lifeless and totally worthless. Unable even to see or hear, to eat or smell, and with no intelligence at all, they have nothing to offer human beings except the nothingness and emptiness that they are.

Despite the repeated warnings found in the Old Testament, many today worship idols of gold and silver just as enthusiastically and energetically as any pagan of old. As Dante said of Charles I of Anjou, "You have made yourself a god of gold and silver./ How else do you differ from idolaters/ Than that they worship one and you a hundred" (*The Divine Comedy*, "Hell," xix, 112-14). Paul writes: "Be sure of this, that no immoral or impure or greedy person, that is, an idolater, has any inheritance in the kingdom of Christ and of God" (Eph 5:5). Yet because of greed and the quest for greater profits, many corporate executives today see no wrong in permitting millions of children to knot carpets in India and

Pakistan, to harvest bananas in Brazil, to salvage rags in Egypt, and to work the cotton fields in Sudan. Paul describes conversion as a twofold process: (1) turning away from idols and (2) serving the true God. "You turned to God from idols to serve the living and true God and to await his Son from heaven, whom he raised from the dead, Jesus, who delivers us from the coming wrath" (1 Thes 1:9-10). "To serve idols" is Paul's shorthand for the worship of powers that demand the allegiance of human beings. The yen, the deutschemark, and the dollar have more worshipers than Marduk ever had, although Venus, goddess of sex, and Bacchus, god of wine, still have their devoted clientele.

Daniel tells the king point-blank: "You have rebelled against the Lord of heaven." Like Nebuchadnezzar, Belshazzar had been a powerful monarch. Like his father, Belshazzar had overstepped the bounds even for an absolute despot. But unlike his father who had learned "that the Most High rules over the kingdom of men and gives it to whom he will" (4:29) and repented of his insolence and self-complacency (4:31-34), Belshazzar remained obstinate, showing no signs of repentance. His sins of arrogance and sacrilege were sins of rebellion—crimes against right order, because, as Daniel says to the king, "the God in whose hand is your life breath and the whole course of your life, you did not glorify" (5:23).

The prophet Nathan also confronted David after the king had committed adultery with Bathsheba, tried to cover up his crime, and then ordered the murder of Uriah, her husband. "Nathan said to David: '. . .Thus says the LORD God of Israel: "I anointed you king of Israel. I rescued you from the hand of Saul. I gave you your lord's house and your lord's wives for your own. I gave you the house of Israel and of Judah. And if this were not enough, I could count up for you still more. Why have you spurned the LORD and done evil in his sight? You have cut down Uriah the Hittite with the sword; you took his wife as your own, and him you killed with the sword of the Ammonites. Now, therefore, the sword shall never depart from your house, because you have despised me and have taken the wife of Uriah to be your wife" ' " (2 Sm 12:7-10). The moment for judgment comes for all sin, including our own.

Daniel Reads and Interprets the Writing on the Wall

Daniel tells the king, "By him [God] were the wrist and hand sent, and the writing set down" (5:24). Like the prophets who had been sent to announce the message of the Lord (Is 6:9; Jer 1:7; Am 7:15), the wrist and hand were sent by God to write down a message of judgment for the unrepentant Belshazzar. Finally after a long period of suspense, Daniel reads the mysterious writing, pronouncing the words "MENE, TEKEL, and PERES." But these words need an interpreter just as the Ethiopian eunuch needed the apostle Philip to instruct him. "Philip ran up and heard him reading Isaiah the prophet and said, 'Do you understand what you are reading?' He replied, 'How can I, unless someone instructs me?' So he invited Philip to get in and sit with him" (Acts 8:30-31).

The cryptic words can have various meanings. Since the end of the last century, scholars have suggested that the words represent three weights or coins: a mina, a shekel (a sixtieth of a mina), and a half mina. These in turn may stand for three kings in that order of significance: Nebuchadnezzar, Belshazzar, and Darius the Mede. Whatever the case regarding the possible meanings, the interpretation of the cryptograms is what is important for our author and for his readers. Taking these three words as Aramaic verb roots, Daniel now interprets them for the panic-stricken Belshazzar. MENE comes from the verb "to count" or "to number." So Daniel tells the king that "God has numbered your kingdom and put an end to it." TEKEL, from the verb "to weigh," means that "you have been weighed on the scales and found wanting." PERES, from the verb "to divide," means that "your kingdom has been divided and given to the Medes and Persians" (5:25-28). In his excellent book on Apocalyptic, S. B. Frost writes about Daniel's interpretation of these three words: "That a kingdom should be weighed in a balance and found wanting is the very stuff of prophecy; that it should be divided is a pronouncement of divine judgment in the very manner of Isaiah; but that it should be *numbered* is the thought of apocalyptic alone. The whole school is impregnated with the conception of periods predetermined by divine decree."

The Lord of history has indeed "numbered" Belshazzar's deeds and those of the mighty Babylonian empire. The king's actions and character were found to be wanting in the scales of God's judgment. The result is that he and his kingdom will be broken up, never to be seen again. "Therefore, they shall be like a morning cloud or like the dew that early passes away, like chaff storm-driven from the threshing floor or like smoke out of the window" (Hos 13:3). Belshazzar could have foreseen God's judgment. As Daniel had reminded him, he knew what God had done to punish the insolence of his father Nebuchadnezzar (5:22). Yet Belshazzar did not accept his moment of grace. He refused to change his ways. He did not learn the lesson God had offered. He proved to be an ethical featherweight by adding to his villainy the sin of sacrilege. *Talis pastor, qualis grex*, "Like leader, so people." The Babylonian empire was indeed vast in extent, and its political influence was immense. But its moral worth was light, with no substance. Its fate was sealed along with Belshazzar's doom.

This is the story of many other empires ever since. God's judgment on hubris and injustice is certain. But the timetable remains known to God alone. There are lessons to be learned from history. Kings and nations come under the sovereign rule of the Lord of history. Kings and nations are not morally autonomous even if they act as if they are accountable to no one but themselves. God will indeed "number" every kingdom, and "weigh" its moral worth, and "divide" what is depraved and give it to someone else. Such is the story of Rome, the greatest empire of the ancient world. The handwriting is clear. It would be foolhardy to believe the divine judgment will be any different on nations today.

Belshazzar Rewards Daniel

Apparently, Belshazzar acknowledges the justice of the divine sentence which Daniel had pronounced against his sacrilege and idolatry. Perhaps in a moment of grace Belshazzar finally saw the errors of his ways and embraces his death as an act of reparation. This may be the reason why Daniel agrees to accept the gifts and honors he had refused earlier (5:17). For by Belshazzar's final order as king his courtiers "*clothed* Daniel *in purple, with a gold collar about his neck, and proclaimed him third in the government of the kingdom*" (5:29). The italicized words occur here for the third, hence the most emphatic, time in the story. That very night "Belshazzar, the Chaldean king, was slain" to be succeeded by Darius the Mede (6:1).

The Evil of Idolatry

After he had profaned the temple vessels for his drinking party, Belshazzar and his carousing guests lifted these sacred chalices in praise of their "gods of silver and gold, bronze and iron, wood and stone, that neither see nor hear nor have intelligence." Idolatry was a direct affront to God who had said to Moses on Mount Sinai, "I, the LORD, am your God, who brought you out of the land of Egypt, that place of slavery. You shall not have other gods besides me. You shall not carve idols for yourselves in the shape of anything in the sky above or on the earth below or in the waters beneath the earth; you shall not bow down before them or worship them" (Ex 20:2-5).

False gods of silver and gold are still worshiped today in the stock exchanges and corporate board rooms of the affluent West. But these gods cannot save, they cannot speak, they cannot satisfy. As the prophet Jeremiah says, "The cult idols of the nations are nothing, wood cut from the forest, wrought by craftsmen with the adze, adorned with silver and gold. With nails and hammers they are fastened, that they may not totter. Like a scarecrow in a cucumber field are they, they cannot speak; they must be carried about, for they cannot walk. Fear them not, they can do no harm, neither is it in their power to do good" (Jer 10:3-5). Though the false gods of silver and gold have nothing to offer, many continue to bow down to them in order to get more and spend more in a vain hope of attaining something wealth can never give.

Profanation of Holy Things

Antiochus IV Epiphanes had also desecrated the Jerusalem temple. "He insolently invaded the sanctuary and took away the golden altar, the lampstand for the light with all its fixtures, the offering table, the cups and the bowls, the golden censers, the

118

curtain, the crowns, and the golden ornament on the facade of the temple. He stripped off everything, and took away the gold and silver and the precious vessels; he also took all the hidden treasures he could find. Taking all this, he went back to his own country, after he had spoken with great arrogance and shed much blood" (1 Mc 1:21-24). Like Belshazzar before him, Antiochus would receive in due time the just recompense for his wickedness and insolence.

Belshazzar committed a sacrilege by misusing the temple vessels for drinking wine in praise of his gods. Paul warns Christians of another profanation. "Whoever eats the bread or drinks the cup of the Lord unworthily will have to answer for the body and blood of the Lord. A person should examine himself, and so eat the bread and drink the cup. For anyone who eats and drinks without discerning the body, eats and drinks judgment on himself" (1 Cor 11:27-29). Paul's reference in that last sentence to "the body" is not to the body of Christ, which every Christian believed was truly present in the eucharist. Rather, it is to the body of Christ comprising all believers. The Corinthians had failed to recognize the body of the Lord present in each member of the community. Indeed in another place, Paul tells them, "When you sin in this way against your brothers and sisters . . . , weak as they are, you are sinning against Christ" (1 Cor 8:12; see Mt 25:31-45). A timely warning to examine ourselves when we are tempted to participate in the eucharist without first honoring our responsibilities to those in need.

XII

"King Darius Signed the Prohibition and Made it Law"

(Daniel 6:2-10)

[2] Darius decided to appoint over his entire kingdom one hundred and twenty satraps, to safeguard his interests; [3] these were accountable to three supervisors, one of whom was Daniel. [4] Daniel outshone all the supervisors and satraps because an extraordinary spirit was in him, and the king thought of giving him authority over the entire kingdom. [5] Therefore the supervisors and satraps tried to find grounds for accusation against Daniel as regards the administration. But they could accuse him of no wrongdoing; because he was trustworthy, no fault of neglect or misconduct was to be found in him. [6] Then these men said to themselves, "We shall find no grounds for accusation against this Daniel unless by way of the law of his God." [7] So these supervisors and satraps went thronging to the king and said to him, "King Darius, live forever! [8] All the supervisors of the kingdom, the prefects, satraps, nobles, and governors are agreed that the following prohibition ought to be put in force by royal decree: No one is to address any petition to god or man for thirty days, except to you, O king; otherwise he shall be cast into a den of lions. [9] Now, O king, issue the prohibition over your signature, immutable and irrevocable under Mede and Persian law." [10] So King Darius signed the prohibition and made it law.

Before Belshazzar was slain, he had given Daniel royal honors and a promotion to "third in the government of the kingdom" (5:29). King Darius, who succeeded to the kingdom, recognized what he had in a man like Daniel. So he appointed Daniel as one of three supervisors to whom the "one hundred and twenty satraps," who would safeguard the royal interests, would be accountable. As in the other stories, it comes as no surprise that "Daniel outshone all the supervisors and satraps because an extraordinary spirit was in him." Elsewhere Daniel is said to have "the spirit of the holy God" (4:5, 6, 15; 5:11), or "the spirit of God" (5:14). The result is that "the king thought of giving him authority over the entire kingdom" (6:4). Thus the stage is set for the drama to follow. It is a story of envy and jealousy leading to conspiracy to do away with innocent Daniel, a story of vindication by God, and of the ultimate destruction of the conspirators in the lions' den which they had prepared for their enemy. This story has the same construction as the one in chapter 3. As in the account of Shadrach, Meshach, and Abednego, the present story develops in a dramatic way, repeating key words and expressions in typical biblical fashion. Thus in the Aramaic original, the expression "the king" appears thirty-one times, "Daniel" twenty-one times, "the kingdom" ten times, "the [lions'] den" ten times, "the lions" nine times.

The Evil of Envy and Jealousy

As often happens when one achieves success, some people become envious and jealous, as is the case here with the two other supervisors and the satraps. Throughout history the twin vices of envy and jealousy have wreaked havoc. Indeed, as we know from the Passion Narratives, "It was out of envy that the chief priests had handed him [Jesus] over" (Mk 15:10; Mt 27:18). "By the envy of the devil, death entered the world, and they who are in his possession experience it" (Wis 2:24). Ben Sira offers this sage comment: "Envy and anger shorten one's life, worry brings on premature old age" (Sir 30:24). Rightly does Iago warn Othello, "O, beware, my lord, of jealousy;/ It is the green-eyed monster, which doth mock/ The meat it feeds on" (Shakespeare, *Othello*, III, iii, 165-67).

The author of Proverbs affirms this keen insight in a somewhat different way: "A tranquil mind gives life to the body, but jealousy rots the bones" (Prv 14:30). "Anger is relentless, and wrath overwhelming—but before jealousy who can stand?" (Prv 27:4). Once during the homily I gave at a wedding, I made the point that jealousy is the only vice from which one gets nothing in return.

The person who steals, for example, gets the stolen goods. But the one who is jealous gets nothing to show for it. After Mass, an elderly woman came to me and said, "Father, you're wrong! The jealous person does get something—stomach ulcers." Wise words indeed.

Jealousy should have no part in the life of the Christian. Genuine love has no room for this vice, for as Paul tells us, "Love is patient, love is kind. It is not jealous, love is not pompous, it is not inflated, it is not rude, it does not seek its own interests, it is not quick-tempered, it does not brood over injury, it does not rejoice over wrongdoing but rejoices with the truth" (1 Cor 13:4-6). Paul lists jealousy among other major sins: "Let us conduct ourselves properly as in the day, not in orgies and drunkenness, not in promiscuity and licentiousness, not in rivalry and jealousy" (Rom 13:13). It may be quite intentional that Paul puts jealousy in the sixth and last place in his list, the number six being, as I pointed out in chapter IV, a number signifying imperfection. Paul says to the Corinthians, "You are still of the flesh. While there is jealousy and rivalry among you, are you not of the flesh, and behaving in an ordinary human way?" (1 Cor 3:3).

The Medes Hate the Outsider Daniel

Another reason for the hatred of the royal courtiers is the fact that Daniel was "the Jewish exile," as his enemies contemptuously refer to him (6:13). His piety was also an irritant. So his enemies conspire to put him to death. Persecution is something the faithful Christian must also be willing to endure. "In fact, all who want to live religiously in Christ Jesus will be persecuted" (2 Tm 3:12). Daniel was, moreover, a foreigner, an outsider. He was different. He was not even a Mede like the other supervisors and satraps. Not only Daniel's position of authority over the entire Median kingdom but also his Jewishness, his otherness, gave rise to suspicion and resentment. Xenophobia—undue fear or contempt of strangers or foreigners—and racism are pernicious bedfellows which bring forth evils of every sort and lead to murderous hate, as in our story.

From earliest times, even among Christians, unfortunately, anti-Jewish sentiment has been a particularly venomous form of xenophobia and racism. The Jews were hated for no other reason than that they were Jews. If they were poor, they were despised. If they were rich, they were considered dishonest and devious. If they were influential, they were criticized. If they were eminent in the arts and sciences, law and medicine, they were envied. In its most extreme form, anti-Jewish hatred led to murderous pogroms in Europe and elsewhere and then to the ultimate obscenity of the Holocaust in Nazi Germany. But in its more common and more subtle form, such hatred corrupts relationships and leads to unjust discrimination and social unrest.

Daniel's Fidelity in Government

A further reason for the hatred and envy of the pagans is Daniel's unimpeachable fidelity. The conspirators had tried their best to find "grounds for accusation against Daniel as regards the administration. But they could accuse him of no wrongdoing; because he was trustworthy, no fault of neglect or misconduct was to be found in him" (6:5). Daniel's enemies could find no evidence to bring a criminal or political charge against him. Three major statements are made here about Daniel's character. First, Daniel was "trustworthy." He was reliable, he was faithful, he was dependable. This calls to mind what Paul says about Christian discipleship. "Thus should one regard us: as servants of Christ and stewards of the mysteries of God. Now it is of course required of stewards that they be found trustworthy" (1 Cor 4:1-2).

Second, Daniel was not negligent. He fulfilled all the obligations of his high government office. He sought no favors because of his position. He did not cut corners. He held himself accountable for his every act. This reminds us of what Jesus said to those who were negligent in their spiritual responsibilities. "Woe to you, scribes and Pharisees, you hypocrites. You pay tithes of mint and dill and cummin, and have neglected the weightier things of the law: judgment and mercy and fidelity. But these you should have done, without neglecting the others" (Mt 23:23).

Third, Daniel was guilty of no misconduct or malfeasance in office. He never abused his power or authority over the entire kingdom. He believed that all power comes from God. He remembered the words of the holy sentinel who had said "that the Most High rules over the kingdom of men: He can give it to whom he will, and set over it the lowliest of men" (4:14). In his trial, Jesus would later rephrase these words for Pilate, "You would have no power over me if it had not been given to you from above" (Jn 19:11).

The Conspirators Trap Daniel

Since Daniel could not be accused of any wrongdoing or incompetence, the conspirators tried another tack—something particularly vicious and cunning. They turned to Daniel's religion and his spiritual practices in order to get him to fall into their trap. The original readers of the story would have related to what was happening to Daniel, for they had experienced similar hatred and persecution at the hands of Antiochus IV Epiphanes. "The king [Antiochus] sent messengers with letters to Jerusalem and to the cities of Judah, ordering them to follow customs foreign to their land; to prohibit holocausts, sacrifices, and libations in the sanctuary, to profane the sabbaths and feast days, to desecrate the sanctuary and the sacred ministers, to build pagan altars and temples and shrines, to sacrifice swine and unclean animals, to leave their sons uncircumcised, and to let themselves be defiled with every kind of impurity and abomination, so that they might forget the law and change all their observances. Whoever refused to act according to the command of the king should be put to death" (1 Mc 1:44-50).

The King's Unjust Decree

The supervisors and satraps "went thronging to the king" and greeted him with the customary salutation, "King Darius, live forever!" Having planned their scheme to the last detail, they tell the king: "All the supervisors of the kingdom, the prefects, satraps, nobles, and governors are agreed that the following prohibition ought to be put in force by royal decree: No one is to address any petition to god or man for thirty days, except to you, O king;

otherwise he shall be cast into a den of lions" (6:8). Such a decree has no parallel in history that we know of. Even the Hellenistic kings who claimed a right to divine honors, such as Antiochus IV, did not prohibit the worship of any other god besides themselves. In our story, however, the point is that Daniel symbolizes the Jewish people, and Darius is a symbol of paganism which demanded an exclusive worship of idols, as in the story of chapter 3.

The conspirators had of course lied when they said "all the supervisors," for Daniel, one of the three supervisors, certainly had no part in suggesting the royal decree. The conspirators use flattery to get the unwitting and naive Darius to go along with their plot. "Now, O king, issue the prohibition over your signature, immutable and irrevocable under Mede and Persian law" (6:9). Unaware of their evil intent, Darius "signed the prohibition and made it law" (6:10). Mighty King Darius proves himself a weakling compared with Daniel, the Jew, who was in control of his own decisions and actions. Reference to the immutability and irrevocability of Mede and Persian law is found also in Esther 1:19 and 8:8. According to the Greek historian Diodorus Siculus, who wrote in the first century B.C., the concept of such law existed in the time of Darius III (335-31 B.C.), the last of the Persian kings.

Daniel Is Caught Praying to God

The rest of the story makes it clear that Darius meant no harm by signing the prohibition. After the conspirators "rushed in and found Daniel praying and pleading before his God" (6:12), they told the king about this violation of the Mede and Persian law. Darius, however, "was deeply grieved at this news and he made up his mind to save Daniel" (6:15). But the conspirators prevailed at last. They talked Darius into enforcing the unjust decree he had made into the law of the land. So Daniel was cast into the lions' den. Despite the king's obvious good will toward Daniel and his noble attempt to save him from the lions, the point remains clear that it was wrong for Darius to sign the immoral law in the first place.

In allowing himself to be persuaded by the flattery of his courtiers, the king showed the flabbiness of his character. He succumbed to the temptation, ever present to rulers in the ancient Near East, of acting like a god. Years before Darius, Nebuchadnezzar had behaved as if he were a god (Dn 4), and Belshazzar learned nothing from his father's errors (Dn 5). When our author wrote the present story, Antiochus IV had tried to force the Jews to worship his dynastic god Baal Shamem, who was identified with Olympian Zeus. Antiochus proclaimed himself the epiphany of that god, taking the epithet Epiphanes ("[god] Manifest") as part of his official name.

Darius proved himself unkingly and spineless in allowing himself to be manipulated by the conspirators. But at least he had good will toward Daniel, "the Jewish exile" (6:14). In sharp contrast, Antiochus IV held the Jews of his day in utter contempt. He did all in his power to abolish Judaism completely from his realm. Like Antiochus IV, Darius passed a law, which in effect forbade the free exercise of religion. Foolishly, he agreed with the conspirators that "No one is to address any petition to god or man for thirty days, except to you, O king." The conspirators had done their work well. Darius fell for their ruse. Perhaps in his vanity and pride he even believed himself to be some kind of divine being who had to be addressed first before anyone could speak to any god or human being.

The Evils of Legal Positivism

But the decree which Darius made into an "immutable and irrevocable" law was unjust, since it was based on legal positivism— the philosophy that an action can be commanded or forbidden simply because the ruling powers say so and make it into a law; morality does not enter into the calculus at all. Darius' law was as immoral as the law which Nebuchadnezzar passed that all must worship his gold idol when the orchestra played (3:4-5). The prophet Isaiah, speaking in the Lord's name, roundly condemns legal positivism and its many evils: "Woe to those who enact unjust statutes and who write oppressive decrees, depriving the needy of judgment and robbing my people's poor of their rights, making widows their plunder, and orphans their prey! What will you do on the day of punishment, when ruin comes from afar? To whom will you flee for help? Where will you leave your wealth, lest it sink beneath the captive or fall beneath the slain? For all this, his wrath is not turned back, his hand is still outstretched!" (Is 10:1-4).

Legal positivism is what lay behind the immoral segregation laws in the United States and the apartheid laws in South Africa that were in force for many years. These laws were enacted to legitimate all sorts of injustices and indignities against the blacks of both countries. In today's world the laws of many governments permit abortions and euthanasia. Accordingly, many people believe that these acts of violence against innocent human life are permissible simply because they are legal. Such laws, however, are not based on sound ethical or moral principles. Human laws can deregulate the airline industry; they cannot deregulate morality. Law does not make right any more than "might makes right."

Unjust laws affecting religion have been common from biblical times to our own day. The result has been persecution and even death for large numbers of believers. Jesus of course warned Christians: "Remember the word I spoke to you, 'No slave is greater than his master.' If they persecuted me, they will also persecute you. If they kept my word, they will also keep yours" (Jn 15:20). "Blessed are they who are persecuted for the sake of righteousness, for theirs is the kingdom of heaven. Blessed are you when they insult you and persecute you and utter every kind of evil against you falsely because of me. Rejoice and be glad, for your reward will be great in heaven. Thus they persecuted the prophets who were before you" (Mt 5:10-12). "They will hand you over to persecution, and they will kill you. You will be hated by all nations because of my name" (Mt 24:9). Early Christians were accused of treason for refusing to worship the emperor, as demanded by Roman law. They were executed either by beheading or by being thrown to the lions for the barbaric entertainment of the crowds. In our story, being thrown into the lions' den at least was not a form of amusement but only a form of punishment. During the long reign of Elizabeth (1558-1603), daughter of Henry VIII and Anne Boleyn, 189 Roman Catholics were put to death for their faith. During the French Revolution a group of sixteen discalced Carmelite nuns from the community at Compiègne in northern France were sentenced to death as counter-revolutionaries and religious fanatics for living as religious under obedience to a superior. Immediately after their brief trial in 1794, they went to the guillotine chanting the *Te Deum*, the Hymn of Praise. The French composer, François Poulenc, immortalized the martyrdom of these nuns in his masterful opera, "Dialogues of the Carmelites" (1957), which was based on a French play with the same name (1948) by Georges Bernanos.

XIII

"The King Ordered Daniel to Be Brought and Cast into the Lions' Den"

(Daniel 6:11-29)

[11] Even after Daniel heard that this law had been signed, he continued his custom of going home to kneel in prayer and give thanks to his God in the upper chamber three times a day, with the windows open toward Jerusalem. [12] So these men rushed in and found Daniel praying and pleading before his God. [13] Then they went to remind the king about the prohibition: "Did you not decree, O king, that no one is to address a petition to god or man for thirty days, except to you, O king; otherwise he shall be cast into a den of lions?" The king answered them, "The decree is absolute, irrevocable under the Mede and Persian law." [14] To this they replied, "Daniel, the Jewish exile, has paid no attention to you, O king, or to the decree you issued; three times a day he offers his prayer." [15] The king was deeply grieved at this news and he made up his mind to save Daniel; he worked till sunset to rescue him. [16] But these men insisted. "Keep in mind, O king," they said, "that under the Mede and Persian law every royal prohibition or decree is irrevocable." [17] So the king ordered Daniel to be brought and cast into the lions' den. To Daniel he said, "May your God, whom you serve so constantly, save you." [18] To forestall any tampering, the king sealed with his own ring and the rings of the lords the stone that had been brought to block the opening of the den.

[19] Then the king returned to his palace for the night; he refused to eat and he dismissed the entertainers. Since sleep was impossible for him, [20] the king rose very early the next morning and hastened to the lions' den. [21] As he drew near, he cried out to Daniel sorrowfully, "O Daniel, servant of the living God, has the God whom you serve so constantly been able to save you from the lions?" [22] Daniel answered the king: "O king, live forever!

²³My God has sent his angel and closed the lions' mouths so that they have not hurt me. For I have been found innocent before him; neither to you have I done any harm, O king!" ²⁴This gave the king great joy. At his order Daniel was removed from the den, unhurt because he trusted in his God. ²⁵The king then ordered the men who had accused Daniel, along with their children and their wives, to be cast into the lions' den. Before they reached the bottom of the den, the lions overpowered them and crushed all their bones.

²⁶Then King Darius wrote to the nations and peoples of every language, wherever they dwell on the earth: "All peace to you! ²⁷I decree that throughout my royal domain the God of Daniel is to be reverenced and feared:

"For he is the living God, enduring forever;
    his kingdom shall not be destroyed,
    and his dominion shall be without end.
²⁸He is a deliverer and savior,
    working signs and wonders in heaven and on earth,
    and he delivered Daniel from the lions' power."
²⁹So Daniel fared well during the reign of Darius and the reign of Cyrus the Persian.

Being one of the three supervisors of the kingdom, Daniel of course knew that Darius had signed the law that "no one is to address a petition to god or man for thirty days, except to the king." Because the law was unjust, however, Daniel engaged in civil disobedience, quietly and unobtrusively. Daniel had the courage to match his convictions. He was willing to pay the price for his non-violent dissent. He was thrown to the lions.

Daniel Disobeys the Unjust Decree

Daniel "continued his custom of going home to kneel in prayer and give thanks to his God in the upper chamber three times a day, with the windows open toward Jerusalem" (6:11). Like other loyal believers ever since, Daniel risked his life in order to follow the practices of his faith. Daniel's unwavering resolve to follow his conscience and worship the God of Israel stands in striking contrast to the indecision of King Darius who allowed himself to be manipulated to sign the unjust law.

Jerusalem was sacred to the Jews because of the temple; that is why Daniel faced in that direction when he prayed. For the Christian, however, there is no special place for worship. Recall the episode of the woman at the well in Samaria. She said to Jesus, "Our ancestors worshiped on this mountain [Gerizim]; but you people say that the place to worship is in Jerusalem." Jesus said to her, "Believe me, woman, the hour is coming when you will worship the Father neither on this mountain nor in Jerusalem. You people worship what you do not understand; we worship what we understand, because salvation is from the Jews. But the hour is coming, and is now here, when true worshipers will worship the Father in Spirit and truth; and indeed the Father seeks such people to worship him" (Jn 4:20-23).

The manner of Daniel's prayer presents a picture of how the Jews prayed in the Diaspora. The roof chamber of a house (1 Kgs 17:19) provided a quiet setting for serious prayer (Acts 10:9). The custom of praying while facing in the direction of the Jerusalem temple or its ruins began during the Babylonian Exile (587-37 B.C.), as we know from 1 Kings 8:44, 48. The first Muslims followed Jewish custom and faced Jerusalem in prayer; but the direction was soon changed toward the Kaaba, their shrine in Mecca. The pious Jew, like Daniel in 6:11, prayed at an open window (Tb 3:11) that faced Jerusalem. Daniel prayed "three times a day"—at dawn, at midday, and toward evening (Ps 55:18). In public prayer, as in a synagogue, people usually prayed standing up. But kneeling down for private prayer, as Daniel does, apparently became a common practice during the Persian period (Ezr 9:5) right into New Testament times (Lk 22:41; Acts 20:36; 21:5).

Daniel's practice of praying at regular intervals each day has been taken up by the Church. In the past the Divine Office was recited at set times during the day by those who had the obligation. Also today in the Office, now called the Liturgy of the Hours, recited by priests, religious, and many lay people, there is a morning, midday, and evening prayer as well as an Office of Readings. The discipline of regular prayer prevents laziness or neglect of this essential part of the spiritual life. It also helps us focus on the presence of God in a world that believes it has no need of God.

The Conspirators Catch Daniel at Prayer

Since Daniel prayed at an open window, his enemies who were spying on him could easily see him violating the royal decree. So they rushed in and caught Daniel in the act—the act of praying. Spies like these are still in our midst. Because of jealousy or envy, personal profit or spite, such informers are ever ready to report on colleagues or even Church members. The effect is still the same— the ruin of another person. The spies now justify their hateful behavior by pretending interest in the king's authority. They remind the king of his decree, but of course fail to say that they themselves conspired to get the decree signed in the first place. They ask the mischievous question, "Did you not decree, O king, that no one is to address a petition to god or man for thirty days, except to you, O king; otherwise he shall be cast into a den of lions?" Darius gives the expected reply, "The decree is absolute, irrevocable under the Mede and Persian law" (6:13).

Daniel Pays the Price for His Fidelity

Though he prayed in private and did not make a public display of his civil disobedience, Daniel had nonetheless violated the law of the realm, which dictated that all, without exception, must conform to the religion of the state. This law was an attempt to deprive Daniel of his freedom. Since Daniel refused to conform, the state demanded that he be crushed. A similar situation prevailed during the reign of Antiochus IV: "A [Jew] could not keep the sabbath or celebrate the traditional feasts, nor even admit that he was a Jew. Moreover, at the monthly celebration of the king's birthday the Jews had, from bitter necessity, to partake of the sacrifices, and when the festival of Dionysus was celebrated, they were compelled to march in his procession, wearing wreaths of ivy" (2 Mc 6:6-7). For refusing to follow the state religion of Rome with its many gods, early Christians were accused of being atheists and suffered martyrdom. Heroes of the faith from earliest times to our own "conquered kingdoms, did what was righteous, obtained the promises; they closed the mouths of lions, put out raging fires, escaped the devouring sword; out of weakness they were made powerful, became strong in battle, and turned back foreign invaders. Women received back their dead through resurrection. Some were tortured and would not accept deliverance, in order to obtain a better resurrection" (Heb 11:33-35).

Once Darius reaffirms that his decree is absolute and irrevocable, the conspirators know they have the king right where they want him. They tell him, "Daniel, the Jewish exile, has paid no attention to you, O king . . . ; three times a day he offers his prayer" (6:14). The reaction of King Darius is instructive. He was "deeply grieved at this news and he made up his mind to save Daniel." His conscience finally comes into play. But it is too late. In forbidding freedom of religion to Daniel, Darius has lost his own freedom, becoming a prisoner of the conspirators. They would not let the king do what he knew to be right. They remind him once again that by Mede and Persian law every royal prohibition or decree is irrevocable. The king was trapped, and he knew it. Because of his ill-advised decree, he had to pronounce judgment: Daniel is to be cast into the lions' den. Recognizing his own folly, however, Darius now prays, saying to Daniel: "May your God, whom you serve so constantly, save you." The king praises Daniel for his fidelity to the Lord and his perseverance in prayer. Irony is at work here. The king's prayer is answered in the dramatic finale of the story.

Daniel in the Lions' Den

There is another irony here. After sealing with his own ring and the rings of his lords the stone over the den, the "divine" king, whose monstrous law is irrevocable, now returns to his palace for the night, not to party like Belshazzar and his court, but to shed tears of bitter sorrow, refusing to eat or be entertained. Conscience-stricken, the king cannot sleep a wink. He has doomed to a cruel death his friend and trusted adviser. Rising very early the next morning, Darius runs to the lions' den. Here the story depicts the king sympathetically. His night of repentance, fasting, and grief prompts him to cry out, "O Daniel, servant of the living God, has the God whom you serve so constantly been able to save you from the lions?" This detail may be based on the ancient Babylonian custom that the victim would be released if he were tortured and had not died by the next day. In his question Darius uses the rich expression "living God," a title which occurs thirty-four times in the Bible, from Deuteronomy 5:26, the first occurrence, to Revelation 7:2, the last. It is this God whom Daniel, the king's loyal supervisor, has served so faithfully. This title adds another irony, for the gods of the pagans are lifeless, "fashioned by the hands of man out of wood and stone, gods which can neither see nor hear, neither eat nor smell" (Dt 4:2; Dn 5:23).

In response to the king's question Daniel could have been vindictive and angry for being treated so shamefully. Instead he answered the king respectfully with the customary greeting, "O king, live forever!" (6:22). This is the same greeting the Chaldeans gave to Nebuchadnezzar in 2:4 and 3:9; the queen gave to Belshazzar in 5:10; and Daniel's enemies gave in 6:7 (cf. 1 Kgs 1:31 and Neh 2:3). Daniel then explains simply and briefly and with no animosity toward the king that he was saved by his God, who "has sent his angel and closed the lions' mouths so that they have not hurt me. For I have been found innocent before him; neither to you have I done any harm, O king!"

Daniel does not even accuse his enemies of their conspiracy against him. He simply lets the king come to his own conclusions about them. Again we see the saving action of God in the lives of those who put their faith in him. In chapter 3, God had sent his angel to drive the raging flames out of the furnace in order to preserve from harm Azariah and his two companions. Here God has sent his angel to deliver Daniel "from the jaws of lions," as we read in 1 Maccabees 2:60. In both cases, the Lord of history and of nature was present and active, doing what seemed to be impossible. Such is the God in whom Daniel and all subsequent believers have put their trust and confidence. This story has inspired many artists, the most notable being Peter Paul Rubens (1577-1640) and Eugène Delacroix (1798-1863), both of whom painted "Daniel and the Lions."

The Conspirators Thrown to the Lions

King Darius rejoices when he hears the voice of his loyal supervisor. Daniel is removed from the lions' den, "unhurt because he trusted in his God" (6:24). Daniel's life of faith reflects the truth of the psalmist's words. "They trust in you who cherish your name, for you forsake not those who seek you, O LORD" (Ps 9:11). Perhaps one of the prayers he recited in his daily devotions is Psalm 55: "Cast your care upon the LORD, and he will support you; never will he permit the just man to be disturbed. And you, O God, will bring them down into the pit of destruction; men of blood and deceit shall not live out half their days. But I trust in you, O LORD" (Ps 55:23-24). The psalmist's words are now fulfilled. The conspirators along with their children and their wives are cast into the lions' den, and the ravenous lions maul them to death and devour them even "before they reached the bottom of the den."

Before his death Mattathias spoke at length to his sons to encourage them to remain faithful in the persecution of Antiochus IV. He gives a brief review of the history of the Chosen People and its glorious ancestors—Abraham, Joseph, Phinehas, Joshua, Caleb, David, and Elijah. He then says, "Hananiah, Azariah and Mishael, for their faith, were saved from the fire. Daniel, for his innocence, was delivered from the jaws of lions. And so, consider this from generation to generation, that none who hope in him shall fail in strength" (1 Mc 2:59-61). These words offer hope, but not a remedy, to those who must face injustice and persecution. Like the original audience of the book, readers today are challenged to make that hope an attitude of their spiritual lives. Deliverance from adversity and death should not be expected simply because one has remained faithful. The Book of Daniel does not offer a solution to the problem of evil and unmerited suffering. It simply accepts the reality of evil and suffering as a mystery to be lived and not a problem to be solved.

Darius' New Decree

Like Nebuchadnezzar in 3:98-100, Darius now writes "to the nations and peoples of every language . . . on the earth." Darius decrees that the God of Daniel must be reverenced and feared throughout the realm. Irony again comes into play. Presumably, this decree of the pagan king becomes immutable, absolute, and irrevocable under Mede and Persian law. Indeed the affirmations

135

Darius makes about God (6:27-28) are indeed absolute and immutable, coming straight out of scripture. The God of Daniel is "the living God," the expression used also in 6:21. He is eternal (Gn 31:33; Jer 10:10; Sir 36:17), and so are his kingdom and dominion (Ps 55:19; 2 Pt 1:11). God is a deliverer (2 Sm 22:2; Ps 40:18) and savior (Ex 15:2; Is 43:11; 1 Chr 16:35), who can work signs and wonders (Dt 26:8; Neh 9:10). It is he who saved Daniel from the lions, for as Judith says in her prayer, "You are the God of the lowly, the helper of the oppressed, the supporter of the weak, the protector of the forsaken, the savior of those without hope" (Jdt 9:11).

Because of his loyalty, Daniel prospered during the reigns of Darius and Cyrus the Persian (6:29). With this verse the first part of the book comes to an end. Cyrus, who is mentioned for the first time in 1:21, appears once again. He is also the reigning king in the fifth and final apocalypse (chaps. 10-12). Cyrus played a significant role in the history of Israel. He allowed the Jews to return from exile in Babylon and to rebuild the temple (Ezr 1:1-4). He is spoken of kindly in Isaiah 44:28: "I say of Cyrus: My shepherd, who fulfills my every wish; he shall say of Jerusalem, 'Let her be rebuilt,' and of the temple, 'Let its foundations be laid.' " In Isaiah 45:1, Yahweh refers to Cyrus as "his anointed . . . whose right hand I grasp." High praise indeed.

In his book, *Daniel, An Active Volcano* (1989), D. S. Russell mentions that early Christians saw in this story many parallels to the passion and resurrection of our Lord Jesus Christ. Like the enemies who were jealous of Daniel, the chief priests, scribes, and leaders of the people conspire out of envy to do away with Jesus (Mk 15:10; Lk 19:47). Like the conspirators who spy on Daniel, Judas presents himself as a spy who will betray Jesus (Mt 26:14-16). Like Darius who spent a sleepless night over the fate of Daniel, Pilate's wife suffered much in a dream and tried to get Jesus released (Mt 27:19). Like Daniel who is found innocent before God, Jesus is declared not guilty by Pilate (Lk 23:4). Like Daniel who was cast into the lions' den, Jesus went down to the lower regions of the earth (Eph 4:9). Like the angel who appears in the lions' den, an angel proclaims that Jesus is risen from the tomb (Mt 28:2-6). Like Darius who rejoiced that Daniel was alive and well, the women go away from the tomb overjoyed (Mt 28:8).

But there are also profound differences between the story of Daniel and the life of Jesus. Daniel's enemies are brutally executed along with their children and their wives. Jesus, dying on the cross, prays for his enemies, "Father, forgive them, they know not what they do" (Lk 23:34). Christians likewise are commanded to love their enemies and to pray for their persecutors (Mt 5:44). Daniel, who is innocent, suffered no hurt from the lions and is rescued from death. Jesus, who is innocent of any crime (Mt 27:4; Lk 23:47; Jn 19:7) and completely sinless (Heb 4:15), suffered excruciating agony in his passion and felt abandoned on the cross before laying down his life for his sheep (Jn 10:15). Daniel is rescued by an angel. Jesus refuses to call down the more than twelve legions of angels that are at his command (Mt 26:53). Clearly, we have a greater than Daniel in Jesus whom we call Lord.

XIV

"Daniel Had a Dream As He Lay in Bed"
(Daniel 7:1-18)

[1]In the first year of King Belshazzar of Babylon, Daniel had a dream as he lay in bed, and was terrified by the visions of his mind. Then he wrote down the dream; the account began: [2]In the vision I saw during the night, suddenly the four winds of heaven stirred up the great sea, [3]from which emerged four immense beasts, each different from the others. [4]The first was like a lion, but with eagle's wings. While I watched, the wings were plucked; it was raised from the ground to stand on two feet like a man, and given a human mind. [5]The second was like a bear; it was raised up on one side, and among the teeth in its mouth were three tusks. It was given the order, "Up, devour much flesh." [6]After this I looked and saw another beast, like a leopard; on its back were four wings like those of a bird, and it had four heads. To this beast dominion was given. [7]After this, in the visions of the night I saw the fourth beast, different from all the others, terrifying, horrible, and of extraordinary strength; it had great iron teeth with which it devoured and crushed, and what was left it trampled with its feet. [8]I was considering the ten horns it had, when suddenly another, a little horn, sprang out of their midst, and three of the previous horns were torn away to make room for it. This horn had eyes like a man, and a mouth that spoke arrogantly. [9]As I watched,

Thrones were set up
　　and the Ancient One took his throne.
His clothing was snow bright,
　　and the hair on his head as white as wool;
His throne was flames of fire,
　　with wheels of burning fire.
[10]A surging stream of fire
　　flowed out from where he sat;

Thousands upon thousands were ministering to him,
and myriads upon myriads attended him.

The court was convened, and the books were opened. [11]I
watched, then, from the first of the arrogant words which the
horn spoke, until the beast was slain and its body thrown into
the fire to be burnt up. [12]The other beasts, which also lost their
dominion, were granted a prolongation of life for a time and a
season. [13]As the visions during the night continued, I saw

One like a son of man coming,
on the clouds of heaven;

When he reached the Ancient One
and was presented before him,

[14]He received dominion, glory, and kingship;
nations and peoples of every language serve him.

His dominion is an everlasting dominion
that shall not be taken away,
his kingship shall not be destroyed.

[15]I, Daniel, found my spirit anguished within its sheath of
flesh, and I was terrified by the visions of my mind. [16]I approached one of those present and asked him what all this meant
in truth; in answer, he made known to me the meaning of the
things: [17]"These four great beasts stand for four kingdoms which
shall arise on the earth. [18]But the holy ones of the Most High
shall receive the kingship, to possess it forever and ever."

In Daniel 2 and 4, Nebuchadnezzar had dreams that terrified him.
In the present chapter Daniel has a terrifying nightmare. This
chapter occupies the central position of the book, and not just
because it is in the middle of the fourteen chapters. It is the most
significant of the book's apocalypses. Like other Jewish apocalypses, it is open-ended, pointing to the future. All was not said in
the past; things of decisive importance are still to come. Like Daniel
2–6, this chapter is written in Aramaic, whereas the last three
apocalypses (Dn 8, 9, and 10–12) are written in Hebrew. The
account of Daniel's dream moreover is a reworking of chapter 2,
the story of Nebuchadnezzar's apocalyptic dream of the statue
made of gold, silver, bronze, and iron with clay tile. Instead of the
four metals in Nebuchadnezzar's dream, four different beasts
appear in Daniel's dream. In both dreams the symbolism is the
same—the metals and the beasts represent the four successive

empires of the Babylonians, Medes, Persians, and Greeks. In 2:34-35, the mysterious stone which demolished the statue, "became a great mountain and filled the whole earth." In the present apocalypse, a mysterious figure in human likeness receives universal dominion after the fourth beast is killed. The symbolism of both chapters depicts the coming of God's kingdom that will supplant the four pagan kingdoms.

Daniel has his awesome dream "in the first year of King Belshazzar of Babylon," the profligate despot who saw the handwriting on the wall in Daniel 5. In the earlier stories, Daniel served as the interpreter of the dreams and visions of other people. Here he is the recipient of a dream that is a divine revelation. Now Daniel himself has need of an interpreting angel (7:15) who tells him the meaning of the beasts and the figure in human likeness. What Daniel saw in the dream was so frightening that it woke him up.

Daniel's Dream

In the vision of the night Daniel saw "the great sea" being whipped up in a cosmic frenzy by "the four winds of heaven." This is no ordinary sea, but a reference to the primeval ocean or chaotic waters that the people of the ancient Near East believed to prevail prior to creation. These are the waters mentioned also in Genesis 1:2 before God spoke his creative word and subdued them. God keeps in check the forces of chaos even in our own world. God alone is in sovereign control. We need fear no power in the heavens or on earth or under the earth, for we can make our own the words of the psalmist: "You still the roaring of the seas, the roaring of their waves and the tumult of the peoples" (Ps 65:8). "More powerful than the roar of many waters, more powerful than the breakers of the sea—powerful on high is the LORD" (Ps 93:4).

On the island called Patmos, the disciple John tells us, "I saw a new heaven and a new earth. The former heaven and the former earth had passed away, and the sea was no more. I also saw the holy city, a new Jerusalem, coming down out of heaven from God, prepared as a bride adorned for her husband" (Rv 21:1-2). In the kingdom of God, there will be no more chaos and disorder. Paul expresses a similar conviction from a Christocentric viewpoint:

140

"For I am convinced that neither death, nor life, nor angels, nor principalities, nor present things, nor future things, nor powers, nor height, nor depth, nor any other creature will be able to separate us from the love of God in Christ Jesus our Lord" (Rom 8:38-39).

The four immense beasts that Daniel saw emerging from the great sea are symbols of chaos, disorder, and mayhem. The Old Testament has various names for these beasts: Leviathan, the coiled serpent, dragon, Rahab. "On that day, The LORD will punish with his sword that is cruel, great, and strong, Leviathan the fleeing serpent, Leviathan the coiled serpent; and he will slay the dragon that is in the sea" (Is 27:1). "Awake, awake, put on strength, O arm of the LORD! Awake as in the days of old, in ages long ago! Was it not you who crushed Rahab, you who pierced the dragon?" (Is 51:9). The imagery here suggests the ultimate victory of God over the forces of evil. Kings and kingdoms come and go. But everlasting is the kingdom of God that has been prepared for those who accept his rule and dominion.

Each of the monstrous beasts, symbolizing an empire, differs from the others. But all the empires came out of the unruly "great sea," for these were the works of darkness and not of God. The first beast was "like a lion, but with eagle's wings" (7:4). This is an accurate depiction of the Babylonian empire. Babylonian art portrayed the empire as a winged lion. The enemies of God and his Chosen People are often called lions. Hence, the psalmist prays, "O God, smash their teeth in their mouths; the jaw-teeth of the lions, break, O LORD!" (Ps 58:7). The two eagle's wings that were plucked represent the Babylonian kings Nebuchadnezzar and Belshazzar. Nebuchadnezzar is portrayed as a lion in Jeremiah 50:17: "A stray sheep was Israel that lions pursued; formerly the king of Assyria devoured her, now Nebuchadnezzar of Babylon gnaws her bones." In Jeremiah 49:22, Nebuchadnezzar is described as an eagle which soars aloft. E. Bickerman writes: "In Babylonian astral geography, lion, bear, and leopard respectively symbolized the south (Babylonia), the north (Media), and the east (Persia)." These are the same three beasts in Daniel's vision.

The second beast was like a ferocious and ravenous bear, which was ordered to get up and "devour much flesh" (7:5). The three tusks in its mouth symbolize its brutality. This is an accurate symbol of the Median kingdom, which was notorious for its cruelty. The bear is next to the lion for its strength and savagery. "I will attack them like a bear robbed of its young, and tear their hearts from their breasts; I will devour them on the spot like a lion, as though a wild beast were to rend them" (Hos 13:8). It is ironic that the symbol of the former Soviet Union is also the bear, for Lenin and Stalin did indeed "devour much flesh" in their purges of political enemies and in the murder of millions of their own people.

The third beast was like a leopard with four wings "like those of a bird" and four heads (7:6). The image of four wings on the back of the leopard further dramatizes the animal's swiftness and agility. The winged leopard aptly symbolizes Persia and its king, Cyrus. Indeed, Isaiah 41:3 describes Cyrus as the warrior whom the Lord raised up to achieve swift victory: "Who has stirred up from the East the champion of justice, and summoned him to be his attendant? To him he delivers the nations and subdues the kings; with his sword he reduces them to dust, with his bow, to driven straw. He pursues them, passing on without loss, by a path his feet do not even tread." The four heads of the leopard are the four Persian kings known to the Bible—Cyrus (Ezr 1:1-2, 7-8; 3:7), Ahasuerus or Xerxes I (Ezr 4:6), Artaxerxes (Ezr 4:7, 11, 23; 6:14), and Darius III Codomannus (Neh 12:22).

It is the fourth beast that is of most interest to Daniel. To highlight his utter revulsion, Daniel, when he introduces the beast, even repeats the phrase, "in the visions of the night." This beast differed from all the others; it was far worse. It could be compared to no known animal on earth: it was "terrifying, horrible, and of extraordinary strength; it had great iron teeth with which it devoured and crushed, and what was left it trampled with its feet" (7:7). This repulsive beast is a fitting symbol of the Greek or Hellenistic kingdom of the Seleucids under whom the author and his first readers were subjects. The most striking feature of this monster is that it had ten horns, which no natural beast possesses. Later Daniel is told that these horns represent ten kings (7:24).

As Daniel looked on, a little horn sprang from the midst of the ten horns, and three of the previous horns were plucked out to make room for it. The "little horn" is the author's contemptuous expression to refer to Antiochus IV Epiphanes, the worst of the Seleucid kings as far as the Jews were concerned. In fact, Antiochus in his climb to power had to overthrow several other royal claimants. This horn had human eyes but a mouth that spoke arrogantly—historically accurate descriptions of Antiochus. Insolence and overweening pride were the hallmarks of this tyrant. As I mentioned in the earlier chapters, Antiochus gave himself the name Epiphanes (meaning "[god] Manifest") and forced others to honor him as a god. In his later years he outdid himself in arrogance by having himself depicted on coins as Olympian Zeus, the principal god of the Greek pantheon, ruler of the heavens, and father of other gods and mortal heroes. In Antiochus IV the forces of chaos and evil reach their apex.

Daniel's Vision of God

Daniel next saw something absolutely astounding. The narrative up to this point has been straight prose. But now the text of 7:9-10 becomes poetry. This passage as well as 7:13-14 and 23-27 are "poetic rhapsodies," as J. A. Montgomery calls them. Daniel witnesses the majestic vision of God, who appears in sharp contrast to the horrible monsters that emerge from the raging chaos. Thrones were being set up, and "the Ancient One took his throne." The scene here is reminiscent of 1 Kings 22:19: "I saw the LORD seated on his throne, with the whole host of heaven standing by to his right and to his left." The abode of God is depicted as serene and dazzling, as opposed to the disorder of the beasts.

God, the Ancient One, wears snow bright clothing; whiteness symbolizes innocence. His white hair represents experience as Lord of the universe. The description of the throne, having "flames of fire, with wheels of burning fire," derives from the exotic visions in Ezekiel 1:4-28 and 10:2-23. In the Bible, fire is a sign of a theophany (Ex 24:17; Dt 4:24; 9:3) and of divine punishment (Pss 50:3; 97:3-4; Rv 20:14). In 7:9-10, fire is mentioned three times, the threefold repetition indicating the superlative nature of this theophany and judgment scene. Countless thousands and myriads minister in loving adoration before the throne of God (Dt 33:3; 1 Kgs 22:19; Is 6:1-3). The esoteric imagery of this scene conveys the awesome majesty and supreme might of the Lord who holds sway over the unruly kingdoms of the beasts.

The Heavenly Court

Court was convened, and the books were opened. There are different kinds of books spoken of in the Bible. In one book are recorded the good and wicked deeds of human beings (Ex 32:32-33; Is 65:6-7; Ps 139:16). Another is "the book of life" (Ps 69:29; Rv 3:5; 13:8; 17:8). "I saw the dead, the great and the lowly, standing before the throne, and scrolls were opened. Then another scroll was opened, the book of life. The dead were judged according to their deeds, by what was written in the scrolls. The sea gave up its dead; then Death and Hades gave up their dead. All the dead were judged according to their deeds. Then Death and Hades were thrown into the pool of fire. (This pool of fire is the second death.) Anyone whose name was not found written in the book of life was thrown into the pool of fire" (Rv 20:12-15). Antiochus IV, the abominable little horn who spoke arrogant words, is thrown into the fire along with the rest of the fourth beast symbolizing the whole Seleucid dynasty (7:11). The other three beasts—the kingdoms of the Babylonians, Medes, and Persians—were granted a reprieve for "a time and a season" (7:12). The probable reason is that they may become states once again until the kingdom of God is established to include them too (as in Is 14:1-2; 49:22-23; Tb 13:11). But we have not seen the last of Antiochus IV. He appears again later in the chapter to "make war against the holy ones," and for a while he is victorious till the Most High pronounces final judgment on him (7:21-27).

The Figure in Human Likeness

Next on the scene comes the mysterious figure in human likeness. The translations usually give "one like a son of man," but that rendering is misleading. The Aramaic simply means "one like a human being." The mysterious figure comes "on the clouds of heaven." On reaching the Ancient One, he "received dominion,

144

glory, and kingship; nations and peoples of every language serve him. His dominion is an everlasting dominion that shall not be taken away, his kingship shall not be destroyed" (7:14). The one like a human being is not to be understood as the Messiah to come even though Jesus often referred to himself as "the son of man." The mysterious figure is a human being in contrast to the pagan kingdoms that are portrayed as beasts. Unlike the beasts that emerge from the chaotic waters and are destroyed, the one in human likeness comes on the clouds of heaven, the domain of God himself, and shares in the divine kingship.

The clue to the identity of the one in human likeness comes later in the chapter. He is the symbol of "the holy people of the Most High," who receive "the kingship and dominion and majesty of all the kingdoms under the heavens" (7:27). These are the men, women, and children who have remained steadfast in their observance of their Jewish faith and practices during the persecution of Antiochus IV when many were martyred. These holy ones will be vindicated and will be given the everlasting authority and kingship that the vicious beasts had claimed for themselves.

In the apocalyptic of this chapter, eschatology ("end-time") corresponds to protology ("beginning-time"). Many of the same expressions are used in both. In the beginning, when God made the heavens and the earth, the chaotic deep and darkness were subdued by God's spirit that swept over the waters. God then spoke his almighty word to create light, which he pronounced good (Gn 1:1-3). In Genesis 1:26-28, God made human beings in his own image and likeness and gave them dominion over the fish of the sea, the birds of the air, the cattle, all the wild beasts, and all the creatures that crawl on the ground. In Daniel 7, the four winds stirred up the great sea of primeval chaos, and four immense beasts emerged. Because of their wickedness and insolence, God pronounced judgment on them and doomed them to destruction. God then bestowed the kingship and dominion on the holy ones of the Most High, thus restoring to his faithful ones what he had granted them at the beginning of creation.

The incarnation of the Son of God is intimately connected with the doctrine of creation (Gn 1). "In the beginning was the Word, and the Word was with God, and the Word was God. He was in the beginning with God. All things came to be through him, and without him nothing came to be. What came to be through him was life, and this life was the light of the human race" (Jn 1:1-4). Creation, incarnation, redemption are all linked in Christ. Chaos and its minions hold no more sway. The Lord is in control. A consoling truth especially when we are in turmoil.

XV

"Judgment Was Pronounced in Favor of the Holy Ones of the Most High"

(Daniel 7:19-28)

[19] But I wished to make certain about the fourth beast, so very terrible and different from the others, devouring and crushing with its iron teeth and bronze claws, and trampling with its feet what was left; [20] about the ten horns on its head, and the other one that sprang up, before which three horns fell; about the horn with the eyes and the mouth that spoke arrogantly, which appeared greater than its fellows. [21] For, as I watched, that horn made war against the holy ones and was victorious [22] until the Ancient One arrived; judgment was pronounced in favor of the holy ones of the Most High, and the time came when the holy ones possessed the kingdom. [23] He answered me thus:

"The fourth beast shall be a fourth kingdom on earth,
    different from all the others;
It shall devour the whole earth,
    beat it down, and crush it.
[24] The ten horns shall be ten kings
    rising out of that kingdom;
    another shall rise up after them,
Different from those before him,
    who shall lay low three kings.
[25] He shall speak against the Most High
    and oppress the holy ones of the Most High,
    thinking to change the feast days and the law.
They shall be handed over to him
    for a year, two years, and a half-year.
[26] But when the court is convened,
    and his power is taken away
    by final and absolute destruction,
[27] Then the kingship and dominion and majesty

of all the kingdoms under the heavens
shall be given to the holy people of the Most High,
Whose kingdom shall be everlasting:
All dominions shall serve and obey him."
[28]The report concluded: I, Daniel, was greatly terrified by my thoughts, and my face blanched, but I kept the matter to myself.

Daniel, and the original readers of the book, were concerned chiefly with the fourth beast, "so very terrible and different from the others, devouring and crushing with its iron teeth and bronze claws, and trampling with its feet what was left" (7:19). What frightened Daniel most of all, however, were the powerful horns on the beast's head. The "ten horns" and, of these ten, the "three horns" that fell before another horn that sprang up, mentioned in 7:8, 20, are ten contemporaries of Antiochus IV Epiphanes. This tyrant was "the horn with the eyes and the mouth that spoke arrogantly, which appeared greater than its fellows" (7:20). The "little horn" (7:8) is the symbol of Antiochus IV. In 7:20 "the horn" and in 7:24 the "other horn" also refer to the same king. It was Antiochus IV who made life miserable for the faithful Jews of our author's day.

Antiochus IV, the Little Horn

In his vision of the night, Daniel sees that Antiochus "made war against the holy ones and was victorious" (7:21). But Antiochus was victorious only for a short while, "until the Ancient One arrived" (7:22). God will not allow wickedness to remain unpunished. The timetable for God to set things right is, of course, unknown. But vindication of the innocent and retribution of the guilty will surely come—in God's own time. The Ancient One, God himself, pronounced judgment "in favor of the holy ones of the Most High," the loyal Jews who observed the law even at risk to their lives. It is these Jews who would possess the kingdom (7:22). In 7:21-22 the author anticipates the fuller explanation of the fourth beast and its horns given in 7:23-27.

Because Daniel "wished to make certain about the fourth beast" (7:19), one of the angelic attendants at God's throne now provides a detailed answer (7:23-27). The fourth beast is the Greek or

Hellenistic kingdom. From the viewpoint of the Jews living as a subject people with no significant political or military power, this kingdom, founded by Alexander the Great, seemed to "devour the whole earth, beat it down, and crush it" (7:23). Alexander had indeed conquered much of the then known world. Daniel's principal interest, however, is not in the "ten horns," or kings of the Greek kingdom, but in the "little horn" (7:8) or "other horn" (7:24) that rises up after them—Antiochus IV whose wickedness is described also in Daniel 8:9-12, where he is likewise called "a little horn," and in 9:26-27 as well as in 11:21-45 where he is described as "a despicable person."

What is summarized briefly in 7:25 is told in detail in 1 Maccabees 1:10-63, 2 Maccabees 5:23-6:11, and Josephus, *Antiquities* xii, 5, 4. Antiochus IV, who began his rule in 175 B.C., was relentless in his policy of Hellenization of the Holy Land. Many Jews went along with this policy in order to get ahead socially and economically. In Jerusalem they built a gymnasium, which was a Greek symbol and center of athletic and intellectual life. Some Jews went so far as to undergo surgery to remove evidence of their circumcision. The reason for having this painful operation was to avoid ridicule, for in the gymnasium men went naked when they participated in sports. These Jews had completely abandoned the covenant of their ancestors and "sold themselves to wrongdoing" (1 Mc 1:15).

But the worst was yet to come. In 169 B.C. Antiochus IV desecrated the temple in Jerusalem, taking as booty the golden altar, the lampstand, the offering table and its utensils, the golden censers, and other sacred items. He also prohibited the offering of holocausts, sacrifices, and libations in the temple. He ordered the people to profane the sabbath and feast days. In the Holy Land he even built pagan altars, temples, and shrines, sacrificing swine and other unclean animals. He forbade circumcision. His intention was to get the Jews to disregard the law of Moses. Because of these edicts against the Jewish religion, many abandoned their faith.

Antiochus perpetrated the ultimate villainy in early December 167 B.C., when he erected the "horrible abomination" (1 Mc 1:54) in the temple in Jerusalem. The abomination was a statue of Olympian Zeus that Antiochus placed right over the great altar of holocausts. This blasphemous shrine is the "horrible abomination," or "desolating sin," of Daniel 8:13; 9:27; 11:31; and 12:11. "The Gentiles filled the temple with debauchery and revelry; they amused themselves with prostitutes and had intercourse with women even in the sacred court. They also brought into the temple things that were forbidden, so that the altar was covered with abominable offerings prohibited by the laws" (2 Mc 6:4-5). Moreover, scrolls containing the law were torn up and burnt. Women who had their sons circumcised were executed with their babies hung from their necks; their families were also killed. "But many in Israel were determined and resolved in their hearts not to eat anything unclean; they preferred to die rather than to be defiled with unclean food or to profane the holy covenant; and they did die. Terrible affliction was upon Israel" (1 Mc 1:62-63).

The persecution of the Jews would last "for a year, two years, and a half-year," or as the Aramaic states literally, "for a time, times, and half time" (7:25), or a total of three and a half years. This number, like other numbers in the book, is primarily symbolic. Seven, as we noted several times above, is the number that symbolizes perfection. So half-seven, or three and a half, symbolizes imperfection itself. Here, however, the period of three and a half years corresponds roughly to the duration of Antiochus IV's persecution, which began in full force with the profanation of the temple on 6 December 167 B.C. (1 Mc 1:54) and came to an end on 14 December 164 B.C. when Judas Maccabeus reconquered Jerusalem and purified the temple (1 Mc 4:52). In 8:14, the duration is given as 1,150 days.

Antiochus Receives God's Judgment

The time for Antiochus to be judged had come at last. In the presence of the Ancient One, the sentence is passed: "His power is taken away by final and absolute destruction" (7:26). This is a reference to the death of Antiochus IV. His demise came about in this way. Antiochus was usually in need of money for his lavish life-style and ambitious programs of Hellenization. So as he "was traversing the inland provinces, he heard that in Persia there was a city called Elymais, famous for its wealth in silver and gold, and that its temple was very rich, containing gold helmets, breastplates, and weapons left there by Alexander, son of Philip, king of Macedonia, the first king of the Greeks. He went therefore and tried to capture and pillage the city. But he could not do so, because his plan became known to the people of the city who rose up in battle against him. So he retreated and in great dismay withdrew from there to return to Babylon" (1 Mc 6:1-4). But he never reached Babylon. He withdrew to Tabae, near Isfahan in Persia, and was struck down with a mysterious disease. "Sick with grief because his designs had failed, he took to his bed. There he remained many days, overwhelmed with sorrow, for he knew he was going to die" (1 Mc 6:8-9). Between 20 November and 19 December 164 B.C. Antiochus died "in bitter grief, in a foreign land" (1 Mc 6:13).

The Everlasting Kingdom of the Most High

For their fidelity to the covenant, "the holy people of the Most High" received "the kingship and dominion and majesty of all the kingdoms under the heavens." The loyal Jews share in the kingdom of the Most High himself. Unlike all the earthly kingdoms that have come and gone, God's kingdom "shall be everlasting: All dominions shall serve and obey him" (7:27). Daniel of course was "greatly terrified" by the vision he had just experienced, and his face "blanched." But he "kept the matter to himself" (7:28). This is a typical device of apocalyptic literature. Predictions of future events are presented as recorded in a secret document long before the events actually take place. The document then becomes known when the predictions recorded in it are about to take place. The document containing the vision of chapter 7 would be revealed to readers in due time, when the Book of Daniel is published. The revelation of the number of pagan kings and their evil empires is described as being given to Daniel "in the first year of King Belshazzar of Babylon" (7:1). But the revelation is not published until after the death of Antiochus IV, some four centuries after Belshazzar. The purpose of this apocalyptic technique, which may strike the contemporary reader as peculiar at best, is not to deceive believers then or now, but rather to bolster the faith of the original

151

readers who understood the reasons of the author. The author employs the literary device of "prophecies after the event" regarding the four kingdoms and their rulers merely as a means to enhance the book's genuine predictions and revelations. The author assures his readers that God in his own time will come to the rescue of his faithful people and give them an eternal kingdom.

The Kingdom of God Inaugurated by Jesus

This kingdom is promised only to the faithful Jews for whom the Book of Daniel was originally composed. As Christians, however, we can see in this promise a glimpse of the kingdom of God that Jesus inaugurated and made available to all people of all times and places, who accept him as Lord. Belonging to the right race or people is not the basis of membership, but being baptized and living out an obedient faith in Jesus as Lord. The kingdom of God is not just about the hereafter but also about the here and now. It is not just about forgiveness and personal salvation but also about involvement in a messy world that has little room for God. Members of the kingdom are called upon to identify and root out the evil in society and to work mightily for justice and peace, especially in the third world. Though the kingdom of God is pure gift, it is a gift that believers must use energetically so that "every tongue [may] confess that Jesus Christ is Lord, to the glory of God the Father" (Phil 2:11).

Some Reflections

Can any of the exotic imagery found in Daniel 7 speak to Christians today? The four pagan kingdoms, which the author speaks of as immense beasts, have come and gone and are mostly forgotten. But the beasts of arrogance and greed, of sensuality and godlessness, are still very much alive. These beasts, like the bear in Daniel's vision, also have power to "devour much flesh" (7:5). Not only our youth but also many adults today yearn for a clear sense of direction in their lives. But without a moral compass they feel lost, adrift in a chaotic sea of sensuality and consumerism, meaninglessness and even hopelessness. Witness the increase in violent crimes, sexual promiscuity, drug and alcohol abuse, infidelity in marriage, broken homes, child abuse. To get some idea of the level of depravity being foisted on society today one need only listen to the obscene and debasing lyrics of the songs and see the suggestive gyrations of the scantily clad singers on MTV. The values and goals of a pagan society cannot and will not satisfy the deepest longings of the heart. Society teaches us the love of power. Jesus teaches us the power of love (Jn 15:9-17). Society teaches us to take control of others. Jesus teaches us to be of service to others, especially the hungry and the homeless (Mt 25:31-40). Society teaches us that to be successful we need to get more and spend more and to hang on to what we have. Jesus teaches us that to enter the kingdom of God we need to let go and to give what we have to the poor (Mt 19:21). The values of Jesus contradict the values of contemporary society, East and West. That is why our society refuses to listen to the demands of Christian love and living. The sad results are obvious to anyone who has eyes to see and ears to hear.

Even the Churches bear responsibility for the moral bankruptcy of contemporary society. Preaching today often seeks to please rather than to challenge, to give solace to the affluent rather than to prick their consciences. As someone once said, "Preaching should comfort the afflicted and afflict the comfortable." In the Sermon on the Mount (Mt 5–7) Jesus spells out clearly the demands of the kingdom of God, a kingdom that far exceeds the one promised to the faithful Jews in Daniel 7.

"Blessed are the poor in spirit, for theirs is the kingdom of heaven" (Mt 5:3). Our society has no sympathy for voluntary poverty; instead, it glorifies the rich. "Blessed are the meek" (Mt 5:5). Our society glamorizes power and status. "Blessed are the merciful" (Mt 5:7). Our society idolizes the ruthless who get ahead at any cost. "Blessed are the clean of heart, for they will see God" (Mt 5:8). Our society encourages sexual indulgence without responsibility. "Blessed are the peacemakers, for they will be called children of God" (Mt 5:9). Our society rewards the arms merchants in the military-industrial complex. Martin Luther King, Jr., who won the Nobel Peace Prize in 1964, said in April 1967, a year before he was assassinated, "A nation that continues year after year

153

to spend more money on military programs than on programs for social uplift is approaching spiritual death." "Blessed are they who are persecuted for the sake of righteousness, for theirs is the kingdom of heaven" (Mt 5:10). Our society promises a "kingdom" without moral accountability, but gives instead a taste of ashes. Paul tells us bluntly: "Do you not know that the unjust will not inherit the kingdom of God? Do not be deceived; neither fornicators nor idolaters nor adulterers nor boy prostitutes nor sodomites nor thieves nor the greedy nor drunkards nor slanderers nor robbers will inherit the kingdom of God" (1 Cor 6:9-10).

XVI

"In My Vision I Saw Myself in the Fortress of Susa"

(Daniel 8:1-27)

[1] After this first vision, I, Daniel, had another, in the third year of the reign of King Belshazzar. [2] In my vision I saw myself in the fortress of Susa in the province of Elam; I was beside the river Ulai. [3] I looked up and saw standing by the river a ram with two great horns, the one larger and newer than the other. [4] I saw the ram butting toward the west, north, and south. No beast could withstand it or be rescued from its power; it did what it pleased and became very powerful.

[5] As I was reflecting, a he-goat with a prominent horn on its forehead suddenly came from the west across the whole earth without touching the ground. [6] It approached the two-horned ram I had seen standing by the river, and rushed toward it with savage force. [7] I saw it attack the ram with furious blows when they met, and break both its horns. It threw the ram, which had not the force to withstand it, to the ground, and trampled upon it; and no one could rescue it from its power.

[8] The he-goat became very powerful, but at the height of its power the great horn was shattered, and in its place came up four others, facing the four winds of heaven. [9] Out of one of them came a little horn which kept growing toward the south, the east, and the glorious country. [10] Its power extended to the host of heaven, so that it cast down to earth some of the host and some of the stars and trampled on them. [11] It boasted even against the prince of the host, from whom it removed the daily sacrifice, and whose sanctuary it cast down, [12] as well as the host, while sin replaced the daily sacrifice. It cast truth to the ground, and was succeeding in its undertaking.

[13] I heard a holy one speaking, and another said to whichever one it was that spoke, "How long shall the events of this vision last concerning the daily sacrifice, the desolating sin which is

placed there, the sanctuary, and the trampled host?" [14]He answered him, "For two thousand three hundred evenings and mornings; then the sanctuary shall be purified."

[15]While I, Daniel, sought the meaning of the vision I had seen, a manlike figure stood before me, [16]and on the Ulai I heard a human voice that cried out, "Gabriel, explain the vision to this man." [17]When he came near where I was standing, I fell prostrate in terror. But he said to me, "Understand, son of man, that the vision refers to the end time." [18]As he spoke to me, I fell forward in a faint; he touched me and made me stand up. [19]"I will show you," he said, "what is to happen later in the period of wrath; for at the appointed time, there will be an end.

[20]"The two-horned ram you saw represents the kings of the Medes and Persians. [21]The he-goat is the king of the Greeks, and the great horn on its forehead is the first king. [22]The four that rose in its place when it was broken are four kingdoms that will issue from his nation, but without his strength.

[23] "After their reign,
      when sinners have reached their measure,
There shall arise a king, impudent
      and skilled in intrigue.
[24]He shall be strong and powerful,
      bring about fearful ruin,
      and succeed in his undertaking.
He shall destroy powerful peoples;
      [25]his cunning shall be against the holy ones,
      his treacherous conduct shall succeed.
He shall be proud of heart
      and destroy many by stealth.
But when he rises against the prince of princes,
      he shall be broken without a hand being raised.
[26]The vision of the evenings and the mornings
      is true, as spoken;
Do you, however, keep this vision undisclosed,
      because the days are to be many."

[27]I, Daniel, was weak and ill for some days; then I arose and took care of the king's affairs. But I was appalled at the vision, which I could not understand.

The present chapter, like chapters 1 and 9–12, is written in Hebrew. The Aramaic part of the book began in 2:4 and concluded at the end of chapter 7. It is probable that the Hebrew parts have been translated from an Aramaic original. This may account for the somewhat inferior literary quality of chapters 8–12. The animal imagery, first introduced in chapter 7, continues here. In fact, by stating "after this first vision, I, Daniel, had another" (8:1), the author deliberately connected this chapter to the preceding one. The present chapter has great importance for the interpretation of the book, for it provides the clearest evidence regarding the identity of the three kingdoms—Median, Persian, and Greek—that follow the Babylonian in chapters 2 and 7.

The Ram and He-Goat

In the present apocalypse Daniel has another vision, the meaning of which is similar in many ways to the one he experienced in chapter 7. The vision, like the earlier one which takes place "in the first year of King Belshazzar" (7:1), occurs during the reign of the same monarch, but in his third year. The scene here is, however, not as frightening as the previous one. Horns play a prominent role in both chapters. The reason is clear. The horn is a natural symbol of power and strength, for in the animal kingdom, horns are both defensive and offensive weapons. The dominant male in a herd uses his horns to fight off any challenger. Furious battles often ensue, even to the death of the weaker animal.

Astrology Then and Now

It is interesting that the ram and the he-goat are also signs in the astrological zodiac. The constellation Aries (a Latin word for ram), located near Taurus and Pisces in the Northern Hemisphere, represents the ram. Aries, the first sign in the zodiac, was believed to protect the Medo-Persian empire. The constellation Capricorn (derived from the Latin words for goat and horn), located near Aquarius and Sagittarius in the equatorial region of the Southern Hemisphere, represents the he-goat. Capricorn, the tenth sign in the zodiac, was believed to be guardian of Greece. These two constellations and the other ten comprising the zodiac were thought to determine the destinies of human beings. Many ancients planned their lives, their hopes, and their battles according to astrological calculations.

Sad to say, superstitions die hard. To the consternation of his generals, Adolf Hitler used to seek the advice of his astrologer to plot strategy during World War II. Ronald Reagan had an astrologer in California whom he consulted regularly even when he was President of the United States. Today millions of people look to the stars and their horoscopes to determine the course of action to take. Many newspapers, including those that are otherwise responsible, carry daily horoscopes. True, many read the horoscope as a harmless curiosity. But all forms of astrology reflect a deep-seated belief that beyond ourselves there is a mysterious force which shapes our lives. The Bible teaches us, however, that the only power "out there" is not in the stars of the heavens but in the One "who made the earth by his power, established the world by his wisdom, and stretched out the heavens by his skill" (Jer 10:12).

The Vision of the Ram

In his vision, Daniel saw himself transported in spirit from Babylon and placed "in the fortress of Susa in the province of Elam . . . beside the river Ulai" (8:2). This fortress was the winter palace of the Median and Persian kings; it was located in the ancient territory of Elam, to the east of Babylonia. The "river Ulai" was actually a canal along the northern side of Susa. Being transported to another place in vision occurs also in Ezekiel 8:3 and 11:1. We learn the identity of the "ram with two great horns, the one larger and newer than the other" (8:3) from 8:20— "the kings of the Medes and Persians." The "larger and newer" horn is a reference to Persia, which indeed was far more powerful and prominent than Media, which it supplanted. Cyrus II the Great (550-30 B.C.) united the Persian and Median kingdoms in 550 B.C.

Daniel "saw the ram butting toward the west, north, and south. No beast could withstand it . . . it did what it pleased and became very powerful" (8:4). This is an accurate description of the Persian empire at its greatest. On the east, it extended as far as India; on

158

the north, to the region of the Caspian Sea; on the west, to the continent of Europe; and on the south, to Egypt. It was the largest empire the world had known to that time. Only with Artaxerxes I (465-24 B.C.) did the Persian empire begin to lose its power. It remained a force to be reckoned with, however, till its last ruler, Darius III Codomanus (335-31 B.C.), who was defeated in battle by the Macedonian Alexander III the Great (336-23 B.C.).

The central point of the apocalypses in chapters 2, 7, 8, 9, and 10–12 is that no earthly kingdom—not even one as mighty as the Persian empire—will long endure. Sooner or later another ruler, ambitious and power hungry, will come along and replace it. This has been the story of nations and empires throughout history. More recent times have seen the demise of the British empire, "on which the sun never set," and of the empire that had been the Soviet Union. It would be foolhardy for powerful nations today, in the east as well as the west, to believe in their hubris that they will not be subject to the same fate.

The Vision of the He-Goat

The "he-goat with a prominent horn on its forehead" who "suddenly came from the west" (8:5) is identified in 8:21 as "king of the Greeks, and the great horn on its forehead is the first king," Alexander the Great. The animal symbolism here is particularly apt. For a ram, representing the Median and Persian kingdoms, could never withstand an attack by a powerful he-goat. Alexander was one of the greatest military commanders of all time. His victories in battle were so swift that the author describes the general as not "touching the ground." Alexander's savage destruction of "the two-horned ram," is graphically described in 8:6-7. Alexander extended his empire, which was greater than the Persian, as far east as the Indus River. There he was forced to stop, not by an enemy but ironically by his own troops who refused to go any further. But even the he-goat with a prominent horn, who "became very powerful," had his horn shattered "at the height of its power" (8:8). This is a pointed reference to Alexander's untimely death. He was felled by a fever and died in Babylon at the age of thirty-three. A timely reminder that the adage "might makes right" is wrong.

159

Moreover, great achievements in the past are no assurance of continued success. The Lord of history is still in charge of human affairs.

The Four Horns and the Little Horn, Antiochus IV

In place of Alexander, "the great horn," four other horns came up on the head of the he-goat. These horns, representing four kingdoms as 8:22 tells us, faced "the four winds of the heavens" (8:8). The reference may be to the division of Alexander's empire among four of his generals. Cassander ruled over Macedonia and Greece; Lysimachus over Thrace; Antigonus over Asia Minor, northern Syria, and the eastern portion of the former Persian empire; and Ptolemy over southern Syria and Egypt. But more likely, the reference is simply to the four points of the compass—north, south, east, and west, as in 11:4.

Our author's concern, however, is only with the "little horn" (8:9) that came out of the Syrian Seleucid dynasty. The little horn is Antiochus IV Epiphanes. Indeed, this archvillain's power "kept growing toward the south" by his invasion of Egypt in 169 and 168 B.C. (Dn 11:25-30; 1 Mc 1:16-19; 2 Mc 5:1-10), "the east" by his attempted invasion of Persia and Parthia in 166 B.C. (1 Mc 3:27-37; 6:1-4), and "the glorious country" (8:9), Palestine, when he made repeated assaults against Jerusalem and other cities (1 Mc 1:20-24; 2 Mc 5:11-21). Antiochus is accurately described as "impudent and skilled in intrigue . . . strong and powerful . . . proud of heart" (8:23-24).

Antiochus' power "extended to the host of heaven," casting down "some of the host and some of the stars" (8:10). The host of heaven usually refers to the stars (Dt 4:19; Jer 31:35). But here the reference is to the Jewish people, many of whom Antiochus persecuted and executed. The loyal Jews are later called "the holy people," or "the people of the holy ones" (8:24 in Hebrew, but transferred to 8:25 in the NAB). These Jews are called "the holy ones of the Most High" in 7:25. Antiochus even "boasted against the prince of the host" (8:11), God himself, who is called "the prince of princes" in 8:25. The tyrant "removed the daily sacrifice" (8:11) of the Jerusalem temple, replacing it with the sacrifice of

Thank you for choosing this book.
If you would like to receive regular information
about New City Press titles, please fill in this card.

Title purchased: ———————————————

Please check the subjects
that are of particular interest to you:

☐ **FATHERS OF THE CHURCH**

☐ **CLASSICS IN SPIRITUALITY**

☐ **CONTEMPORARY SPIRITUALITY**

☐ **THEOLOGY**

☐ **SCRIPTURE AND COMMENTARIES**

☐ **FAMILY LIFE**

☐ **BIOGRAPHY / HISTORY**

Other subjects of interest: ———————————

(please print)

Name:———————————————————

Address: ———————————————————

———————————————————————

———————————————————————

NEW CITY PRESS
202 CARDINAL RD.
HYDE PARK NY 12538

swine and other unclean animals (1 Mc 1:44-47), to which 8:12 alludes.

Desecration of the Temple

Antiochus' worst crime was the desecration of the Jerusalem temple by erecting over the altar of holocausts the statue of Olympian Zeus. This pagan idol is called "the desolating sin" in 8:13 and the "horrible abomination" in 1 Maccabees 1:54 and Daniel 9:27; 11:31; 12:11. When a holy one—in this case an angel—asked how long the abomination would last, the answer was: "For two thousand three hundred evenings and mornings; then the sanctuary shall be purified" (8:14). The reference is to the number of evening and morning sacrifices; hence, this number divided by two amounts to 1,150 days, a little more than three years, or the amount of time the abomination remained in the temple—from 6 December 167 B.C. till 14 December 164 B.C.

Gabriel Explains the Vision

Daniel of course is baffled by the vision he has just experienced. A manlike figure then appears; it is the angel Gabriel. Another angel speaking with a human voice tells Gabriel to explain the vision to Daniel, who, as expected in the angelic presence (10:7-11), falls "prostrate in terror." Gabriel explains that "the vision refers to the end time" (8:15-17), the time of retribution. He proceeds to explain the meaning of the two-horned ram and the he-goat with the various horns (8:20-24), an explanation we examined above. Now we learn what is to happen to the treacherous Antiochus IV, the "little horn." God's "appointed time" has come, as it always will. The angel assures Daniel and all the readers of the book that "there will be an end" (8:19) to human perversity and arrogance.

Because Antiochus rose up "against the prince of princes," God himself, "he shall be broken without a hand being raised" (8:25). It was not a human hand that brought down the villain but the divine hand that also crashed the statue in 2:34, 45, and wrote the writing on the wall in 5:5. The reference is to the death of the tyrant

161

in a land not his own (1 Mc 6:1-16). In 2 Maccabees, the story is embellished and dramatized. Antiochus "was seized with excruciating pains in his bowels and sharp internal torment, a fit punishment for him who had tortured the bowels of others with many barbarous torments" (2 Mc 9:5-6). "The body of this impious man swarmed with worms, and while he was still alive in hideous torments, his flesh rotted off, so that the entire army was sickened by the stench of his corruption. Shortly before, he had thought that he could reach the stars of heaven, and now, no one could endure to transport the man because of this intolerable stench" (2 Mc 9:9-10). "So this murderer and blasphemer, after extreme sufferings, such as he had inflicted on others, died a miserable death in the mountains of a foreign land" (2 Mc 9:28).

The relish with which the author of 2 Maccabees tells this story may not be Christian, but the principal point he makes is still valid: God will not allow colossal evil either of nations or of individuals to go unpunished. The timetable for divine intervention, however, remains unknown. The time allotted to even the most powerful nations is limited. Their destinies are not written in the stars but are determined by the Lord in whose presence "the nations are as nought, as nothing and void he accounts them" (Is 40:17). At the end of the revelation Gabriel tells Daniel to keep the vision secret (8:26)—something Daniel decided to do on his own at the conclusion of the vision in chapter 7.

Reflections on the Kingdom of God

Yet with the purification and reconsecration of the temple on 14 December 164 B.C. (1 Mc 4:52-54), the kingdom promised in 7:27 had not yet come to the Jews. It was the teaching of Jesus that transformed Old Testament expectation of the kingdom of God. The kingdom will not come about by force of arms but will be a free gift to those who repent and believe and recognize their need for God. "Jesus began to preach and say, 'Repent, for the kingdom of heaven is at hand' " (Mt 4:17). "Blessed are the poor in spirit, for theirs is the kingdom of heaven" (Mt 5:3). Righteousness and the willingness to suffer for it are hallmarks of membership in the kingdom. "Blessed are they who are persecuted for the sake of righteousness, for theirs is the kingdom of heaven" (Mt 5:10).

Doing the will of God in loving service of each other is essential; lip service will not do. "Not everyone who says to me, 'Lord, Lord,' will enter the kingdom of heaven, but only the one who does the will of my Father in heaven" (Mt 7:21). Only the childlike and humble of heart can enter the kingdom. It is not open to the high and the mighty who experience no need for God. "Amen, I say to you, whoever does not accept the kingdom of God like a child will not enter it" (Mk 10:15). The rich who feel self-sufficient will have problems. "For it is easier for a camel to pass through the eye of a needle than for a rich person to enter the kingdom of God" (Lk 18:25).

The kingdom of God is already present in the lives of believers but its fullness is yet to come. "Asked by the Pharisees when the kingdom of God would come, [Jesus] said in reply, 'The coming of the kingdom of God cannot be observed, and no one will announce, "Look, here it is," or, "There it is." For behold, the kingdom of God is among you' " (Lk 17:20-21). The kingdom demands a right set of priorities. "For the kingdom of God is not a matter of food and drink, but of righteousness, peace, and joy in the holy Spirit" (Rom 14:17).

Christians can take hope from reading the Book of Daniel. There is indeed "the appointed time" set by God who will bring evil to an end. How and when the divine intervention will take place remain known to God alone. The time of the second coming of the Lord—the *parousia*—also is unknown, as Jesus clearly tells us. "But of that day or hour, no one knows, neither the angels in heaven, nor the Son, but only the Father. Be watchful! Be alert! You do not know when the time will come. . . . What I say to you, I say to all: 'Watch!' " (Mk 13:32-33, 37). While remaining alert and watchful, ever faithful to the demands of God's kingdom, we should keep in mind what Paul tells us: "We walk by faith, not by sight" (2 Cor 5:7). We entrust our lives to our loving Father, confident that in his own good time the mysteries of life and death will be made clear. "At present we see indistinctly, as in a mirror, but then face to face. At present I know partially; then I shall know fully, as I am fully known" (1 Cor 13:12).

XVII

"Gabriel, the One Whom I Had Seen Before in Vision, Came to Me in Rapid Flight"

(Daniel 9:1-27)

¹It was the first year that Darius, son of Ahasuerus, of the race of the Medes, reigned over the kingdom of the Chaldeans; ²in the first year of his reign I, Daniel, tried to understand in the scriptures the counting of the years of which the LORD spoke to the prophet Jeremiah: that for the ruins of Jerusalem seventy years must be fulfilled.

³I turned to the Lord God, pleading in earnest prayer, with fasting, sackcloth, and ashes. ⁴I prayed to the LORD, my God, and confessed, "Ah, Lord, great and awesome God, you who keep your merciful covenant toward those who love you and observe your commandments! ⁵We have sinned, been wicked and done evil; we have rebelled and departed from your commandments and your laws. ⁶We have not obeyed your servants the prophets, who spoke in your name to our kings, our princes, our fathers, and all the people of the land. ⁷Justice, O Lord, is on your side; we are shamefaced even to this day: the men of Judah, the residents of Jerusalem, and all Israel, near and far, in all the countries to which you have scattered them because of their treachery toward you. ⁸O LORD, we are shamefaced, like our kings, our princes, and our fathers, for having sinned against you. ⁹But yours, O Lord, our God, are compassion and forgiveness! Yet we rebelled against you ¹⁰and paid no heed to your command, O LORD, our God, to live by the law you gave us through your servants the prophets. ¹¹Because all Israel transgressed your law and went astray, not heeding your voice, the sworn malediction, recorded in the law of Moses, the servant of God, was poured out over us for our sins. ¹²You carried out the threats you spoke against us and against those who governed us, by bringing upon us in Jerusalem the greatest calamity that has ever occurred

under heaven. [13]As it is written in the law of Moses, this calamity came full upon us. As we did not appease the LORD, our God, by turning back from our wickedness and recognizing his constancy, [14]so the LORD kept watch over the calamity and brought it upon us. You, O LORD, our God, are just in all that you have done, for we did not listen to your voice.

[15]"Now, O Lord, our God, who led your people out of the land of Egypt with a strong hand, and made a name for yourself even to this day, we have sinned, we are guilty. [16]O Lord, in keeping with all your just deeds, let your anger and your wrath be turned away from your city Jerusalem, your holy mountain. On account of our sins and the crimes of our fathers, Jerusalem and your people have become the reproach of all our neighbors. [17]Hear, therefore, O God, the prayer and petition of your servant; and for your own sake, O Lord, let your face shine upon your desolate sanctuary. [18]Give ear, O my God, and listen; open your eyes and see our ruins and the city which bears your name. When we present our petition before you, we rely not on our just deeds, but on your great mercy. [19]O Lord, hear! O Lord, pardon! O Lord, be attentive and act without delay, for your own sake, O my God, because this city and your people bear your name!"

[20]I was still occupied with my prayer, confessing my sin and the sin of my people Israel, presenting my petition to the LORD, my God, on behalf of his holy mountain—[21]I was still occupied with this prayer, when Gabriel, the one whom I had seen before in vision, came to me in rapid flight at the time of the evening sacrifice. [22]He instructed me in these words: "Daniel, I have now come to give you understanding. [23]When you began your petition, an answer was given which I have come to announce, because you are beloved. Therefore, mark the answer and understand the vision.

[24]"Seventy weeks are decreed
        for your people and for your holy city:
Then transgression will stop and sin will end,
        guilt will be expiated,
Everlasting justice will be introduced,
        vision and prophecy ratified,
        and a most holy will be anointed.
[25]Know and understand this:
From the utterance of the word
        that Jerusalem was to be rebuilt
Until one who is anointed and a leader,
        there shall be seven weeks.

During sixty-two weeks
it shall be rebuilt,
With streets and trenches,
in time of affliction.
26 After the sixty-two weeks
an anointed shall be cut down
when he does not possess the city;
And the people of a leader who will come
shall destroy the sanctuary.
Then the end shall come like a torrent;
until the end there shall be war,
the desolation that is decreed.
27 For one week he shall make
a firm compact with the many;
Half the week
he shall abolish sacrifice and oblation;
On the temple wing shall be the horrible abomination
until the ruin that is decreed
is poured out upon the horror."

Right from the start, we notice that this chapter is different from the preceding two and from the final apocalypse (10:1–12:13). Here is no vision to be followed by interpretation. Instead, we find Daniel trying to understand the "seventy years" Jeremiah spoke of concerning the restoration of Jerusalem after its destruction by the Babylonians in 587 B.C. In Jeremiah 25:11-14, the prophet speaks of seventy years being allotted to Babylon's domination. Then in a letter that can be dated to 594 B.C. Jeremiah prophesied: "Thus says the LORD: Only after seventy years have elapsed for Babylon will I visit you and fulfill for you my promise to bring you back to this place" (Jer 29:10). According to Zechariah 1:12-16, the period refers apparently to the time between the destruction of the temple in 587 B.C. and its reconstruction in 520-15 B.C. But this explanation did not satisfy our author. He was looking for the end of persecution and the rededication of the temple which Antiochus IV Epiphanes had desecrated in December 167 B.C. Hence, he portrays Daniel seeking understanding in prayer. Only in answer to his prayer (9:3-19), which takes up the major portion of the chapter, does Daniel experience a vision of the angel Gabriel, who comes to give the interpretation of Jeremiah's prophecy.

Daniel Prays for Understanding

The fictional setting of this chapter is the first year of Median King Darius, whom we first met in 6:1 and in the story of Daniel in the lions' den (6:2-29). Daniel has been reading "the scriptures," literally, "the Books," containing the prophecy of Jeremiah. This is the first mention in the Bible of a special collection of sacred books, probably of the prophetic corpus, which at that time had already been accepted as a discrete portion of what would become the Old Testament. This chapter was composed about 167-66 B.C. Some time after 117 B.C., the grandson of Ben Sira (Sirach) published a translation into Greek of his grandfather's book. In the Foreword to his translation the grandson writes of "the law, the prophets, and the rest of the books" (or the Writings). These designations would later be used for the threefold division of the Jewish Bible. The full canon of the Bible, however, would not be defined until Christian times.

Daniel's Prayer of Lament

Daniel's prayer is curious, for it is not a personal prayer for enlightenment regarding the seventy weeks, as we might expect. Rather, it is a liturgical prayer, one of the most impressive in the entire Old Testament. It is a humble confession of the nation's sins and a poignant plea for mercy and deliverance. In many respects, it is similar to the prayer of Azariah in 3:25-45. The prayer is written in good classical Hebrew, unlike the other Hebrew portions of the book, which were probably translated from an Aramaic original. Some scholars conclude, therefore, that the prayer is an older composition, which was inserted into the chapter by a later editor. But it is also probable that our author himself added an older prayer here in order to remind the community of its responsibility for the adversities the nation had experienced. The author no doubt made the prayer his own, for he earnestly sought the deliverance of Jerusalem from the domination of Antiochus IV.

Daniel turns to the Lord God, "pleading in earnest prayer, with fasting, sackcloth, and ashes" (9:3). According to Exodus 34:28 and Acts of the Apostles 13:2, fasting is a preparation for a revelation. Daniel at the end of his prayer would receive a divine message from Gabriel. At the beginning of his public ministry Jesus also fasted (Mt 4:2). Sackcloth and ashes were used as a form of penance in biblical times (Is 58:5; Jer 6:26; Jon 3:6; Jdt 4:11; Est 4:3; 1 Mc 3:47; Mt 11:21). Daniel's prayer is a mosaic of expressions taken over mostly from the older biblical books. After beginning with "Ah, Lord, great and awesome God" (Dt 7:21; 10:17; Neh 1:5; 9:32; Ps 89:8), Daniel proclaims his faith in divine mercy for those who love God and keep the covenant by observing the commandments (9:4). God is ever true to his word; his mercy is always present to those who are faithful to him.

Daniel's Confession of the Nation's Sins

Daniel now confesses the sins committed by the Chosen People in the Holy Land as well as in the Diaspora, "in all the countries to which [God has] scattered" them (9:5-14). God had warned the people repeatedly that he would curse and destroy them if they did not heed his voice (Lv 26:14-39; Dt 27:14-26; 28:15-68). Daniel acknowledges that it was not the Babylonians who destroyed the kingdom of Judah, but rather God himself who brought "upon us in Jerusalem the greatest calamity that has ever occurred under heaven" (9:12; cf. 1:1-2). Because kings and people alike refused to repent by turning back from their wickedness, "the LORD kept watch over the calamity and brought it upon us." Daniel then praises God for being righteous and true to his word: "You, O LORD, our God, are just in all that you have done, for we did not listen to your voice" (9:14; cf. Bar 2:9; Tb 3:2; Ps 145:17). The psalmist expresses a similar conviction: "I know, O LORD, that your ordinances are just, and in your faithfulness you have afflicted me" (Ps 119:75).

Daniel Appeals for Mercy

Daniel now affirms his faith in the God "who led [his] people out of the land of Egypt with a strong hand" (Ex 13:3, 9, 14, 16; Dt 5:15; 6:21; 7:8; 9:26; 26:8; Jer 32:21). Frankly confessing the sin and guilt of the whole people, including himself (9:15, 20), he now appeals to God's mercy. Though the people have become "the reproach of all [their] neighbors" on account of their "sins and the crimes of [their] ancestors," Daniel begs the Lord to allow his anger and wrath to turn "away from [his] holy city Jerusalem, [his] holy mountain" (9:16; cf. Is 27:13; 66:20; Jl 4:17; Zec 8:3). Speaking in his own name, Daniel finally prays: "Hear . . . O God, the prayer and petition of your servant; and for your own sake, O Lord, let your face shine upon your desolate sanctuary. . . . O Lord, pardon! O Lord, be attentive and act without delay, for your own sake, O my God, because this city and your people bear your name!" (9:17, 19). The God of Israel is a God who is close to his people, a God who can be addressed with candor and confidence. Daniel reminds God that coming to the rescue of his Chosen People is something the Lord should do "for [his] own sake," a phrase repeated twice (cf. Pss 25:11; 79:9; 109:21; 143:11; Bar 2:14). Jerusalem and the Chosen People should be spared because they bear God's name— an idea adapted from Psalm 79:9. The people, aware of their great sin, rely not on their own righteousness, as if they could earn God's grace, but only on God's "great mercy." The rhetorical effect in 9:19 is striking—the threefold (hence emphatic) repetition of "O Lord," followed by imperative verbs, "hear . . . pardon . . . be attentive and act without delay."

Many of us today have lost a sense of sin and responsibility for the crime, poverty, and corruption facing our cities, our nations, and our world. But we have all "sinned, been wicked and done evil; we have rebelled and departed from [God's] commandments and . . . laws" (9:5). Nor have we obeyed "God's servants the prophets" (9:6, 10) who plead with us, "Turn back, each of you, from your evil way and from your evil deeds; then you shall remain in the land which the LORD gave you and your fathers, from of old and forever" (Jer 25:5). Instead of turning back to God in humble prayer and sincere repentance, however, we have turned our backs on God. We have sought for solutions to our problems in social and political action alone as if the demands of God do not matter in human affairs. But confessing our sinfulness, turning away from our personal and institutional evil, and embracing a life of righteousness based on God's law are essential if we are to survive as a people.

The Bible teaches us loudly and clearly that God has a stake in our world. God is not simply a God "out there," utterly transcendent and beyond us, but also a God "right here," totally immanent and involved in our lives. Recall the words of Jesus: "Jerusalem, Jerusalem, you who kill the prophets and stone those sent to you, how many times I yearned to gather your children together, as a hen gathers her young under her wings, but you were unwilling! Behold, your house will be abandoned, desolate" (Mt 23:37-38). The Lord is concerned about our cities too. He deplores drug and alcohol abuse, sexual promiscuity, homelessness, marital irresponsibility, lack of reverence for all human life, crime in high places and low, exploitation of the poor to enrich the wealthy, racial and sexual discrimination, political and social corruption.

Daniel singles out kings, princes, and ancestors for special blame (9:8). These are the political and spiritual leaders responsible for promoting the welfare of the community. Though they, like the rest of us, must give an accounting to the Lord, we must never hesitate to tell them that they are accountable also to us for what they have done or have failed to do. But we must bear in mind that we also are part of the problem. We are accountable for our complicity in the greed and unjust (but often legal) business practices of many corporations. Unless all of us—leaders and people alike—are willing to repent and to follow the way of the Lord, our house too will be abandoned, desolate.

Spiritual Dimensions of Daniel's Prayer

We may now summarize in five points the spiritual message of Daniel's prayer—a message also found elsewhere in the Bible. First, the Lord is a "great and awesome God" (9:4). God is to be reverenced and acknowledged for what he is—the supreme Being, maker of heaven and earth. Fear of the Lord, an expression found scores of times in the Old Testament, involves the attitude of respect and love one should have for God as for a parent, and the moral obligations following from that love. "And now, Israel, what does the LORD, your God, ask of you but to fear the LORD, your God, and follow his ways exactly, to love and serve the LORD, your God, with all your heart and all your soul" (Dt 10:12; cf. Mal 1:6).

170

The New Testament adds another truth: "God is love" (1 Jn 4:16). God's love was proved beyond question when Jesus died for us on the cross (Jn 3:16).

Second, God alone is the one who saves. In the Exodus, God led his people out of the land of slavery in Egypt (9:15) to the Promised Land of freedom (Ex 13:3, 14; Dt 5:6; 6:21-23). We too can find salvation and freedom only in God (Gal 5:1; 1 Pt 2:16). Our technology and gadgets may satisfy our physical and emotional needs for the moment, but only God can fulfill the deepest longings of our spirit.

Third, God is righteous (9:7). This means that God always does what is right and just. But it also means God will always act in accordance with his nature, which is characterized by his steadfast love and holiness. God also demands righteousness and holiness of us. "Speak to the whole Israelite community and tell them: Be holy, for I, the LORD your God, am holy" (Lv 19:2). Jesus tells us, "Be perfect, just as your heavenly Father is perfect" (Mt 5:48).

Fourth, God is a just judge (9:11-14) who will not leave sin unpunished (Lv 26:14-39; Dt 28:15-68; Mt 25:41-46; Lk 10:13-15). The wrath of God is a corollary of this truth. Presumption is a serious sin. "We know the one who said: 'Vengeance is mine; I will repay,' and again: 'The Lord will judge his people.' It is a fearful thing to fall into the hands of the living God" (Heb 10:30-31).

Fifth, the Lord is a God of hope and mercy (9:9, 17-19). He will look with compassion and loving forgiveness on those who repent of their sins and turn back to him (Ex 34:6; Dt 4:31; 7:9; Eph 2:4-7). We are never beyond hope unless we think we are hopeless, in which case we will fulfill our own expectation.

Daniel's Prayer Is Answered

Daniel's prayer is now answered without delay. The angel Gabriel, whom Daniel had first seen in 8:16, appears to him "in rapid flight"—a phrase that probably lies behind the tradition in Christian art of depicting angels as human beings with wings. It is the time of "the evening sacrifice" (9:21), or mid-afternoon. Gabriel gives Daniel the "understanding" that he had sought regarding the "seventy years" spoken of by Jeremiah (9:2, 22).

171

Gabriel was sent because Daniel is "beloved" (9:23), a title an angel uses also in 10:11, 19. Understanding God's will and having the courage to do it is the essence of prayer. Often we think of prayer, however, as asking God to do what we want. But that is not prayer; that is manipulation. We may complain that God has not listened to us because he has not done what we prayed for. But God's refusal and silence may be precisely the answer to our prayer. As Oscar Wilde once dryly observed: "When the gods wish to punish us they answer our prayers" (*An Ideal Husband*, Act II).

Daniel now learns that the "seventy years" (9:24) are actually "seventy weeks" of years, or 490 years, "when transgression will stop" and "a most holy will be anointed" (9:24)—a reference to the Holy of Holies in the temple reconsecrated in 164 B.C. As I mentioned before, numbers in the Bible are used primarily for symbolic purposes. Hence, we should not take the seventy weeks of years literally; they symbolize a lengthy period of time: seven (a perfect number) times ten (a round number). The first seven weeks of years, forty-nine years, are fairly accurate: from 587 B.C., the destruction of Jerusalem, to 539 B.C., when the "anointed leader," Cyrus the Great (Is 45:1) ended the Babylonian Exile. The "sixty-two weeks" of years (9:25) are only a rough approximation. At the end of that time, "an anointed [was] cut down," a reference to the murder of the high priest Onias III in 171 B.C. (2 Mc 4:1-38). "The people of a leader" and the destruction of "the sanctuary" (9:26) refer to the Syrians led by Antiochus IV and their plundering of the temple in 167 B.C. (1 Mc 1:29-35). For "one week" of years, from about 171 to 164 B.C., Antiochus made "a firm compact with the many," those Jews who compromised their faith by accepting Hellenistic ways (1 Mc 1:11-15). For "half a week" of years Antiochus had abolished "sacrifice and oblation" and set up "the horrible abomination," the statue of Olympian Zeus, right in the temple itself. The abomination remained in the temple from 6 December 167 to 14 December 164 B.C., approximately the three and a half years mentioned here.

What is noteworthy is that the author tried to understand Jeremiah's prophecy in terms of his own second-century B.C. situation. The sixth-century B.C. time-frame for the Daniel narratives is, of course, a literary fiction that the author employs in order to affirm his conviction that God is in control. The biblical books do not have meaning only for their original recipients. What Daniel is doing here is also what the New Testament does when it reinterprets many of the predictions and expectations of the Old Testament in the light of Jesus Christ. Thus, Matthew 1:22-23 quotes the prophecy of Isaiah 7:14, which in the Septuagint reads, "The virgin shall be with child and bear a son, and they shall name him Emmanuel," and interprets the text as applying to the virginal birth of Jesus. Isaiah's original prophecy in the eighth century B.C., however, referred to the birth of Hezekiah, the son of Ahaz. Throughout history, Christians have been led by the Holy Spirit to seek from the ancient words of scripture light and guidance for the situations they faced. This does not imply, however, that the Bible provides a celestial calculus for determining the course of current world events, as some fundamentalists claim.

Coming of the End

Because the text tells us, "the end shall come like a torrent; until the end there shall be war, the desolation that is decreed" (9:26), many fundamentalist Christians have tried to calculate "the end" and the "war, the desolation," in terms of contemporary events. Hal Lindsay, for example, in his vastly popular book, The Late Great Planet Earth (1970), writes that the Bible contains over five hundred prophecies concerning the end-time. Among these, he writes, are the establishment of the State of Israel in 1948 (predicted in Ezekiel 38-40), the return of Jerusalem to Israeli control in 1967 (Zec 12-14), the conversion of Africa to communism (Dn 11:35-45), the rise of a new Roman Empire in the form of the European Economic Community (Dn 7:17), and the apostasy of many of the churches (2 Pt 2:1). On the basis of what he reads into the Bible, Lindsay also provides plans and maps of the campaigns that will take place in World War III.

John F. Walvoord of Dallas Theological Seminary published a book ominously entitled Armageddon, Oil and the Middle East (1991). He wrote that the events in the Persian Gulf crisis (1990-91) were fulfillments of the promise of the Second Coming of Christ. The book, which sold over a million copies, made the New

York Times best seller list. This kind of tea leaf exposition, which does violence to God's inspired word, may strike us as exegetically witless and theologically worthless. But many radio and television evangelists preach such fantasies to millions of people. In 1990, Pat Robertson, for example, told viewers of his "700 Club" TV program that the war with Iraq and other events in the Middle East were happening because, as he claimed, "It's exactly what the Bible said." Jack Van Impe informed his national TV audience that biblical prophecies pointed to events in Iraq and the Persian Gulf as the prelude to the biblical Battle of Armageddon, symbol of the final destruction of the forces of evil (Rv 16:12-16). Interpretations of this kind call to mind Shakespeare's famous words: "In religion/ What damned error but some sober brow/ Will bless it, and approve it with a text, / Hiding the grossness with fair ornament" (*Merchant of Venice*, III, ii, 77-80).

More alarming, however, is what *Newsweek* magazine reported some years ago: Because of the popularity of his book Lindsay had given a lecture at the Pentagon, and according to Lindsay, with the approval of President Ronald Reagan. What is dangerous about the wrong-headed and ungrounded interpretations of Lindsay and others like him is that some people take it seriously with potentially disastrous consequences. "Predictions" like Lindsay's tend to become self-fulfilling "prophecies."

The inspired author of the Book of Daniel, however, tells us nothing about the timetable of "the end." He merely teaches that there will be an end to wickedness, but that end will come in God's own time, and not according to our misguided and self-serving calculations.

XVIII

"In the Third Year of Cyrus, King of Persia, a Revelation Was Given to Daniel"

(Daniel 10:1–11:1)

[1] In the third year of Cyrus, king of Persia, a revelation was given to Daniel, who had been named Belteshazzar. The revelation was certain: A great war; he understood it from the vision. [2] In those days, I, Daniel, mourned three full weeks. [3] I ate no savory food, I took no meat or wine, and I did not anoint myself at all until the end of the three weeks.

[4] On the twenty-fourth day of the first month I was on the bank of the great river, the Tigris. [5] As I looked up, I saw a man dressed in linen with a belt of fine gold around his waist. [6] His body was like chrysolite, his face shone like lightning, his eyes were like fiery torches, his arms and feet looked like burnished bronze, and his voice sounded like the roar of a multitude. [7] I alone, Daniel, saw the vision; but great fear seized the men who were with me; they fled and hid themselves, although they did not see the vision. [8] So I was left alone, seeing this great vision. No strength remained in me; I turned the color of death and was powerless. [9] When I heard the sound of his voice, I fell face forward in a faint.

[10] But then a hand touched me, raising me to my hands and knees. [11] "Daniel, beloved," he said to me, "understand the words which I am speaking to you; stand up, for my mission now is to you." When he said this to me, I stood up trembling. [12] "Fear not, Daniel," he continued; "from the first day you made up your mind to acquire understanding and humble yourself before God, your prayer was heard. Because of it I started out, [13] but the prince of the kingdom of Persia stood in my way for twenty-one days, until finally Michael, one of the chief princes, came to help me. I left him there with the prince of the kings of Persia, [14] and came to make you understand what shall happen to your people in the days to come; for there is yet a vision concerning those days."

¹⁵While he was speaking thus to me, I fell forward and kept silent. ¹⁶Then something like a man's hand touched my lips; I opened my mouth and said to the one facing me, "My lord, I was seized with pangs at the vision and I was powerless. ¹⁷How can my lord's servant speak with you, my lord? For now no strength or even breath is left in me." ¹⁸The one who looked like a man touched me again and strengthened me, saying, ¹⁹"Fear not, beloved, you are safe; take courage and be strong." ²⁰When he spoke to me, I grew strong and said, "Speak, my lord, for you have strengthened me." "Do you know," he asked, "why I have come to you? Soon I must fight the prince of Persia again. When I leave, the prince of Greece will come; ²¹but I shall tell you what is written in the truthful book. No one supports me against all these except Michael, your prince, ¹¹:¹standing as a reinforcement and a bulwark for me."

We now come to the last, and longest, apocalypse of the book, 10:1–12:13. It is divided into three parts: the prologue recounting the angel's appearance to Daniel and their opening dialogue (10:1–11:1); the revelation of things to come from the Persian period to the time of Antiochus IV Epiphanes (11:2-45); and the epilogue depicting a final scene and the angel's parting words to Daniel (12:1-13). We shall devote a chapter to each of these parts. This apocalypse is the climax of the book, for it supplies many details that were lacking in the first four apocalypses (chaps. 2, 7, 8, 9), which also describe what is to happen to the faithful Jews at the end of the evil age. As in the earlier apocalypses, the present vision seems to describe the future course of history. What we actually have is a narrative of selected events before and during the lifetime of our author, who lived during the persecution of Antiochus IV. By means of the literary device of "prophecies after the event," the author declared his conviction that God is Lord of history and will vindicate those who remain loyal to him.

Daniel Receives a Revelation

Daniel experiences this revelation "in the third year of Cyrus, king of Persia" (10:1), or 536 B.C., the fictional date to provide the setting for the coming prophecies. Since Daniel began his career "in the third year of . . . Jehoiakim, king of Judah" (1:1), or 606 B.C., the total number of years of Daniel's ministry would be the biblically perfect number of seventy. Thus, Daniel receives his most perfect as well as longest and most detailed revelation in his seventieth year of service.

Daniel, "who had been named Belteshazzar," a name he received in the Babylonian court (1:7), is overwhelmed by the revelation he is about to receive. "The revelation [literally, the word] was certain," or absolutely trustworthy, for it came from the Lord of history. It concerned "a great war," from which the loyal people would emerge victorious. Thanks to the divine help he would receive from the angelic figure, Daniel understood the revelation "from the vision" (10:1) to come. But he prepared himself thoroughly for this last and detailed revelation. He mourned or did penance "three weeks," literally, "three weeks of days" (10:2, 3), to distinguish "weeks [of years]" in 9:24-27.

The number three has symbolic value, denoting the superlative degree. Some examples: In order to emphasize the transcendent holiness of God, the seraphim cried one to the other, "Holy, holy, holy is the LORD of hosts! All the earth is filled with his glory!" (Is 6:3). When David learned the news of the death of his son, he repeated his son's name three times as he wept, "My son Absalom! My son, my son Absalom! If only I had died instead of you, Absalom, my son, my son!" (2 Sm 19:1). In the vision of heavenly worship, the four living creatures, each with six wings like the seraphim in Isaiah 6:2, exclaim day and night, "Holy, holy, holy is the Lord God almighty, who was, and who is, and who is to come" (Rv 4:8). The twenty-one days of Daniel's fast are the total of three times seven (the number for perfection as in 3:19; 4:13, 20, 22, 29). Thus, the duration of Daniel's penance was perfect in every respect. He fasted from the rich fare of meat and wine, only eating bread and drinking water. Because anointing with oil was a luxury (Am 6:6) as well as a sign of rejoicing, it was given up in periods of mourning (2 Sm 14:2; Is 61:3; Jdt 10:3) and fasting (Mt 6:17).

Spiritual exercises of prayer and fasting have a long history (Ezr 8:23; Neh 1:4; Tb 12:8; Ps 35:13; Bar 1:5). Thus we read, "While they were worshiping the Lord and fasting, the Holy Spirit said,

'Set apart for me Barnabas and Saul for the work to which I have called them.' Then, completing their fasting and prayer, they laid hands on them and sent them off" (Acts 13:2-3). "They appointed presbyters for them in each church and, with prayer and fasting, commended them to the Lord in whom they had put their faith" (4:23). Prior to ordination, candidates for major orders make a retreat of several days to prepare themselves for the ministry ahead. Retreats and periods of prayer and penance have also become common for other Christians who want to lead a more examined spiritual life with God. Such exercises help to focus our attention and to examine whether our life-style is in accord with the gospel.

In keeping with a convention of apocalyptic literature, the author gives a precise date to Daniel's vision: "the twenty-fourth day of the first month" (10:4), the month called Nisan (Neh 2:1), mid-March to mid-April. Standing on the bank of the Tigris River, Daniel witnessed a dazzling sight: "A man dressed in linen with a belt of fine gold around his waist. His body was like chrysolite, his face shone like lightning, his eyes were like fiery torches, his arms and feet looked like burnished bronze, and his voice sounded like the roar of a multitude" (10:4-5). The priests wore linen, a ritually pure fabric (Ex 39:27-29; Lv 6:3). The angels are clothed in linen in Revelation 15:6, as are the Bride of the Lamb (Rv 19:8) and the heavenly armies (Rv 19:14). The gold belt is an indication of the angel's lofty status. The description of his body derives mainly from Ezekiel 1 where the four living creatures or cherubim are described. The identification of this angel is not certain, but it is probably Gabriel, who also appeared in 8:15-16 and 9:21-27.

The Vision Terrifies Daniel

The awesome vision, which Daniel alone saw, charged the atmosphere around him so much that the men who were with him knew that something extraordinary was happening; so they fled in terror (10:7). Left alone, Daniel now "turned the color of death," and hearing the angel's roaring voice, he fell "forward in a faint" (10:8-9). Falling face to the ground is the usual response to a divine or angelic apparition (8:16-18; Jos 5:14; Ez 1:28; Rv 1:17). Daniel's reactions call to mind a similar vision that Saul of Tarsus experienced on the road to Damascus. "On his journey, as [Saul] was nearing Damascus, a light from the sky suddenly flashed around him. He fell to the ground and heard a voice saying to him, 'Saul, Saul, why are you persecuting me?' He said, 'Who are you, sir?' The reply came, 'I am Jesus, whom you are persecuting. Now get up and go into the city and you will be told what you must do.' The men who were traveling with him stood speechless, for they heard the voice but could see no one" (Acts 9:3-7). Mystics like Francis of Assisi and John of the Cross, Hildegarde of Bingen and Teresa of Avila, as well as countless others have also had overwhelming experiences of the Lord breaking into their lives. For most of us, however, the divine inbreak is not as dramatic but is nonetheless real. We can see Jesus in the faces of the hungry, the thirsty, the stranger, the homeless, and the prisoner (Mt 25:31-40).

Moreover, faith puts us in personal contact with the living God who enables us to transcend our natural capabilities and to become examples of upright living in a society with little room for anything or anyone beyond the empirical. We can be consoled by the words of the Lord to the Apostle Paul, who had prayed to be relieved of "a thorn in the flesh": "My grace is sufficient for you, for power is made perfect in weakness." We can then make our own Paul's response: "I will rather boast most gladly of my weaknesses, in order that the power of Christ may dwell with me" (2 Cor 12:7, 9).

The Angel Consoles Daniel

A hand, presumably the angel's, now touches Daniel reassuringly. The angel addresses Daniel as "beloved" in 10:11 and 19, exactly what Gabriel calls him in 9:23, and urges him to stand up and to understand what he is about to hear. Reassured but still trembling, Daniel stood up (10:10-11). The angel says, "Fear not, Daniel," at the beginning of his opening speech (10:12) and for emphasis repeats the expression near the end (10:19). In the Bible when God or one of his servants says to a person, "fear not," or "do not be afraid," a revelation usually follows (cf. Gn 15:1; Ex 14:13; Jos 1:9; Is 7:4-7; 35:4; 41:10, 13-14; 43:1, 5; Jer 30:10; 46:27; Bar 4:27; Tb 12:17; Mt 28:10; Lk 1:13, 30; 12:32; Rv

11:17). The angel informs Daniel that his prayer was heard from the time he "made up [his] mind to acquire understanding and humble [himself] before God" (10:12).

Searching out the will of God in humility and prayer is a prerequisite for an understanding of the divine plan. Though God is utterly transcendent and awesome, he tells us time and time again in scripture not to be afraid but to trust him. Our faith does not give us all the answers, which is a blessing in disguise. For if we had all the answers, we would often be obnoxious and impossible to live with. But faith does give us the firm assurance that our life in this messy world does make sense, for God is in charge in his quiet and mysterious way. No earthly power can nullify the divine will. We must do all we can, of course, to promote the kingdom of God in our pagan society; but we should leave the outcome and the timetable in the hands of the Lord.

Daniel's fear is a normal reaction in the presence of the supernatural. The awareness of the holy underscores one's unworthiness. Recall the story of Simon, James, and John. When Jesus told Simon to go out into deep water and lower the nets for a catch, Simon answered that they had labored all night but caught nothing. Nevertheless, Simon did as he was told. They caught such a great number of fish that their nets were tearing. "When Simon Peter saw this, he fell at the knees of Jesus and said, 'Depart from me, Lord, for I am a sinful man.' For astonishment at the catch of fish they had made seized him and all those with him, and likewise James and John, the sons of Zebedee, who were partners of Simon. Jesus said to Simon, 'Do not be afraid; from now on you will be catching human beings'" (Lk 5:8-10). When we feel just as unworthy for the tasks of our vocation, the Lord who called us will give us the strength we need. We are not alone. The Lord is ever at our side. We must trust him, for he has never failed in his promises.

Michael, Israel's Guardian Angel

The angel was sent by God to give Daniel the understanding he sought in prayer (10:12). But when the angel started out, he was detained. So he tells Daniel, "The prince of the kingdom of Persia stood in my way for twenty-one days, until finally Michael, one of the chief princes, came to help me. I left him there with the prince of the kings of Persia" (10:13). "Twenty-one days" is precisely the duration of Daniel's three-week fast (10:3). Thus, the author emphasizes the connection between Daniel's spiritual exercises and the help the angel received from Michael. "The prince of the kings of Persia," mentioned twice here, is the tutelary or guardian angel of Persia.

Michael, however, is the guardian angel of the Jewish people. He receives the titles "one of the chief princes" (10:13), "your prince" (10:21), and "the great prince, guardian of your people" (12:1). The implication is that Michael as protector of the Chosen People could easily hold the prince of Persia in check. The very name "Michael"—which means "Who is like God?"—suggests the dignity and power of the angel. Thus, the people of God have in Michael a powerful intercessor in the heavenly court. In Jude 9, Michael is called "archangel," which corresponds to the expression "great prince" in 12:1. In Revelation 12:7-9, Michael is leader of the angels who do battle against the huge dragon and its angels. Though there are forces of evil at work in our world thanks to original sin and our personal sins, we know from faith that God and his angels will prevail. So we need not fear. As Paul writes: "What will separate us from the love of Christ? Will anguish, or distress, or persecution, or famine, or nakedness, or peril, or the sword? . . . No, in all these things we conquer overwhelmingly through him who loved us. For I am convinced that neither death, nor life, nor angels, nor principalities, nor present things, nor future things, nor powers, nor height, nor depth, nor any other creature will be able to separate us from the love of God in Christ Jesus our Lord" (Rom 8:35, 37-39).

In the Garden of Gethsemane, Jesus prayed, "Father, if you are willing, take this cup away from me; still, not my will but yours be done" (Lk 22:42). This is a perfect prayer. The text continues: "And to strengthen him an angel from heaven appeared to him. He was in such agony and he prayed so fervently that his sweat became like drops of blood falling on the ground" (Lk 22:43-44). Like Daniel, Jesus had prayed for understanding in his crushing agony. The Father for his own mysterious reasons did not remove the cup of suffering and death. But in answer to Jesus' prayer, the Father sent an angel to strengthen him. In our moments of crisis and need we can also be certain of our heavenly Father's help to strengthen and console us. Jesus himself has assured us of his assistance and presence: "Behold, I am with you always, until the end of the age" (Mt 28:20). God is not indifferent to our situation. God does listen to our prayers. We are not alone in a chaotic world. God is in charge though he may choose to remain silent for a time. We have but to trust in God's word and to wait for his consolation. "Peace I leave with you; my peace I give to you. Not as the world gives do I give it to you. Do not let your hearts be troubled or afraid" (Jn 14:27).

The Angel Touches Daniel Again

Daniel is still overwhelmed by the appearance of the angel (10:15-17). So the angel gives him another strengthening touch, saying, "Fear not, beloved, you are safe; take courage and be strong" (10:18-19). The angel then gives him a preview of what is to come. After the angel leaves to fight the prince of Persia, "the prince of Greece will come" (10:20), a reference to the Seleucid dynasty and its notorious tyrant Antiochus IV. The angel now will tell Daniel "what is written in the truthful book [or book of truth]" (10:21). This book is God's record of what has happened and what is still to come. Other texts speak of God's book as a ledger of a person's moral decisions and destiny (Ex 32:32-33; Mal 3:16; Tb 12:12; Pss 56:9; 139:16; Lk 10:20).

Touch is mentioned three times in this episode (10:10, 16, 18), the number three denoting emphasis. Indeed, touch is a healing and comforting power in human relationships. When two blind men asked Jesus for a cure, he touched their eyes and restored their sight (Mt 9:27-30). When the disciples heard the voice from the cloud at the Transfiguration, they fell prostrate in terror. "But Jesus came and touched them, saying, 'Rise, and do not be afraid' " (Mt 17:7). Jesus never hesitated to use touch in ministering to others (Mt 8:3, 15; 20:34; Mk 1:41; 7:33; Lk 5:13; 7:14; 22:51). "People were bringing children to [Jesus] that he might touch them" (Mk 10:13). Jesus not only recognized the value of touching others; he also allowed himself to be touched (Mt 9:20-21; 14:36; Mk 3:10;

Lk 6:19; 24:39). Unfortunately, many today are reluctant to extend the touch of a hand to another person for fear of being misunderstood or even accused of sexual harassment or worse.

XIX

"By Stealth and Fraud He Shall Seize the Kingdom"

(Daniel 11:2-4, 21-45)

[2] Now I shall tell you the truth. "Three kings of Persia are yet to come; and a fourth shall acquire the greatest riches of all. Strengthened by his riches, he shall rouse all the kingdom of Greece. [3] But a powerful king shall appear and rule with great might, doing as he pleases. [4] No sooner shall he appear than his kingdom shall be broken and divided in four directions under heaven; but not among his descendants or in keeping with his mighty rule, for his kingdom shall be torn to pieces and belong to others than they.

[21] "There shall rise in his place a despicable person, to whom the royal insignia shall not be given. By stealth and fraud he shall seize the kingdom. [22] Armed might shall be completely overwhelmed by him and crushed, and even the prince of the covenant. [23] After allying with him, he shall treacherously rise to power with a small party. [24] By stealth he shall enter prosperous provinces and do that which his fathers or grandfathers never did; he shall distribute spoil, booty, and riches among them and devise plots against their strongholds; but only for a time. [25] He shall call on his strength and cleverness to meet the king of the south with a great army; the king of the south shall prepare for battle with a very large and strong army, but he shall not succeed because of the plots devised against him. [26] Even his table companions shall seek to destroy him, his army shall be overwhelmed, and many shall fall slain. [27] The two kings, resolved on evil, shall sit at table together and exchange lies, but they shall have no success, because the appointed end is not yet.

[28] "He shall turn back toward his land with great riches, his mind set against the holy covenant; he shall arrange matters and return to his land. [29] At the time appointed he shall come again

to the south, but this time it shall not be as before. [30]When ships of the Kittim confront him, he shall lose heart and retreat. Then he shall direct his rage and energy against the holy covenant; those who forsake it he shall once more single out. [31]Armed forces shall move at his command and defile the sanctuary stronghold, abolishing the daily sacrifice and setting up the horrible abomination. [32]By his deceit he shall make some who were disloyal to the covenant apostatize; but those who remain loyal to their God shall take strong action. [33]The nation's wise men shall instruct the many; though for a time they will become victims of the sword, of flames, exile, and plunder. [34]When they fall, they shall receive a little help, but many shall join them insincerely. [35]Of the wise men, some shall fall, so that the rest may be tested, refined, and purified, until the end time which is still appointed to come.

[36]"The king shall do as he pleases, exalting himself and making himself greater than any god; he shall utter dreadful blasphemies against the God of gods. He shall prosper only till divine wrath is ready, for what is determined must take place. [37]He shall have no regard for the gods of his ancestors or for the one in whom women delight; for no god shall he have regard, because he shall make himself greater than all. [38]Instead, he shall give glory to the god of strongholds; a god unknown to his fathers he shall glorify with gold, silver, precious stones, and other treasures. [39]To defend the strongholds he shall station a people of a foreign god. Whoever acknowledges him he shall provide with abundant honor; he shall make them rule over the many and distribute the land as a reward.

[40]"At the appointed time the king of the south shall come to grips with him, but the king of the north shall overwhelm him with chariots and horsemen and a great fleet, passing through the countries like a flood. [41]He shall enter the glorious land and many shall fall, except Edom, Moab, and the chief part of Ammon, which shall escape from his power. [42]He shall extend his power over the countries, and not even the land of Egypt shall escape. [43]He shall control the riches of gold and silver and all the treasures of Egypt; Libya and Ethiopia shall be in his train. [44]When news from the east and the north terrifies him, he shall set out with great fury to slay and to doom many. [45]He shall pitch the tents of his royal pavilion between the sea and the glorious holy mountain, but he shall come to his end with none to help him."

We now come to the bulk of the last apocalypse of the book. This chapter describes in veiled and allusive language the intrigues and wars, intermarriages and alliances between the rulers of Syria and of Egypt. Our author refers to these rulers as "the king of the north" and "the king of the south." These kings fought frequent battles over Palestine, for it was the land bridge between Egypt and Asia Minor (modern Turkey). But the author provides the clearest and fullest information about the reign of Antiochus IV Epiphanes, because the author lived through that brutal period. The author's purpose is didactic. So he employs the literary device of "prophecy after the event" to convey to his readers his own unshaken faith in the God of revelation who alone determines the destinies of nations and peoples.

History is not a haphazard series of events but a working out of the divine plan. Believers are called upon to trust in God especially in times of persecution. Though the apocalypse seems to provide a timetable for divine intervention, it is clear that the author and editors of the book left the date open (12:11-12). Unfortunately, however, some fundamentalist Christian evangelists have read into this chapter predictions of such events of recent times as the dissolution of the Soviet Union, the 1991 Gulf War, various upheavals in Red China and the Middle East, and the rise of the European Economic Community. But as I indicated above in chapter XVII, such a reading does a disservice to the inspired word of God and to the reader who takes the Bible seriously.

The Persian Age to Alexander the Great

The angel now tells Daniel "the truth" regarding what is to come. He gives a summary of the history from the Persian period down to our author's own day (11:2-45). The identities of the "three kings of Persia," who follow Cyrus the Great (550-30 B.C.), are not certain, for the Persian empire had a total of eleven kings. The "fourth" king, who "shall acquire the greatest riches of all" (11:2), may be Xerxes I (486-65 B.C.), who had fabulous wealth, or else may simply symbolize the wealth of the Persian empire in general. The "powerful king" who does "as he pleases" (11:3) is Alexander the Great (336-23 B.C.), the he-goat with a great horn in 8:5-8, 21.

186

After his untimely death, at the age of thirty-three, his empire was broken up and "divided in the four directions under heaven" by four of his generals, "but not among his descendants" (11:4)—a dim-witted half-brother and two sons, all of whom were done away with by the generals. We need not go into detail regarding the battles and fortunes of the early Seleucids in the north and the Ptolemies in the south, the two divisions of Alexander's empire of interest in the chapter (11:5-20). The author's principal concern, however, was the reign of the Seleucid monarch Antiochus IV Epiphanes, who receives the lion's share of space (11:21-45).

Antiochus IV's Usurpation of the Throne

Our author has nothing but contempt for Antiochus, "a despicable person," called "a sinful offshoot" in 1 Maccabees 1:10, "an arrogant and terrible man" in 4 Maccabees 4:15. After the murder of Seleucus IV Philopator (187-75 B.C.), his son Demetrius became the legitimate successor to the throne. Instead, however, Seleucus' brother, Antiochus IV, seized the kingdom by "stealth and fraud" and later murdered his nephew Demetrius (11:21). In 175 B.C. Antiochus consolidated his control by crushing the "armed might" of his Seleucid rivals. "The prince of the covenant" (11:22) is the legitimate high priest Onias III, who vigorously opposed the Hellenization policies of Antiochus. So Antiochus deposed him and installed as high priest Onias' brother Jason, who had offered the tyrant a huge bribe in exchange for the honor. Jason enthusiastically supported the Hellenization of the Holy Land. The story is told in 2 Maccabees 4:7-17.

The author now alludes to Antiochus' double-dealing, treachery, and intrigue (11:23-27). Antiochus plundered the wealth of the "prosperous provinces" and was far more liberal than any of his predecessors in distributing "spoil, booty, and riches" (11:24) to his friends and supporters (1 Mc 3:30). In 169 B.C. he waged war against the inferior forces of his nephew Ptolemy VI Philometor, who was easily defeated thanks to the foolish advice he received from two of his counsellors, "his table companions" (11:25-26). Meanwhile powerful nobles in Alexandria had transferred their allegiance to Philometor's brother, crowning him ruler with the name Ptolemy VII Physcon. In the ensuing struggle for power, Antiochus pretended support for Philometor who had been captured in the war ("the two kings . . . shall sit at table together and exchange lies"), thereby seeking to weaken Egypt by strengthening the rivalry between his two nephews. But Antiochus' scheme did not work; "the appointed end" for Egypt was not yet (11:27).

Antiochus had to "turn back toward his land" because he had to settle some unrest that occurred when the rumor spread that he had died. On the way north to Antioch, his capital, he plundered the Jerusalem temple once again (11:28), putting to death thousands of Jews and enslaving others (2 Mc 5:5-20). In the meantime his Egyptian nephews Ptolemy VI and Ptolemy VII had been reconciled and were now reigning conjointly. So in 168 B.C. Antiochus "at the time appointed" came "again to the south" in hopes of controlling Egyptian affairs once more; "but this time it . . . [was not] as before" (11:29). He reached Alexandria where "ships of the Kittim," the Romans, confronted him. The Roman consul Gaius Popillius Laenas humiliated Antiochus and forced him to retreat north.

Antiochus' Reign of Terror

In his rage Antiochus again plundered what was left of Jerusalem, leaving unharmed only those who had forsaken the covenant (11:30). This time, however, he was determined to put an end to the Jewish religion. He abolished "the daily sacrifice," and in December 167 B.C. he set up "the horrible abomination" (11:31), the statue of Olympian Zeus over the altar of holocausts in the temple. He also burned "scrolls of the law," the Torah, and forbade circumcision and every other practice of the Jewish faith, putting to death any who defied his unjust laws (1 Mc 1:54-63; 2 Mc 6:1-2). Many Jews, who "were disloyal to the covenant" by their accommodations with the Hellenizing policies of Antiochus, now completely apostatized. Others, however, remained "loyal to their God" (11:32). These suffered bloody persecution for three years, until 164 B.C. when the temple was rededicated.

The nation's "wise men" (11:33; Hebrew *maskilim*), a term occurring also in 11:35 and 12:3, 10, are the faithful Jewish leaders who opposed Hellenization. These are later called in Greek *hasidaioi*, "Hasideans," a word derived from Hebrew *hasidim*, "pious ones" (1 Mc 2:42; 7:13; 2 Mc 14:6). Since even the high priest Jason and other priests had gone along with Hellenization (2 Mc 4:7-16), many ordinary Jews were wondering if they too should adjust their values to the new ways. Accordingly, the wise leaders instructed "the many, or multitude" not to compromise but to remain steadfast in their faith. Their fidelity would "for a time" make them "victims of the sword, of flames, exile, and plunder" (11:33). "When they fall, they shall receive a little help"—a reference to the Maccabean resistance under Mattathias and his son Judas (1 Mc 2:15-28, 42-48; 3:10-26; 4:1-25).

The expression, "a little help," emphasizes our author's lack of enthusiasm for military intervention. Many Jews who had followed the ways of Hellenization for economic and social gains now joined the Maccabean resistance "insincerely," that is, in order to save their own necks. For Mattathias and Judas dealt harshly with apostate Jews (1 Mc 2:44-46; 3:5-8). Some of "the wise men" would fall, "so that the rest may be tested, refined, and purified." The persecution would last only till the time "appointed" (11:35) by the Lord of history. Our author clearly favored non-violent resistance over military action. The suffering and death of the faithful Jews would be the means God would use to test, refine, and purify the rest of the people. As James A. Montgomery observes in his commentary, this verse is the earliest expression of the idea that "the blood of martyrs is the seed of the Church."

Non-violent resistance has also been the philosophy of such effective leaders as Mahatma Gandhi (1869-1948). He is universally honored for his non-violent struggles against British rule to achieve social justice and political independence for India. Today he is called the father of his country. Dr. Martin Luther King, Jr. (1929-68), is another outstanding example. An eloquent Baptist minister, he became a forceful leader of the civil rights movement in the United States from the mid-1950s to his death. Even when faced with violence himself, he never resorted to violence. He won the Nobel Peace Prize in 1964 for applying principles of non-violent resistance to the fight for racial equality and justice. He once wrote: "Now and then one develops a conviction in one's life which is so valuable and full of meaning that one clings to it to the end. If all Negroes in the United States were converted to violence, I would prefer to remain the sole and solitary voice to preach that this is the wrong way." Like Gandhi before him, King paid the price for his conviction. He was assassinated by his enemies.

Antiochus IV attacked "the prince of the covenant," the legitimate high priest (11:22), and then "the holy covenant" itself (11:30), because the covenant is what made the Jews different from everybody else. The demands of the covenant made them dissidents in a pagan society. Loyal Jews would not compromise their faith in order to acquiesce to the tyrannical policy of Hellenization. Hence, Antiochus launched an all-out attack against them. But even at risk of their lives, many remained faithful, refusing to conform to the laws of the state.

Unfortunately, Jews have been persecuted throughout the centuries, even by Christians, simply because they were Jews. Any form of anti-Jewish sentiment is, however, immoral and is to be deplored, especially by Christians who are themselves people of the covenant. "[Jesus] is mediator of a new covenant" (Heb 9:15; cf. Mt 26:28; 1 Cor 11:25). Christians who are true to their name must also be dissidents in a pagan society when the laws of the state are at variance with the laws of God. Because a practice is legal does not make it moral. The laws that validated racial segregation in the United States and in South Africa are a case in point. Legal abortion is another. Christians must be willing to pay the price for their convictions, as martyrs have always done from antiquity to our own day. Christians will never be popular for the stands they take on moral issues. The words of our Lord Jesus are a prediction of that. "Remember the word I spoke to you, 'No slave is greater than his master.' If they persecuted me, they will also persecute you. If they kept my word, they will also keep yours" (Jn 15:20).

Many Jews endorsed Antiochus' policies of Hellenization. They were mainly from the wealthy and priestly classes who would suffer great losses if they opposed the government. Some no doubt acted in good faith, convinced that they could adjust and adapt the practices of their ancestral faith to the new ways of Greek culture and philosophy. But our author was among those who viewed all

190

such attempts as religious and moral compromises with devastating consequences. Accommodation to the mores and values of a pagan society is the perennial temptation of Christians too. In order to get ahead socially and economically we live by standards that are incompatible with the gospel. We may engage in the externals of Christian faith, like prayer and liturgy, and receive the sacraments regularly. We even make retreats and days of recollection. We read and study scripture and speak about our Christian faith as something important. But our life-style bespeaks a set of values and priorities that are not much different from those of a non-Christian. Success and accumulation of wealth are many people's primary motivations. The result is a less than convincing witness to our professed faith. Adult Christians are sometimes shocked by the pagan attitudes and goals of their children. But children pick up most of their attitudes and goals from their parents.

Antiochus IV did not stop with persecuting the Jewish religion and desecrating the temple. In his arrogance he added to his name the epithet "Epiphanes," which means "[god] Manifest." On coins he put the title "theos," meaning "god," next to his name and had his portrait resemble the image of Olympian Zeus, the principal god of the Greek pantheon, ruler of the heavens, and father of other gods and mortal heroes. Thus Antiochus made "himself greater than any god." For monotheistic Jews these were "dreadful blasphemies against the God of gods" (11:36), the true God of Israel, whom Deuteronomy 10:17 describes as "the God of gods, the LORD of lords, the great God, mighty and awesome." Antiochus did not even have "regard for the gods of his ancestors or for the one in whom women delight," the fertility god Tammuz, called Adonis by the Greeks. The reason is that Antiochus made "himself greater than all" (11:37). Instead of honoring Apollo, one of his ancestral gods, Antiochus worshiped and identified himself with Olympian Zeus, "the god of strongholds" (11:38). The Romans equated Zeus with the god of their fortress in Rome. Antiochus was lavish and provided "with abundant honors" (11:39) those who promoted his policies (1 Mc 2:18; 2 Mc 7:24).

The cult of the fertility god Tammuz/Adonis and the goddess of love Venus is still quite alive today. Television and radio, magazines and videos, all pour out their homage to these "deities." But these gods can only titillate; they cannot save or give meaning. Zeus, "the god of strongholds," like Mars, the Roman god of war, is still venerated by the major powers. The military-industrial complex makes huge profits from the manufacture and sale of weapons of destruction.

The Death of Antiochus IV

Up to 11:39 our author has given us a somewhat veiled history of Antiochus' life as "prophecy after the event." Now he gives what seems to be a forecast of events leading to Antiochus' death, which would happen after the publication of the book (11:40-45). But none of the material given here corresponds to anything we know from other sources. The author, using the biblical convention of imaginative prediction, is nonetheless speaking with authority under divine inspiration. What is being taught here is not the accuracy of those details, which come from the author's creative imagination based on Antiochus' past interventions in Egypt and elsewhere, but the certainty that God will intervene "at the appointed time" (11:40). Since Antiochus committed many of his worst atrocities in Palestine, the author places the locale of the tyrant's death in the hill country to the west of Jerusalem, "between the sea," the Mediterranean, and "the glorious holy mountain," Mount Zion, site of the temple (11:45). Some of these details are based on the apocalyptic struggle between good and evil depicted in Ezekiel 38:1–39:20. As a matter of historical record, however, Antiochus spent his last days seeking to raise money by plundering the wealthy temple of Artemis in Elymais. Repulsed by the angry inhabitants, Antiochus was forced to retreat to Tabae, near Isfahan in Persia, where he was stricken by a mysterious illness and died a miserable death in 164 B.C. (1 Mc 6:1-16). Indeed, there was "none to help him" (11:45), or as 8:25 put it, he was broken, "without a hand being raised."

XX

"Many of Those Who Sleep in the Dust of the Earth Shall Awake"

(Daniel 12:1-12)

[1] "At that time there shall arise
    Michael, the great prince,
    guardian of your people;
It shall be a time unsurpassed in distress
    since nations began until that time.
At that time your people shall escape,
    everyone who is found written in the book.
[2] Many of those who sleep
    in the dust of the earth shall awake;
Some shall live forever,
    others shall be an everlasting horror and disgrace.
[3] But the wise shall shine brightly
    like the splendor of the firmament,
And those who lead the many to justice
    shall be like the stars forever.

[4] "As for you, Daniel, keep secret the message and seal the book until the end time; many shall fall away and evil shall increase."

[5] I, Daniel, looked and saw two others, one standing on either bank of the river. [6] One of them said to the man clothed in linen, who was upstream, "How long shall it be to the end of these appalling things?" [7] The man clothed in linen, who was upstream, lifted his right and left hands to heaven; and I heard him swear by him who lives forever that it should be for a year, two years, a half-year; and that, when the power of the destroyer of the holy people was brought to an end, all these things should end. [8] I heard, but I did not understand; so I asked, "My lord, what follows this?" [9] "Go, Daniel," he said, "because the words are to be kept secret and sealed until the end time. [10] Many shall be

refined, purified, and tested, but the wicked shall prove wicked; none of them shall have understanding, but the wise shall have it. [11]From the time that the daily sacrifice is abolished and the horrible abomination is set up, there shall be one thousand two hundred and ninety days. [12]Blessed is the man who has patience and perseveres until the one thousand three hundred and thirty-five days. [13]Go, take your rest, you shall rise for your reward at the end of days."

We come now to the final section of this long apocalypse that began in 10:1. Here the author expresses his firm conviction in the ultimate vindication of the Jews who had suffered persecution in the reign of terror instigated by Antiochus IV. We should understand 12:1-13 as continuing the prediction of 11:40-45, the imaginative forecast of the tyrant's death. These present verses, however, contain a revelation that is far more significant and consoling than the death of Antiochus. What the author teaches is that the righteous who persevere to the end will receive their reward, not in the present life but in the life to come where they shall live forever.

The Victory of the Righteous

The first four verses (12:1-4) contain the concluding words of the angel's lengthy revelation that began in 10:20. Michael, whom we first met in 10:13 and again in 10:21, appears for the third time to add solemnity to the scene (12:1). As I pointed out before, threefold repetition indicates the superlative degree or emphasis. Thus, the mention of Michael's name three times in this apocalypse highlights the importance of his role in protecting the People of God. The angel tells Daniel that Michael, who earlier had been described as "one of the chief princes" (10:13) and "your prince" (10:21), is indeed "the great prince, guardian of your people" (12:1). Sent by God, Michael, who had earlier overcome the princes of Persia and Greece (10:13, 20-21), now arises to defend and deliver the Israel of faith—the loyal Jews who were persecuted and martyred when they could have saved their lives and their fortunes by abiding by the unjust laws of Antiochus. Unlike the angel who had lots to say to Daniel (10:11–12:4), Michael has no speaking part in the unfolding drama. His presence, however, in this final scene speaks eloquently of the importance of his role as guardian of God's people.

The phrase, "that time," also occurs three times, and in a single verse (12:1). The third, hence most emphatic, occurrence highlights the statement about the end time to come. The expression, "at that time," repeated twice, at the beginning and end of the verse, is found especially in the prophets (Jer 3:17; 4:11; 8:1; 31:1; Jl 4:1-2; Zeph 1:12; 3:19-20; Mt 24:21). It is an eschatological phrase that is used deliberately here to evoke in the readers the certainty regarding the divine intervention to come in the future known to God alone. But before God steps in, there will be "a time unsurpassed in distress since nations began until that time." This is not only a reference to the persecution of Antiochus IV—a persecution that for the author, who lived through it, was indeed unsurpassed. The quoted words are also a literary convention the sacred authors employ to portray the upheavals which, according to the Bible, will accompany the time when God steps into human history to right all wrongs (Ex 9:18; Jer 30:7; Jl 2:1-2; Mt 24:29-31; Mk 13:19; Rv 16:18).

But Daniel's people "shall escape, everyone who is found written in the book" (12:1). In 10:21, mention is made of "the book of truth," a record of the revelation the angel is about to give. One of the Dead Sea Scrolls contains these words: "(Deliver your people) . . . every one who is written in the book of life (or of the living)." The expression, "the book of life," occurs also in Psalm 69:29. The New Testament also speaks of this book in which are inscribed the names of the faithful followers of the Lord (Phil 4:3) and a record of their conduct. "I saw the dead, the great and the lowly, standing before the throne, and scrolls were opened. Then another scroll was opened, the book of life. The dead were judged according to their deeds, by what was written in the scroll" (Rv 20:12; cf. 3:5; 13:8; 17:8; 20:15; 21:27). Only those Jews who have remained unshaken in their faith despite persecution have their names "written in the book." They shall indeed escape from their misery and pain.

Doctrine of the Resurrection

Now we come to the most important, and most discussed, verse of the book (12:2)—the teaching on the resurrection. "Many of those who sleep in the dust of the earth shall awake;/ Some shall live forever, others shall be an everlasting horror and disgrace" (12:2). No matter what the trials and tribulations of the past, there will be an end. God will intervene. He will save his people and reward them beyond their greatest expectations. Here for the first time is a clear teaching on life after death. In the earlier biblical books, Sheol or the netherworld was the final resting place for all mortals—saints and sinners alike. Sheol was not a place of retribution for the virtuous or for the wicked. It was simply viewed as the abode of the dead. Reward for righteousness and punishment for the sin were meted out only in the present life (Lv 26:1-39; Dt 28:1-68). Relics of this idea are still with us—in the so-called Puritan work ethic.

In Sheol the dead had a dull, dark, listless survival totally devoid of anything resembling life. Sheol was simply "the land of oblivion" (Ps 88:13) where one was cut off even from God. "My couch is among the dead, like the slain who lie in the grave, whom you remember no longer and who are cut off from your care" (Ps 88:6). "Anything you can turn your hand to, do with what power you have; for there will be no work, nor reason, nor knowledge, nor wisdom in the netherworld where you are going" (Qoh 9:10). "Give, take, and treat yourself well, for in the netherworld there are no joys to seek" (Sir 14:16). The dead could not even praise God, and life without praise was not worthy of the name. "For among the dead no one remembers you; in the netherworld who gives you thanks?" (Ps 6:6).

There has been much discussion about 12:2. Opinions range from resurrection for all people (good and bad, Jew and non-Jew) to resurrection for only the Jewish martyrs. But this much seems certain. At least two groups of people will receive after death recompense for their deeds: (1) the Jews who remained true to their faith despite persecution; these will be rewarded in the resurrection where they "shall live forever"; and (2) the Jews who gave up their faith rather than suffer for it; after death, these will remain in the grave where they will rot away and be "an everlasting horror and disgrace." In describing the punishment of the wicked, our author had in mind the last verse of Isaiah: "They shall go out and see the corpses of the men who rebelled against me; their worm shall not die, nor their fire be extinguished; and they shall be abhorrent to all mankind" (Is 66:24). Since the author was writing for fellow Jewish believers, it is not likely that he had intended to teach anything regarding retribution after death for non-Jews.

Some scholars have argued that resurrection is taught also in Isaiah 26:19: "But your dead shall live, their corpses shall rise; awake and sing, you who lie in the dust. For your dew is a dew of light, and the land of shades gives birth." But it is more probable that this text merely promises a restoration to the nation after its defeat, as in the vision of the people's dry bones that come back to life in Ezekiel 37:11-14. The text of Daniel 12:2, however, is the first sure teaching on resurrection, at least for the faithful Jews. This teaching becomes even more explicit a few years later in 2 Maccabees 7:7-23; 12:38-46; 14:45-46.

The Wisdom of Solomon, written after Daniel and 2 Maccabees, teaches that the older biblical doctrines on death, Sheol, and earthly reward for virtue and punishment for wickedness (Dt 28:1-68) are not the full story. After death the righteous will be rewarded with immortality (Wis 3:4; 4:1; 8:13, 17; 15:3) and incorruption (Wis 2:23; 6:18, 19). "The souls of the righteous are in the hand of God" (Wis 3:1). Human beings are immortal not because of the native immortality of the soul, as Plato taught. Rather, immortality is a pure gift that God grants to those who are righteous (Wis 6:17-20). The fate of the wicked is less clear, but they "shall be utterly laid waste and shall be in grief and their memory shall perish" (Wis 4:19). Later Jewish literature and of course the New Testament are more explicit regarding retribution for the wicked as well as the virtuous. The teaching of Jesus in Matthew 25:31-46 is a good example.

Regarding the mystery of death, the "Pastoral Constitution on the Church in the Modern World" (*Gaudium et Spes*) of Vatican II, states: "It is in the face of death that the riddle of human existence becomes most acute. Not only are human beings tormented by pain and by the advancing deterioration of their bodies, but even more so by a dread of perpetual extinction. They rightly follow the intuition of their hearts when they abhor and repudiate the absolute ruin and total disappearance of their own persons" (#18). "Through Christ and in Christ, the riddles of sorrow and death grow meaningful. Apart from his gospel, they overwhelm us. Christ has risen, destroying death by his death. He has lavished life upon us so that, as children in the Son, we can cry out in the Spirit: Abba, Father! (Rom 8:15; Gal 4:6)" (#22).

Death is part of life. All living creatures must come to an end. But death for those who believe in the Lord Jesus, who rose from the dead, is not the end of their existence. Death is a transition from this mortal life to life immortal with God. So we can exclaim with Paul: " 'Death is swallowed up in victory. Where, O death, is your victory? Where, O death, is your sting?' The sting of death is sin, and the power of sin is the law. But thanks be to God who gives us the victory through our Lord Jesus Christ" (1 Cor 15:54-57). Paul also declared, "The Spirit itself bears witness with our spirit that we are children of God, and if children, then heirs, heirs of God and joint heirs with Christ, if only we suffer with him so that we may also be glorified with him. I consider that the sufferings of this present time are as nothing compared with the glory to be revealed for us" (Rom 8:16-18).

Special Reward for the Wise Leaders

Our author now speaks of the fate of "the wise" (Hebrew *maskilim*), mentioned in this apocalypse the emphatic number of three times (11:35; 12:3, 10). These will receive special glory in the resurrection, for they "shall shine brightly like the splendor of the firmament." The wise steadfastly upheld the law of Moses and vigorously opposed the policy of Hellenization. They also were in the forefront of the non-violent resistance, thus leading "the many to justice." For their courage in the face of extreme peril to their lives, "the wise" will be distinguished from the rest of the martyrs, for they "shall be like the stars forever" (12:3). The stars here, as in Job 38:7, probably symbolize the angels. Thus, these stalwart leaders would share in the splendor of the angels themselves.

After completing the revelation, the angel tells Daniel to "keep secret the message and seal the book until the end time." Gabriel had given Daniel a similar order in 8:26. The "end time" is evidently a reference to the time of publication of the book when other faithful Jews could read this apocalypse and so be motivated to remain loyal to their faith. The sealing of a book was serious business (Is 29:11). Only authorized persons could break the seal. "I saw a scroll in the right hand of the one who sat on the throne. It had writing on both sides and was sealed with seven seals. . . . I shed many tears because no one was found worthy to open the scroll or to examine it. One of the elders said to me, 'Do not weep. The lion of the tribe of Judah, the root of David, has triumphed, enabling him to open the scroll with its seven seals' " (Rv 5:1, 4-5).

Epilogue

Daniel now sees two angels, "standing on either bank of the river" (12:5), first mentioned in 10:4. The reason for these two is that testimony given under oath required two or three witnesses (Dt 19:15). One angel asks the other, "who was clothed in linen," the "how long" question, which we first saw in 8:13, regarding "the end of these appalling things" (12:6). The other raises not only his right hand, the customary one in oaths, but also his left, to add solemnity; he swears that it should be for "a year, two years, a half-year." This is the identical expression given in 7:25; in 9:27, the same time span is given as "half the week" of years. The "destroyer of the holy people," Antiochus IV, and his persecution would then come to an end (12:7). Daniel hears but does not understand this message; so he asks for enlightenment (12:8).

The angel simply tells Daniel to go his way, for "the words are to be kept secret and sealed until the end time" (12:9)—the same instructions given in 12:4. The angel speaks again of the persecution in which many Jews will be "refined, purified, and tested"—words used only of "the wise" in 11:35. The "wicked" are the Jews who compromised their faith; they have no understanding of God's ways in permitting the persecution to take place. But "the wise" do understand (12:10). Next the angel gives the amount of time in which "the horrible abomination" (the statue of Zeus, as in 8:13) would remain in the temple: 1,290 days (12:11). The time given in 8:14 is 1,150 days. Actually, the statue was removed after 1,103 days when the temple was reconsecrated (1 Mc 4:52-53). In 12:12 the angel blesses those who persevere 1,335 days. It may be that different editors of the book are responsible for these numbers. But more likely, the numbers are used symbolically, as in most other cases. The original readers no doubt understood the symbolism here, but it eludes us today. Finally, the angel tells Daniel to take his rest, in the grave (Is 57:1-2). But that will not be the end of Daniel, for he will rise to receive his "reward at the end of days" (12:13). Thus, the final apocalypse comes to a close. As Moses Stuart has observed in his old commentary (1850), this conclusion is "an assurance full of comfort to him, who was now very far advanced in life; and full of comfort to all who walk in his steps, and are animated by his spirit."

Concluding Remarks

The many obscurities of language and symbolism in these five apocalypses serve as timely reminders that the Book of Daniel should not be read as a collection of predictions regarding recent or current events. Fundamentalist Christians and television evangelists, however, have read into these apocalypses all sorts of things that have happened throughout history up to our own day, including the Gulf crisis in 1990-91 and the tragedy in Waco, Texas, where David Koresh and many of his Branch Davidian followers were burnt to death in 1993. As we approach the turn of the millennium, fundamentalists have already begun to come forward with even more prognostications about "the end" being near. They see in the "thousand years" of Revelation 20:1-6 a reference to the year 2000. But the expression, "a thousand years," like other numbers in Revelation and the rest of the Bible, is not to be taken literally but symbolically as the long interval between Satan's being "tied up" (symbol of Jesus' life-death-resurrection victory over the forces of evil and death itself) and the end of the world. The "end" is known to God alone, as Jesus forcefully reminded us. "But of that day and hour no one knows, neither the angels of heaven, nor the Son, but the Father alone" (Mt 24:36).

It would be consummate arrogance for anyone to misuse the Bible to suggest a more precise timetable.

XXI

"A Very Beautiful and God-fearing Woman, Susanna"

(Daniel 13:1-27)

¹In Babylon there lived a man named Joakim, ²who married a very beautiful and God-fearing woman, Susanna, the daughter of Hilkiah; ³her pious parents had trained their daughter according to the law of Moses. ⁴Joakim was very rich; he had a garden near his house, and the Jews had recourse to him often because he was the most respected of them all.

⁵That year, two elders of the people were appointed judges, of whom the Lord said, "Wickedness has come out of Babylon: from the elders who were to govern the people as judges." ⁶These men, to whom all brought their cases, frequented the house of Joakim. ⁷When the people left at noon, Susanna used to enter her husband's garden for a walk. ⁸When the old men saw her enter every day for her walk, they began to lust for her. ⁹They suppressed their consciences; they would not allow their eyes to look to heaven, and did not keep in mind just judgments. ¹⁰Though both were enamored of her, they did not tell each other their trouble, ¹¹for they were ashamed to reveal their lustful desire to have her. ¹²Day by day they watched eagerly for her. ¹³One day they said to each other, "Let us be off for home, it is time for lunch." So they went out and parted; ¹⁴but both turned back, and when they met again, they asked each other the reason. They admitted their lust, and then they agreed to look for an occasion when they could meet her alone.

¹⁵One day, while they were waiting for the right moment, she entered the garden as usual, with two maids only. She decided to bathe, for the weather was warm. ¹⁶Nobody else was there except the two elders, who had hidden themselves and were watching her. ¹⁷"Bring me oil and ointments," she said to the maids, "and shut the garden doors while I bathe." ¹⁸They did as

she said; they shut the garden doors and left by the side gate to fetch what she had ordered, unaware that the elders were hidden inside.

[19] As soon as the maids had left, the two old men got up and hurried to her. [20] "Look," they said, "the garden doors are shut, and no one can see us; give in to our desire, and lie with us. [21] If you refuse, we will testify against you that you dismissed your maids because a young man was here with you."

[22] "I am completely trapped," Susanna groaned. "If I yield, it will be my death; if I refuse, I cannot escape your power. [23] Yet it is better for me to fall into your power without guilt than to sin before the Lord." [24] Then Susanna shrieked, and the old men also shouted at her, [25] as one of them ran to open the garden doors. [26] When the people in the house heard the cries from the garden, they rushed in by the side gate to see what had happened to her. [27] At the accusations by the old men, the servants felt very much ashamed, for never had any such thing been said about Susanna.

We now come to the Appendix of the book with the three charming narratives of Susanna (chap. 13), Bel (14:1-22), and the Dragon (14:23-42). Unlike the homiletic stories of chapters 1–6, these are entertaining folktales with all the elements of a good short story— characterization, suspense, plot, and denouement. Susanna is unique because the action takes place in the local Jewish community and court, and not in the pagan royal courts, as in the other stories. Susanna is also the first detective story in world literature; and as courtroom drama, it anticipates by over two thousand years the Perry Mason and Matlock mysteries and other popular television shows and movies. Susanna is a story of a woman's conjugal chastity triumphing over the lust and deceit of two male elders of the Jewish community.

The story may also be read as a parable. The two lawless elders, one of whom Daniel calls "offspring of Canaan" (13:56), would symbolize the apostate Jews, especially under Antiochus IV Epiphanes, who tried to get the loyal Jews, symbolized by Susanna, to abandon their religion. The prophets often called apostasy from the Lord "fornication" and "adultery" (Is 1:21; 57:3; Jer 3:8-9; 5:7; 13:27; Ez 6:9; 23:27; Hos 2:4). Thus, Susanna's courageous response to the two lechers—"If I yield, it will be my death; if I refuse, I cannot escape your power. Yet it is better for me to fall into your power without guilt than to sin before the Lord" (13:22-23)— would express exactly the conviction of the Jews who were martyred rather then give up their faith.

The story of Susanna has captivated artists throughout the ages. Of all the women in the Old Testament, Susanna is probably the most depicted in art. Catacomb frescoes from the second to the fourth centuries represent various scenes from the story. One of the most striking paintings, found in the Cemetery of Pretestato, is a mid-fourth-century work in which Susanna is portrayed as a lamb between two wolves. The early seventeenth-century frescoes of Baldassare Croce in the Church of Santa Susanna, Rome, cover the whole story.

The three stories in the Appendix have come down to us in Greek. But today most scholars agree that Hebrew is the original language. Unfortunately, the Hebrew text is no longer extant. Most translations are based upon the Theodotion form of the stories. In the Septuagint form, there are differences, some of which will be noted in my commentary.

Susanna's Virtue

Right at the outset, as in any good short story, we get the setting, which is Babylon, and then the characters of the narrative. In Hebrew, Joakim, the name of Susanna's husband (13:1), means "Yahweh will establish." This name gives us a hint as to the outcome of the story when the Lord "will establish" the innocence of Susanna. Her name in Hebrew means "lily." In the catacombs of Domitilla and Callistus and in the mosaics at Ravenna, flowers signified the state of the saints in heaven, the lily symbolizing virginity. In the late Middle Ages, the lily represented purity, Christ, Mary, and particularly the Annunciation. In Susanna's case, the lily indeed symbolizes her purity. Like Sarah (Tb 6:2) and Judith (Jdt 8:7-8), Susanna was very beautiful (13:2, 32). She was the daughter of Hilkiah, which in Hebrew means "Yahweh is my portion." Her pious parents honored their responsibilities by training her in the "law of Moses" (13:3; see Dt 4:9; 6:6-7). Like Joseph,

Job, Tobit, and Judith, Susanna was very rich, and her husband had great respect in the Jewish community (13:4). But her wealth and status did not distract her from her religious obligations. She was a "God-fearing woman," which means she was wise and observed the commandments. For as Ben Sira observes, "Those who fear the LORD disobey not his words; those who love him keep his ways. Those who fear the LORD seek to please him, those who love him are filled with his law" (Sir 2:15-16).

The Wicked Elders and Their Conspiracy

Now the plot thickens. Into this scene of family serenity and bliss enter two wicked "elders of the people," who had been appointed judges (13:5). These men were supposed to be paragons of justice and righteousness (Lv 19:15). Instead, they were corrupt to the core. As the old Latin proverb puts it: *Corruptio optimi pessima*, "Corruption of the best is the worst." These elders, being leaders of the community, also enjoyed hospitality in the house of Joakim (13:6). In the afternoon Susanna used to take a walk in the garden. The two elders, seeing her every day, "began to lust for her," suppressing "their consciences," not allowing "their eyes to look to heaven," and not keeping in mind "just judgments" (13:8-9). The sequence here is often the same as in our own fall into sin: temptation, suppressing the voice of conscience, refusing to consider the spiritual effects of our action, and ignoring the just judgment of God. Ashamed of their lustful desire, neither told the other about their designs on Susanna. Each tried to get the other to get out of the way so that they could satisfy their lust alone with her. But both came back to the garden; now it was useless to conceal their intentions. So they shamelessly "admitted their lust," and conspired to meet her when she was by herself (13:10-14). Sinners love company.

The wisdom literature of the Old Testament was brutally frank in warning about temptations and sins of the flesh. "Lust indulged starves the soul, but fools hate to turn from evil" (Prv 13:19). "Go not after your lusts but keep your desires in check. If you satisfy your lustful appetites they will make you the sport of your enemies" (Sir 18:30-31). Keen observers of the human scene, the sages knew that sexual appetites do not go away with age. "Three kinds of men I hate; their manner of life I loathe indeed: A proud pauper, a rich dissembler, and an old man lecherous in his dotage" (Sir 25:2). Often the advice of the biblical authors in sexual matters was self-serving and pragmatic, for they realized that we need as many motives as possible to keep the commandments. Sexual sins were not only contrary to God's will but were also contrary to a person's best interests. "Entertain no thoughts against a virgin, lest you be enmeshed in damages for her. Give not yourself to harlots, lest you surrender your inheritance. Gaze not about the lanes of the city and wander not through its squares. Avert your eyes from a comely woman; gaze not upon the beauty of another's wife. Through woman's beauty many perish, for lust for it burns like fire" (Sir 9:5-8). Ever the realist, Ben Sira knew his own weaknesses; so he says a prayer that we could all take to heart: "A brazen look allow me not; ward off passion from my heart. Let not the lustful cravings of the flesh master me, surrender me not to shameless desires" (Sir 23:5-6).

The Attempted Rape

Now the scene is set for entrapping Susanna. On a hot day she decides to take a bath in the garden pool. A perfectly innocent thing to do, for she thought she was alone except for her two maids who usually accompanied her. But the two lecherous men had hidden in the garden to watch her. She asked the maids to bring "oil and ointments" for use after her bath (cf. 2 Sm 12:20; Ru 3:3; Jdt 10:3). Oil was often perfumed to make a fragrant ointment (Mt 26:7). She then tells the maids to shut the garden doors to preserve her modesty while she bathed. The maids did as they were told, leaving by a side gate, presumably the servants gate, "unaware that the elders were hidden inside" (13:18). After the maids left, the two old "peeping Toms" ran up to Susanna, reminding her that the garden doors were shut, so that no one can see them.

In their attempted rape, they ordered Susanna to give in to their sinful passion, telling her "to lie with us" (13:20), literally, "to be with us"—the author's delicate euphemism for sexual intercourse (Gn 39:10; 2 Sm 13:20). If she refused, they threatened to testify against her that she dismissed her maids because a young man "was with" her (13:21), the same euphemism as before. Their threat of accusing Susanna of the capital crime of adultery with a young man, if she refused to submit to them, constitutes serious force. Hence, their crime is attempted rape and not seduction, as is often assumed by scholars. Seduction occurs when one induces or persuades another to have sexual intercourse. That is hardly the case here. What is especially contemptible is that the two men abused their power and authority as elders of the Jewish community in their attempt to rape Susanna. As Lord Acton once astutely remarked, "Power tends to corrupt and absolute power corrupts absolutely" ("Letter to Bishop Mandell Creighton" [April 5, 1887]). Sad to say, history knows of many others in religious institutions who have exploited their power and status to gain the trust and confidence of those to whom they were sexually attracted in order to rape or seduce them. The strong words of Jesus come to mind: "Things that cause sin will inevitably occur, but woe to the person through whom they occur. It would be better for him if a millstone were put around his neck and he be thrown into the sea than for him to cause one of these little ones to sin" (Lk 17:1-2).

Susanna's Refusal to Submit to Rape

Despite the threats of the two elders, Susanna refused to submit to their attempted rape. She tells them what they as elders should have known, even though in their burning passion they preferred not to think of it. If she yielded to their lust, it would mean death for her (13:22) as well as for them, for in the law of Moses, which Susanna learned from her pious parents (13:3), the punishment for failure to cry out during an attempted rape was death for both the man and the woman (Dt 22:23-24). She chooses to become the victim of the vicious plot of the two lechers, telling them courageously: "It is better for me to fall into your power without guilt than to sin before the Lord" (13:23). Susanna chose to be falsely accused of adultery "without guilt" (13:3) rather than to commit the actual crime of adultery for which the penalty was death (Lv 20:10; Dt 22:22; Jn 8:5). When the wife of Potiphar tried to seduce Joseph, who, like Susanna, was "strikingly handsome in countenance and body," Joseph refused her advances, saying, "How could I commit so great a wrong and thus stand condemned before God?" (Gn 39:9). There comes a moment of decision in moral matters when one must take a stand even at great personal risk.

Susanna cried out with a loud voice because she was threatened with rape. Her shriek is in keeping with the law in Deuteronomy. "If within the city a man comes upon a maiden who is betrothed, and has relations with her, you shall bring them both out to the gate of the city and there stone them to death: the girl because she did not cry out for help though she was in the city, and the man because he violated his neighbor's wife. Thus shall you purge the evil from your midst" (Dt 22:23-24). Thus, Susanna cried out to seek help. The old men also shouted, but their cry was to fulfill their threat to falsely accuse Susanna of adultery. Then one of them opened both garden doors. Hearing the cries from the garden, the people in the house "rushed in by the side gate to see what had happened to her" (13:26). The two lechers accused Susanna exactly as they had threatened to do. The servants "felt very much ashamed, for never had any such thing been said about Susanna" (13:27).

Some Reflections

Sex is a powerful force in our lives, no matter what our age. It is a force that needs to be held in check. If we do not control our sexual impulses and appetites, they will control us and debase us. Today the crisis that Susanna faced has changed only in the details. Sexual harassment is an unfortunate fact of life. Some men and women have used their power or position like the two elders—to obtain sexual gratification from their subordinates. In order to loosen the moral inhibitions of a person reluctant to yield to pressure for sexual favors, others have used alcohol or drugs, or have appealed to the slogan, "Everybody does it." Equally deplorable is the use of sex to obtain from superiors advancement in employment or career.

We should also keep in mind what Jesus says about lustful glances: "You have heard that it was said, 'You shall not commit adultery.' But I say to you, everyone who looks at a woman with lust has already committed adultery with her in his heart" (Mt 5:27-28). This does not mean that looking at and admiring a person's beauty and physical attributes is immoral. We read, for example, of Judith's beauty: "She was beautifully formed and lovely to behold" (Jdt 8:7). And Esther receives these compliments: "She glowed with the perfection of her beauty and her countenance was as joyous as it was lovely" (Est D:5). Obviously, the sacred authors who wrote these words appreciated and celebrated the beauty of women. For after all, God is the one who made the bodies of women and men beautiful. And God knows we are not blind. So when we admire and praise a person's beauty we admire and praise the Lord who created it. "From the greatness and the beauty of created things their original author, by analogy, is seen" (Wis 13:5).

Accordingly, looking at a beautiful person is not wrong. What can lead us into sin is our lack of self-control and our failure to keep our desires in check. For, as Jesus has told us, "From within people, from their hearts, come evil thoughts, unchastity, theft, murder, adultery, greed, malice, deceit, licentiousness, envy, blasphemy, arrogance, folly. All these evils come from within and they defile" (Mk 7:21-23). In our relationships with others, we should keep in mind the words of Titus 1:15: "To the clean all things are clean, but to those who are defiled and unbelieving nothing is clean; in fact, both their minds and their consciences are tainted."

XXII

"She Trusted in the Lord Wholeheartedly"

(Daniel 13:28-63)

[28] When the people came to her husband Joakim the next day, the two wicked elders also came, fully determined to put Susanna to death. Before all the people they ordered: [29] "Send for Susanna, the daughter of Hilkiah, the wife of Joakim." When she was sent for, [30] she came with her parents, children and all her relatives. [31] Susanna, very delicate and beautiful, [32] was veiled; but those wicked men ordered her to uncover her face so as to sate themselves with her beauty. [33] All her relatives and the onlookers were weeping.

[34] In the midst of the people the two elders got up and laid their hands on her head. [35] Through her tears she looked up to heaven, for she trusted in the Lord wholeheartedly. [36] The elders made this accusation: "As we were walking in the garden alone, this woman entered with two girls and shut the doors of the garden, dismissing the girls. [37] A young man, who was hidden there, came and lay with her. [38] When we, in a corner of the garden, saw this crime, we ran toward them. [39] We saw them lying together, but the man we could not hold, because he was stronger than we; he opened the doors and ran off. [40] Then we seized this one and asked who the young man was, [41] but she refused to tell us. We testify to this." The assembly believed them, since they were elders and judges of the people, and they condemned her to death.

[42] But Susanna cried aloud: "O eternal God, you know what is hidden and are aware of all things before they come to be: [43] You know that they have testified falsely against me. Here I am about to die, though I have done none of the things with which these wicked men have charged me."

[44] The Lord heard her prayer. [45] As she was being led to execution, God stirred up the holy spirit of a young boy named

Daniel, ⁴⁶ and he cried aloud: "I will have no part in the death of this woman." ⁴⁷All the people turned and asked him, "What is this you are saying?" ⁴⁸He stood in their midst and continued, "Are you such fools, O Israelites! To condemn a woman of Israel without examination and without clear evidence? ⁴⁹Return to court, for they have testified falsely against her."

⁵⁰Then all the people returned in haste. To Daniel the elders said, "Come, sit with us and inform us, since God has given you the prestige of old age." ⁵¹But he replied, "Separate these two far from one another that I may examine them."

⁵²After they were separated one from the other, he called one of them and said: "How you have grown evil with age! Now have your past sins come to term: ⁵³passing unjust sentences, condemning the innocent, and freeing the guilty, although the Lord says, 'The innocent and the just you shall not put to death.' ⁵⁴Now, then, if you were a witness, tell me under what tree you saw them together." ⁵⁵"Under a mastic tree," he answered. "Your fine lie has cost you your head," said Daniel; "for the angel of God shall receive the sentence from him and split you in two." ⁵⁶Putting him to one side, he ordered the other one to be brought. "Offspring of Canaan, not of Judah," Daniel said to him, "beauty has seduced you, lust has subverted your conscience. ⁵⁷This is how you acted with the daughters of Israel, and in their fear they yielded to you; but a daughter of Judah did not tolerate your wickedness. ⁵⁸Now, then, tell me under what tree you surprised them together." ⁵⁹"Under an oak," he said. "Your fine lie has cost you also your head," said Daniel; "for the angel of God waits with a sword to cut you in two so as to make an end of you both." ⁶⁰The whole assembly cried aloud, blessing God who saves those that hope in him. ⁶¹They rose up against the two elders, for by their own words Daniel had convicted them of perjury. According to the law of Moses, they inflicted on them the penalty they had plotted to impose on their neighbor: ⁶²They put them to death. Thus was innocent blood spared that day.

⁶³Hilkiah and his wife praised God for their daughter Susanna, as did Joakim her husband and all her relatives, because she was found innocent of any shameful deed. ⁶⁴And from that day onward Daniel was greatly esteemed by the people.

The two elders, whose attempted rape had failed, now do what they had threatened to do. They falsely accuse Susanna of committing adultery with a young man in the garden. Since they were judges in the community as well as elders, the assembly believed them and condemned Susanna to death. At the last moment Daniel shows up to rescue the innocent woman. The elders are then put to death instead.

The Elders Bear False Witness against Susanna

The poet William Congreve once wrote: "Heaven has no rage like love to hatred turned,/ Nor hell a fury like a woman scorned" (*The Mourning Bride*, I, i [1697]). These words describe exactly the feelings of "the two wicked elders," literally, "the two elders full of lawless intentions" (13:28). These men had been entrusted with upholding the law of Moses. Not only have they violated their sacred trust by their attempted rape, but they are also "fully determined to put Susanna to death" in order to cover up their crime. They summoned her to appear before all the people. She comes with "her parents, children, and all her relatives" (13:30).

Being a woman of refinement and great beauty (13:31), Susanna was "veiled," but the lawless men ordered her to be unveiled, "so as to sate themselves with her beauty" (13:31). All who saw this humiliation of Susanna wept (13:33). In the Septuagint form of the story, Susanna is stripped and exposed naked for the crowd to see—the punishment for women who had committed adultery (Hos 2:4-12; Ez 16:37-39). The two elders "got up" (the same verb is used in 13:19 to describe their action in the garden) and "laid their hands on her" (13:34)—the ritual required when witnesses testified in a capital crime (Lv 24:14). The irony here is striking, for this is the only time the two lechers, who had conspired to have sexual contact with Susanna, actually touch her. In tears, Susanna "looked up to heaven, for she trusted in the Lord wholeheartedly" (13:35). Her actions contrast sharply with the actions of the lawless elders, who in 13:9 had "suppressed their consciences" and did not "look to heaven."

The two elders now give their false testimony under oath, accusing "this woman," literally "this one" (13:36), of committing adultery with a young man in the garden. They said they could not lay hold of the young man, because he was too strong for them; so he escaped from the garden. But they did seize "this one" (13:40), but she refused to identify the young man. The two elders never refer to Susanna by name, but use rather the Greek pronoun "this one." In the present context "this one" implies contempt as if to suggest that Susanna is nothing more than a sexual object for them. Neither is the pornographer interested in the name or personhood of the women and men he depicts lasciviously; they are to be viewed merely as sexual toys. The two elders finish their perjured testimony by affirming solemnly, "We testify to this" (13:41). Believing them because "they were elders and judges of the people," the assembly condemned Susanna to death.

Susanna's Prayer for Deliverance

Susanna, who had earlier "looked up to heaven" and "trusted in the Lord" (13:35), now takes the stand in her own defense and testifies in prayer, appealing to the Judge of all. God knows not only "what is hidden" but also "all things before they come to be" (13:42)—a truth clearly stated also in Sirach 42:18, though many translations, which follow the Greek instead of the Hebrew, miss the point. God knows, as Susanna reminds him, that the lawless elders have testified falsely against her. She concludes by affirming solemnly that she is innocent of the charges made against her (13:43).

God hears her prayer, stirring up "the holy spirit of a young boy named Daniel" (13:45), who comes to her rescue. The very name Daniel means "God is my judge." He cries aloud, "I will have no part in the death of this woman" (13:46). He then upbraids the people for condemning Susanna without proper cross-examination and clear evidence (cf. Dt 19:15-20). He orders them to return to court. This scene is behind Shylock's famous lines when Portia, disguised as the young judge Balthazar, seems to favor his case: "A Daniel come to judgment! Yea, a Daniel!/ O wise young judge, how I do honour thee!" (Shakespeare, *The Merchant of Venice*, IV, i, 222-23).

What is of special interest is that the person God stirred up to deliver Susanna was not one of the upright elders of the community, but rather a young boy named Daniel. In antiquity, the young were taught to know their place and to keep their mouth shut in the presence of their elders. "Young man, speak only when necessary, when they have asked you more than once. Be brief, but say much in those few words, be like the wise man, taciturn. When among your elders be not forward, and with officials be not too insistent" (Sir 32:7-9). The reason is that the young were thought to lack the experience necessary for attaining understanding and wisdom. "So with old age is wisdom, and with length of days understanding" (Jb 12:12). That is why Ben Sira says to the young, "Frequent the company of the elders; whoever is wise, stay close to him" (Sir 6:34).

But in our story, God chooses a young boy to save Susanna. God "stirred up the holy spirit" of Daniel (13:45); in 4:5 and 5:11, Daniel is said to possess "the spirit of the holy God," and in 5:14, "the spirit of God." So Daniel stands up courageously in the midst of the entire community, including all the good elders who were thought to be wise, and calls them "fools" for condemning "a woman of Israel without examination" (13:48). With his God-given wisdom Daniel then successfully prosecutes the two wicked elders. God chooses whom he wills for his purposes. Our expectations cannot restrict God's choices or manner of action. The prophet Isaiah gives us the reason: "For my thoughts are not your thoughts, nor are your ways my ways, says the LORD. As high as the heavens are above the earth, so high are my ways above your ways and my thoughts above your thoughts" (Is 55:8-9). That is why the young should take heart when they are called by God for a particular task. Obstacles appear formidable. But God never calls us to do his work without giving us the grace and strength to bring it to completion. The call of the young man Jeremiah to become a prophet is an outstanding example (Jer 1:4-10).

Daniel's Cross-Examination

Daniel now conducts his famous cross-examination of the two lawless elders. The other elders ask Daniel to sit in judgment with them since God had given him "the prestige of old age" (13:50)—wisdom. Daniel orders the two men to be separated from each other. He summoned one of them, accusing him of growing "evil

213

with age" (13:52)—in stark contrast with the proverb that one becomes wise with age (Jb 12:12; Sir 6:18). Daniel accuses the elder of serious crimes of injustice: "passing unjust sentences, condemning the innocent, and freeing the guilty" (13:53), all of which are condemned in Exodus 23:6-7. Next comes Daniel's famous question: Under what tree did the elder see Susanna and the young man lying together? The elder answered, "Under the mastic tree [Greek *schinos*]." Daniel replies: Your lie has cost you your head, for the angel of God "shall split you in two" [Greek *schisei*]. The wordplay in the Greek words *schinos* and *schisei* is deliberate and ironic to imply that the elder has pronounced the death sentence on himself.

Next Daniel brings in the other elder, calling him "offspring of Canaan," a reference to the sexual sins of Canaan in Genesis 9:20-27 and Leviticus 18:24-30. He accuses the elder of sexual sins with the daughters of Israel; but Susanna, "a daughter of Judah," refused to yield to his lust. Daniel then asks this elder the same question regarding the tree where the alleged crime took place. The answer was: "Under an oak [Greek *prinos*]." Daniel again replies: Your lie has cost you your head, for the angel of God shall "cut you in two" [Greek *prisai*]. Once more the ironic wordplay in Greek indicates the elder's punishment. The contradiction between the perjured statements of the two elders is dramatized by the contrast between the mastic tree, which is quite small, and the oak, which is very large.

The Vindication of Susanna and Punishment of the Elders

At the conclusion of Daniel's brilliant cross-examination, "the whole assembly cried aloud, blessing God who saves those that hope in him." Indeed, Susanna was a woman who trusted in the Lord (13:35) and hoped in him (13:60). Being a "God-fearing woman" (13:2), Susanna followed the injunctions of Ben Sira: "You who fear the LORD, trust in him, and your reward will not be lost. You who fear the LORD, hope for good things, for lasting joy and mercy" (Sir 2:8-9). The assembly passed judgment on the two perjured elders. "According to the law of Moses, they inflicted on them the penalty they had plotted to impose on their neighbor:

They put them to death" (13:61-62). The law is found in the Pentateuch: "If an unjust witness takes the stand against a person to accuse him of a defection from the law, the two parties in the dispute shall appear before the LORD in the presence of the priests or judges in office at that time; and if after a thorough investigation the judges find that the witness is a false witness and has accused his kin falsely, you shall do to him as he planned to do to his kin. Thus shall you purge the evil from your midst" (Dt 19:16-19).

Thus was the innocent blood of Susanna spared that day. Her whole family—her father Hilkiah and her mother, her husband and all her relatives—joined in praise of God because Susanna "was found innocent of any shameful deed" (13:63). God did indeed come to her rescue. And because of the brilliant courtroom tactics, which proved that the lawless elders had lied about Susanna, Daniel became "greatly esteemed by the people" (13:64). The young Daniel, whom God had raised up for the occasion, had proved to be wiser than any of the older members of the community.

Alas, predicaments like Susanna's often do not have a happy ending. The vindication of the innocent does not always happen in the present life. Corrupt judges and juries have accepted bribes to convict the innocent or acquit the guilty. Yet the Old Testament is unambiguous in its condemnation of such abuses of power. "You shall keep away from anything dishonest. The innocent and the just you shall not put to death, nor shall you acquit the guilty" (Ex 23:7). "You shall not distort justice; you must be impartial. You shall not take a bribe; for a bribe blinds the eyes even of the wise and twists the words even of the just" (Dt 16:19). The abuse of power in sexual matters is equally grievous and condemned by God. When King David at the height of his power had committed adultery with Bathsheba and made her pregnant, he tried to cover up his crime by getting her husband Uriah the Hittite to sleep with her. When Uriah refused to do so, David had him murdered, so that he could have Bathsheba to himself. But the Lord did not allow David to get away with his multiple crimes, but punished him severely (2 Sm 11:2–12:12).

XXIII

"The Babylonians Had an Idol Called Bel"

(Daniel 14:1-22)

[1] After King Astyages was laid with his fathers, Cyrus the Persian succeeded to his kingdom. [2] Daniel was the king's favorite and was held in higher esteem than any of the friends of the king. [3] The Babylonians had an idol called Bel, and every day they provided for it twelve bushels of fine flour, forty sheep, and six measures of wine. [4] The king worshiped it and went every day to adore it; but Daniel adored only his God. [5] When the king asked him, "Why do you not adore Bel?" Daniel replied, "Because I worship not idols made with hands, but only the living God who made heaven and earth and has dominion over all mankind." [6] Then the king continued, "You do not think Bel is a living god? Do you not see how much he eats and drinks every day?" [7] Daniel began to laugh. "Do not be deceived, O king," he said; "it is only clay inside and bronze outside; it has never taken any food or drink." [8] Enraged, the king called his priests and said to them, "Unless you tell me who it is that consumes these provisions, you shall die. [9] But if you can show that Bel consumes them, Daniel shall die for blaspheming Bel." Daniel said to the king, "Let it be as you say!" [10] There were seventy priests of Bel, besides their wives and children.

When the king went with Daniel into the temple of Bel, [11] the priests of Bel said, "See, we are going to leave. Do you, O king, set out the food and prepare the wine; then shut the door and seal it with your ring. [12] If you do not find that Bel has eaten it all when you return in the morning, we are to die; otherwise Daniel shall die for his lies against us." [13] They were not perturbed, because under the table they had made a secret entrance through which they always came in to consume the food. [14] After they departed the king set the food before Bel, while Daniel ordered his servants to bring some ashes, which they scattered through the whole temple; the king alone was present. Then they went outside, sealed the closed door with the king's ring, and departed. [15]The priests entered that night as usual, with their wives and children, and they ate and drank everything.

[16]Early the next morning, the king came with Daniel. [17]"Are the seals unbroken, Daniel?" he asked. And Daniel answered, "They are unbroken, O king." [18]As soon as he had opened the door, the king looked at the table and cried aloud, "Great you are, O Bel; there is no trickery in you." [19]But Daniel laughed and kept the king from entering. "Look at the floor," he said; "whose footprints are these?" [20]"I see the footprints of men, women, and children!" said the king. [21]The angry king arrested the priests, their wives, and their children. They showed him the secret door by which they used to enter to consume what was on the table. [22]He put them to death, and handed Bel over to Daniel, who destroyed it and its temple.

The stories of Bel and the Dragon, which conclude the Book of Daniel, are biting satires on the folly and futility of idol worship. The mocking of idols and their makers is a common motif in the Old Testament (Pss 115:4-8; 135:15-18; Is 40:18-20; 44:9-20; 46:6-7; Bar 6; Hab 2:18-19; Wis 13:1-16:1). The scathing words of Jeremiah 10:3-5 are typical: "For the cult idols of the nations are nothing, wood cut from the forest, wrought by craftsmen with the adze, adorned with silver and gold. With nails and hammers they are fastened, that they may not totter. Like a scarecrow in a cucumber field are they, they cannot speak. They must be carried about, for they cannot walk. Fear them not, they can do no harm, neither is it in their power to do good."

The narrative of Bel, like that of Susanna, is also an interesting and clever detective story. Daniel appears again at the royal court, as in the stories of chapters 1–6, this time in the court of Cyrus the Persian, the monarch mentioned in 1:21; 6:29; and 10:1. Like Susanna, this story is well constructed in terms of characterization, plot, suspense, and denouement; and it is entertaining as well.

Daniel Refuses to Worship the Idol Bel

Cyrus the Persian captured the kingdom of the last Median ruler, Astyages (585-50 B.C.). In 539 B.C. he seized Babylon, the setting for the stories of Bel and the Dragon. We were told in 6:29 that Daniel "fared well . . . in the reign of Cyrus the Persian." So in 14:2, Daniel is described as "the king's favorite." He is held in higher esteem than any of "the friends of the king"—an expression for those who held top positions in the court (1 Mc 10:20; 13:36; 15:32; Jn 19:12). In the Septuagint form, 14:2 reads: "There was once a priest, Daniel by name, the son of Abal, a favorite of the king of Babylon." Since the text of 1:3 and 6 says nothing about the priesthood of Daniel, this reading may represent an earlier version of the story before it was attached as an appendix to the book.

The god Bel (in Hebrew *ba'al*, meaning "master, lord") became identified with the chief Babylonian deity Marduk, also called Merodach (Is 46:1; Jer 50:2; 51:44). The mocking of idolatry begins right at the outset. Babylonian documents speak of the food and drink sacrifices offered to the gods. According to certain inscriptions, Nebuchadnezzar made available huge amounts of food and drink for Bel. Here the Babylonians provided Bel with daily rations of twelve bushels of fine flour, forty sheep, and "six measures of wine" (14:3), more than fifty gallons. Bel had some appetite and thirst! On an inscription Cyrus claimed that he was ordained by Bel to rule over Babylon. Perhaps that is why the author tells us that the king worshiped the idol every day. Earlier in the book, Nebuchadnezzar had ordered, under penalty of death, that all nations and peoples should "fall down and worship the golden statue" he had made (3:4-6). Daniel's loyal companions Shadrach, Meshach, and Abednego refuse to comply with the king's command and so are thrown into the fiery furnace. But as a matter of historical record (Ezr 1:1-4; 6:3-5), the Persians were more enlightened than the Babylonians, allowing and supporting freedom of religion. Cyrus is called "the champion of justice" (Is 41:2) and even "Yahweh's friend" (Is 48:14). That is why Daniel without risk to his life can tell the king that he adores "only his God" (14:4), the true God of Israel.

The King Questions Daniel

When asked why he does not adore Bel, Daniel tells the king, "Because I worship not idols made with hands, but only the living

God who made heaven and earth and has dominion over all mankind" (14:5; cf. Ex 20:11; Ps 146:6; Acts 14:15; Rv 14:7). The expression, "the living God," occurs also in 6:21, 27 and dozens of other times in the Bible. The king retorts, "You do not think Bel is a living god? Do you not see how much he eats and drinks every day?" (14:6). There is delicious irony in these questions. Since Bel needs to eat and drink so much every day, the implication is that if he does not receive these provisions, he would not survive! Daniel cannot suppress a deriding laugh—an action that indicates he is indeed "the king's favorite." For if he were not, laughing at a king as powerful as Cyrus would have been an impertinence of the first order, which would have cost Daniel his head. He tells the king that the idol is "only clay inside and bronze outside" and "has never taken any food or drink" (14:6). This is another of the many polemics in the Bible against idol worship.

Does Bel Consume the Daily Provisions?

The king summons the priests and orders them to tell him who consumes all the provisions given to the idol. They must answer under penalty of death. If the priests can show that Bel consumes the provisions, then Daniel will die "for blaspheming Bel"(14:7-8). Daniel calmly agrees to this condition. There were "seventy priests of Bel" (14:10); the number symbolizes perfection or fullness. But the combined intelligence of the seventy priests in devising their secret door into the temple is no match for the wisdom God had given to Daniel to detect their ruse. So even though the priests have the "perfect" odds of seventy to one against Daniel, they still lose out in the end. This brings to mind the dramatic odds the prophet Elijah faced when he challenged the 450 prophets of Baal to prove that Yahweh alone is God, and not Baal (1 Kgs 18:19-40).

Inside the temple of Bel, the priests told the king they were going to leave, and they ask him to set out the usual food and wine. They ask him to shut the door and seal it with his signet ring. Then they say, "If you do not find that Bel has eaten it all when you return in the morning, we are to die; otherwise Daniel shall die for his lies against us" (14:12). Irony again comes into play, for the priests had just passed the death sentence on themselves.

The Secret Door of the Temple

Now we learn why the priests "were not perturbed." They had a secret entrance through which they entered the temple each night to consume the idol's daily provisions. The priests now leave the temple. The king sets out the provisions before the idol. Being "the king's favorite" (14:2), Daniel feels at liberty to order his servants to scatter ashes throughout the temple. Only the king saw Daniel do this (14:14). The two men then left the temple, and the king sealed the closed door, as King Darius and his lords had sealed with their rings the stone that covered the lions' den (6:18). That night the priests and their wives and children entered as usual and "ate and drank everything" (14:15). It took seventy priests and their wives with their presumably many children to consume the enormous amounts of food and wine set out for Bel. This is another ironic detail to emphasize the folly of believing in a god who needs so much simply to stay alive. What is interesting is that Daniel does not receive any direct assistance from God, as in other stories of the book. To prove that the idol is not a god but a mere creation of human hands, Daniel simply uses the intelligence God had blessed him with (1:17-20) and his skills as a detective to uncover the fraud perpetrated by the priests of Bel.

God has called all of us to do his work in whatever vocation we may have. But like Daniel in this story, we should not expect direct divine inspiration to tell us what we should do or not do. Indeed, God expects us to use our own intelligence and talents as well as our Christian imagination in planning our life and in doing his will. The great inventor Thomas Alva Edison (1847-1931) once wrote: "Genius is one per cent inspiration and ninety-nine per cent perspiration." Somewhat the same is true if we substitute the words "Christian life" for "genius," and "divine inspiration" for "inspiration." Divine inspiration can come to us in various ways, some of which may surprise us. The Bible of course is a privileged place in which we can learn more about God's will for us. Prayerful reading of scripture will sharpen our sensitivities to spiritual and moral values in our life. We will be challenged, cajoled, and shamed into admitting our weakness, our sins, our need for Someone and some thing higher than the satisfaction of the needs of the moment. But we will also receive the quiet prompting of the Spirit who will guide our mind and imagination to seek out what needs our attention.

We need not fear even when faced with those who persecute us, for as Jesus tells us, "When they hand you over, do not worry about how you are to speak or what you are to say. You will be given at that moment what you are to say. For it will not be you who speak but the Spirit of your Father speaking through you" (Mt 10:19-20). We must also be open to the fact that God speaks to us through the voices of other people—parents, spouse, children, homilist, counsellor, friend, foe—who may open up to us possibilities we never have thought of. But the rest is up to us. We must use our ingenuity and raise our own sweat in doing God's will.

The Deceit of the Priests Revealed

Early the next morning, the king asked Daniel if the seals to the temple door had been broken. Daniel gave of course the obvious answer: The seals were unbroken. When the king opened the door and saw that the table of offerings was empty, he cried out, "Great are you, O Bel; there is no trickery in you" (14:18). As in 14:7, Daniel, unable to contain himself at the gullibility of the king, burst out laughing (14:19). The Septuagint form is more graphic: "Daniel laughed heartily and said to the king, 'Come see the deception of the priests, Your Majesty.' " Being on such good terms with the king, Daniel kept him from entering the temple. Since the king had seen only what he wanted to see—the empty table—he did not bother to look at the floor of the temple. So Daniel has to tell the king to look down at the floor and asks, "Whose footprints are these?" The king in amazement says, "I see the footprints of men, women, and children" (14:19-20). He finally gets the point that he has been deceived by the priests. He arrests the priests and their families and puts them all to death. He gives the idol to Daniel who destroys it and its temple. So ends this delightful story. But the battle over idols still rages.

Some Reflections

As I noted above, the name Bel derives from the word for "master, lord." Today the idols of consumerism and hedonism, self-indulgence and status-seeking, materialism and greed—all try to lord it over us in their claims on our allegiance. These idols demand far more than the daily provisions of fine flour, sheep, and wine that the pagans offered to Bel. Today's idols make increasing demands on our time and our energy, our intelligence and our will, our personal life and our family life. What they offer in return are empty promises for a "better life"—more buying sprees, a bigger house in a better neighborhood, high-tech gadgets, labor-saving devices, expensive vacations. What they cannot offer is what we seek most—a sense of belonging, meaning, direction, and purpose in our life.

The secret to a happy life is learning to let go. That is why saints like Francis of Assisi and Therese of Lisieux were so free and so intensely human. Advertisers—the high priests of today's idolatry—know very well that we are creatures more of desire than of need. So they utilize all the alluring resources of the media to motivate us to desire more and more and then some. But unless we control our desires, our desires will control us. And the results of giving in to our desires are not what we expect. We find ourself ill at ease and bored, tired and frustrated. Our life is cluttered with our toys. Yet joy seems to evade us. We never seem to have enough time for ourselves, our spouse, our children. Jesus makes the point forcefully: "No one can serve two masters. He will either hate one and love the other, or be devoted to one and despise the other. You cannot serve God and mammon. Therefore I tell you, do not worry about your life, what you will eat or drink, or about your body, what you will wear. Is not life more than food and the body more than clothing?" (Mt 6:24-25).

Like the king who at first did not see the footprints in the ashes, we tend to see only what we want to see, and nothing more. The result is that we miss much that is vital in our life. Our tunnel vision, our material expectations, and our self-seeking passions restrict our field of view. What we need is a wide-angle lens to perceive the fullness and richness of the reality around us and within us. A full and satisfying life does not consist in what we *have* and *where* we live, but in what we *are* and *how* we live.

Daniel's favored position with the king did not prevent him from speaking his mind when faced with the question of idol worship. Daniel had the courage of his convictions and acted on them without fear of the consequences. We too will have occasions to speak up in moral matters like abortion and euthanasia, life-style and values, social justice, civil rights, and homelessness. Standing up and being counted may get our head knocked off, figuratively or even literally, as in the case of Archbishop Romero in El Salvador. Other stalwart Christians were persecuted, imprisoned, and even murdered for their defense of economic, social, and civil rights for the dispossessed in South Africa, the United States, and Central and South America. Such Christians have followed the example of John the Baptist who was beheaded precisely because he spoke out fearlessly against the adulterous marriage of Herod and Herodias, wife of his brother Philip (Mt 14:3-11).

What will be our response? Will we act or will we waffle? When tempted to say nothing at all about issues that demand a Christian response, we should keep in mind a proverb I once heard: "Silence isn't always golden; sometimes it's just plain yellow."

XXIV

"There Was a Great Dragon Which the Babylonians Worshiped"

(Daniel 14:23-42)

²³There was a great dragon which the Babylonians worshiped. ²⁴"Look!" said the king to Daniel, "you cannot deny that this is a living god, so adore it." ²⁵But Daniel answered, "I adore the Lord, my God, for he is the living God. ²⁶Give me permission, O king, and I will kill this dragon without sword or club." "I give you permission," the king said. ²⁷Then Daniel took some pitch, fat, and hair; these he boiled together and made into cakes. He put them into the mouth of the dragon, and when the dragon ate them, he burst asunder. "This," he said, "is what you worshiped."

²⁸When the Babylonians heard this, they were angry and turned against the king. "The king has become a Jew," they said; "he has destroyed Bel, killed the dragon, and put the priests to death." ²⁹They went to the king and demanded: "Hand Daniel over to us, or we will kill you and your family." ³⁰When he saw himself threatened with violence, the king was forced to hand Daniel over to them. ³¹They threw Daniel into a lions' den, where he remained six days. ³²In the den were seven lions, and two bodies and two sheep had been given to them daily. But now they were given nothing, so that they would devour Daniel.

³³In Judea there was a prophet, Habakkuk; he mixed some bread in a bowl with the stew he had boiled, and was going to bring it to the reapers in the field, ³⁴when an angel of the Lord told him, "Take the lunch you have to Daniel in the lions' den at Babylon." ³⁵But Habakkuk answered, "Babylon, sir, I have never seen, and I do not know the den!" ³⁶The angel of the Lord seized him by the crown of his head and carried him by the hair; with the speed of the wind, he set him down in Babylon above the den. ³⁷"Daniel, Daniel," cried Habakkuk, "take the lunch

God has sent you." [38]"You have remembered me, O God," said Daniel; "you have not forsaken those who love you." [39]While Daniel began to eat, the angel of the Lord at once brought Habakkuk back to his own place.

[40]On the seventh day the king came to mourn for Daniel. As he came to the den and looked in, there was Daniel, sitting there! [41]The king cried aloud, "You are great, O Lord, the God of Daniel, and there is no other besides you!" [42]Daniel he took out, but those who had tried to destroy him he threw into the den, and they were devoured in a moment before his eyes.

We now come to the final portion of the book. The story of the Dragon (14:23-42) is a variant on the story of Daniel in the lions' den found in chapter 6. As in the story of Bel, Daniel is a non-conformist. He refuses to worship the great dragon even though everybody else was doing it, for the Babylonians believed it to be a living god. Because he slays the dragon with the king's permission, the Babylonians force the king to hand Daniel over to them. They cast Daniel into the lions' den where he is again saved by God. The setting is the same as in the story of Bel: the court of King Cyrus; Daniel again is a privileged member of that court.

Daniel Receives Permission to Slay the Dragon

This story presumes the earlier one about Bel, as 14:28 makes clear. In fact, the Septuagint form begins, "In that place there was a great dragon . . ." (14:23). The Greek word for "dragon" can also mean "serpent." In the ancient Near East, there was a widespread mythology and cult of serpents. The serpent, a phallic symbol, represented fertility and life. The serpent was also a cosmic figure, identified with the monster of chaos (Is 27:1; cf. Jb 7:12; Ps 74:13-14; Ez 32:2). It is not certain what the author is making fun of here. He may be mocking either the worship of an actual serpent, or the mythological serpent/chaos-monster that, according to Babylonian belief, Bel/Marduk had killed in battle. On the Ishtar Gate of Babylon there was a serpent-headed dragon, which was believed to be the guardian spirit of the gate. That may be the reason why in our story the Babylonians are said to worship the dragon. In later apocalyptic literature the dragon was the symbol of evil and of Satan or the devil (Rv 12:3-9; 13:2-4; 20:2-3).

The king says to Daniel, "Look! you cannot deny that this [dragon] is a living god, so adore it" (14:24). The Septuagint form and other ancient versions are more graphic: "You cannot say it [the dragon] is bronze. See, it is alive. He eats and drinks, so adore it." Just because the serpent-dragon is alive, the king believes it is a "living god." But Daniel would have nothing to do with such nonsense. So being "the king's favorite," with a position higher than "any of the friends of the king" (14:2), he calmly answers, "I adore the Lord, my God, for he is the living God" (14:25). The God of Israel is the only true, living God. This living God cannot be represented by an animal or any other image. Then Daniel asks for permission to kill this dragon "without sword or club," and the king, being kindly disposed toward Daniel, gives permission (14:26).

Daniel Slays the Dragon

In Babylonian mythology, Bel/Marduk had to use weapons of war to subdue and slay the serpent/chaos-monster. Now Daniel, armed only with his faith and confidence in God, approaches the serpent/dragon without any weapons at all. He uses only the common substances of "pitch, fat, and hair" that "he boiled together and made into cakes," feeding them to the dragon, which then "burst asunder." Standing over the loathsome carcass, Daniel says to the king, "This is what you worshiped" (14:27).

The peculiar nature of this account does not strain credulity or detract from its effectiveness. In fact, these exotic details add to the overall entertainment value of the author's caustic satire on idolatry. The audience can easily imagine how this bizarre concoction of pitch, fat, and hair—none of which in fact are poisonous to a serpent—would swell up in the dragon's belly and burst it open. The Old Testament calls pagan idols the handiwork of human beings (Dt 27:15; Is 2:8; 31:7; Pss 115:4; 135:15; Wis 14:8); and animals, including serpents, were the handiwork of God (Gn 1:24-25; 3:1). Neither a man-made idol nor a living creature, therefore, can be "a living god," as the king believed. Daniel proves that point dramatically in the stories of Bel and the Dragon.

The Babylonians Throw Daniel to the Lions

When the Babylonians find out what had happened to the dragon, they went in anger to the king, accusing him of becoming a Jew, for "he has destroyed Bel, killed the dragon, and put the priests to death" (14:28). Calling the king a Jew is an ironic detail that adds to the enjoyment of the story, for it anticipates what the king will say at the end: "You are great, O Lord, the God of Daniel, and there is no other besides you!" (14:41). Our author depicts Cyrus in a favorable light (cf. Is 44:28 and 45:1). The "bad guys" are the Babylonians who force the king's hand, threatening to kill him and his family if he does not hand Daniel over to them. As a matter of historical record, however, Cyrus' control over Babylon was absolute; no one would have dared to challenge him. But our author is unconcerned about historical precisions; he is telling his story for only one purpose—to ridicule pagan idolatry. So the king gives in to their demand. They throw Daniel into a den where there were "seven lions" (14:32) and where he remains seven days (14:40). In the earlier story, Daniel had remained in the lions' den only overnight (6:19-20). The author again uses "seven" to symbolize "perfection" or "totality" in the number of lions and the number of days in the den, thus dramatizing the extreme danger Daniel faced. The lions were fed each day with two human bodies and two sheep—a fairly substantial diet. The bodies presumably were those of criminals. In fact, the Septuagint form adds some interesting details: "Conspirators against the king were given to [the lions]. Every day [the lions] were given two bodies of those condemned to death. The crowd threw Daniel into the lions' pit so that he might be eaten up and have no burial." Denial of burial was the ultimate disgrace (1 Kgs 21:23-24; Am 2:1). Thus, the lions in the den provided an effective deterrent to potential law-breakers. For the first six days that Daniel was in the den, the lions were given nothing to eat, so that "they would devour Daniel" (14:32). Daniel should have been a tempting morsel. For as Cervantes accurately observed, "There is no sauce in the world like hunger" *(Don Quixote de la Mancha* [1605-16]).

227

God Provides Lunch for Daniel and Rescues Him

Now the author gives his story more strange (and comic) details. A certain prophet named Habakkuk was preparing lunch for the reapers in the field when an angel of the Lord orders him to take this food to Daniel "in the lions' den at Babylon." There is no reason to assume that this prophet is the same as the Habakkuk whose book is found among the Prophets. Normally, in the Bible, prophets do not provide food service. But since a prophet is one who is sent by God to speak or act in his behalf, Habakkuk is indeed a prophet because he is fulfilling God's mission—to deliver lunch to Daniel. When Habakkuk protests that he has never seen Babylon and knows nothing of the lions' den, "the angel of the Lord seized him by the crown of his head and carried him by the hair; with the speed of the wind, he set him down in Babylon above the den" (14:36).

Here is the first instance of fast food service and even faster delivery—by air! More than two thousand years later, Domino's Pizza at its best cannot deliver its products that fast. This is the first instance also of round trip travel by air; one-way air travel is described in 1 Kings 18:12; 2 Kings 2:11, 16; and Ezekiel 8:3. As the prophet does not speak on his own behalf but only on God's behalf, so in like manner when the prophet acts, he acts on God's behalf and not on his own. That is why Habakkuk says to Daniel, "Take the lunch God has sent you." Daniel of course is grateful for this food, for he had not eaten in "six days" (14:31). So he praises God both for providing the lunch and for keeping the lions from having him for lunch: "You have remembered me, O God; you have not forsaken those who love you" (14:38). Like Susanna who trusted in the Lord (13:35) and hoped in him and so was saved (13:60), Daniel confesses that God remembers those who love him. The Old Testament teaches that God remembers his faithful people who turn to him in their troubles (Gn 8:1; 30:22; Lv 26:45; Nm 10:9; Ps 98:3; Bar 5:5).

In the conclusion of the story, King Cyrus is again portrayed sympathetically. On the seventh day the king came to the den to mourn, for he was convinced that the seven hungry lions would surely have devoured Daniel. But when the king looked into the

den, he saw Daniel sitting there unharmed. Like King Nebuchadnezzar in 2:47; 3:95-96; 4:31-32, and King Darius in 6:27-28, King
Cyrus now makes a confession of faith in the God of Israel: "You
are great, O Lord, the God of Daniel, and there is no other besides
you!" (14:41). The king knows the Old Testament too, for he uses
expressions that are found in such texts as Exodus 20:3; Deuteronomy 5:7; Isaiah 44:8; 45:5, 21; Wisdom 12:13. There is of course
no evidence at all that mighty King Cyrus, a polytheist, would
make such a profession of orthodox Jewish faith. But this would
not in the least have bothered the author, or his original audience.
His intention was to lampoon pagan idolatry and to show the
grandeur of Jewish faith and practice. He makes good use of
exaggeration and esoteric details to add interest and provide
amusement.

The king now removes Daniel and throws "those who had tried
to destroy him" into the lions' den—a punishment to fit their
crime. The ravenous lions devour them "in a moment before his
eyes" (13:42). Thus the pagans lose out again, as in all the other
stories of the book.

The account of Daniel in the lions' den, found here and in
chapter 6, has captivated the imagination not only of artists but
also of homilists. One of the most memorable is the delightful
homily on prayer written in 337 by the Syriac father Aphraat. In
extolling Daniel's spirit of prayer, he adds some colorful and
charming details to the familiar story: "Daniel prayed, and his
prayer shut the mouths of the voracious lions. . . . The lions
stretched out their paws and caught Daniel so that he did not hit
the ground. They embraced him and kissed his feet. When Daniel
got up in the den to pray, they followed Daniel's example and
stretched out their paws to heaven. . . . Although the pit was
completely covered and sealed, a bright light shone inside. And so
the lions rejoiced, for they saw this light because of Daniel. When
Daniel wanted to lie down and sleep, the lions stretched themselves
out so that he could sleep on their backs and not on the ground."
Aphraat concludes: "Every one of our righteous ancestors when
faced with adversity took up the weapon of prayer and through
prayer were delivered from that adversity." A point worth taking
to heart.

Some Reflections

The blatant parody of idolatry in the story of the Dragon may strike today's reader as naive and artless. But this and the other stories in the book have given encouragement and a degree of comic relief to the original audience—a persecuted people with no political clout and little economic opportunity. Hellenistic culture and religious practices, including polytheism and idolatry, had made pervasive inroads even among the Jewish community (1 Mc 1:11-15; 2 Mc 4:7-17). Stories like these reminded the loyal Jews of their glorious heritage, which is far superior to pagan religions with their lifeless idols and numerous gods and goddesses that cannot bring salvation.

Daniel confronts paganism head on and without fear. Confident of God's help, he does not just ignore the serpent-dragon but takes concrete measures to destroy it. Without Daniel's active intervention, the dragon would not have "burst asunder." Today the dragon of sex and pleasure has far more adherents than the old Babylonian idol. What can we do to explode this dragon so that people can see they are worshiping a worthless idol, a god that promises much but can give nothing beyond the satisfaction of the moment? Do we have the courage and conviction to take a stand and confront the powers in the media that influence our society and culture? Do we speak out forcefully in moral issues like pornography, television violence and suggestive programing, and lack of concern for the poor and homeless? As Oliver Goldsmith has reminded us: "Silence gives consent" (*The Good-Natur'd Man* [1768]).

The prophet Ezekiel has given us this salutary admonition: "If I say to the wicked man, You shall surely die; and you do not warn him or speak out to dissuade him from his wicked conduct so that he may live: That wicked man shall die for his sin, but I will hold you responsible for his death" (Ez 3:18). In other words, we cannot avoid our personal accountability by asking Cain's question, "Am I my brother's keeper?" (Gn 4:9). We are indeed our brother's and our sister's keeper. We have a moral duty to combat the widespread paganism in our society and culture. We believe in a God of love as well as a God of righteous anger, who will not be mocked by human arrogance, greed, and insensitivity to the poor. God forewarned the Chosen People, "If you transgress the covenant of the LORD, your God, which he enjoined on you, serve other gods and worship them, the anger of the LORD will flare up against you and you will quickly perish from the good land which he has given you" (Jos 23:16; cf. Dt 28:15-68). The people did not observe the Sinai Covenant. So as they had been told, God destroyed the nation by means of the Babylonians in 587 B.C.

Ancient Rome decayed from within long before it was destroyed by enemies from without. Can we in the West presume that our fate will be different? What gives us hope is that God "will not sweep away the innocent with the guilty" (Gn 18:23-32). The power of good can overcome the power of evil. Indeed, Paul tells us: "Do not be conquered by evil but conquer evil with good" (Rom 12:21). What we need most of all is the courage and wisdom of Daniel.

I conclude with three stanzas of "A Psalm of Life" by the American poet Henry Wadsworth Longfellow (1807-82):

> Tell me not, in mournful numbers,
>   Life is but an empty dream!—
> For the soul is dead that slumbers,
>   And things are not what they seem.
> Life is real! Life is earnest!
>   And the grave is not its goal;
> Dust thou art, to dust returnest,
>   Was not spoken of the soul. . . .
> Lives of great men all remind us
>   We can make our lives sublime,
> And, departing, leave behind us
>   Footprints on the sands of time.

Select Bibliography

Anderson, R. A. *Signs and Wonders: A Commentary on the Book of Daniel*. International Theological Commentary. Grand Rapids: Eerdmans, 1984.

Boice, J. M. *Daniel: An Expositional Commentary*. Grand Rapids: Zondervan, 1989.

Boyer, P. *When Time Shall Be No More: Prophecy Belief in Modern American Culture*. Cambridge, MA: Harvard University Press [Belknap], 1992.

Campbell, D. K. *Daniel, God's Man in a Secular Society*. Grand Rapids: Discovery House, 1988.

Collins, J. J. *Daniel: A Commentary on the Book of Daniel*. Hermeneia. Minneapolis: Fortress, 1993.

Davies, P. R. *Daniel. Guides to Biblical Scholarship*. Old Testament Guides. Sheffield: JSOT Press, 1985.

Frost, S. B. *Old Testament Apocalyptic: Its Origin and Growth*. London: Epworth Press,1952.

Hammer, R. *The Book of Daniel*. Cambridge/New York: Cambridge University Press, 1976.

Hartman, L. F., and A. A. Di Lella. *The Book of Daniel*. Anchor Bible 23. Garden City, NY: Doubleday, 1978.

Heaton, E. W. *The Book of Daniel: Introduction and Commentary*. Torch Bible Commentaries. London: SCM Press, 1964.

Goldingay, J. *Daniel*. Word Biblical Commentary. Dallas: Word Books, 1989.

Lacocque, A. *The Book of Daniel*. Atlanta: John Knox, 1979.

————. *Daniel in His Time. Studies on Personalities of the Old Testament*. Columbia, SC: University of South Carolina Press, 1988.

Mendel, A. P. *Vision and Violence*. Ann Arbor, MI: University of Michigan Press, 1992. Mendel's book focuses strictly on the antecedents of American apocalypticism. After a brief historical survey (Old Testament, antiquity, medieval, reformation, age of reason, the scientific revolution, counterculture, Fundamentalism), he then turns to an examination of apocalyptic in American politics (the Red Scare, etc.).

Morris, L. *Apocalyptic*. Grand Rapids, MI: Eerdmans, 1972.

Russel, D. S. *Daniel*. Edinburgh: Saint Andrew, 1989.

————. *Daniel*. Daily Study Bible Series. Philadelphia: Westminster, 1981.

————. *Daniel: An Active Volcano*. Edinburgh: Saint Andrew, 1989. A splendid book of reflections on Daniel.

————. *Divine Disclosure: An Introduction to Jewish Apocalyptic*. Minneapolis: Fortress, 1992.

Towner, W. S. *Daniel*. Interpretation Commentary. Atlanta: John Knox, 1984.

Wilson, Larry W. *Eighteen End-time Bible Prophecies*. Brushton, NY: TEACH Services, 1992.